C000259532

Molière on Stage

Molière on Stage

What's So Funny?

Robert W. Goldsby

ANTHEM PRESS
LONDON · NEW YORK · DELHI

Anthem Press
An imprint of Wimbledon Publishing Company
www.anthempress.com

This edition first published in UK and USA 2012
by ANTHEM PRESS
75-76 Blackfriars Road, London SE1 8HA, UK
or PO Box 9779, London SW19 7ZG, UK
and
244 Madison Ave. #116, New York, NY 10016, USA

Copyright © Robert W. Goldsby 2012

The author asserts the moral right to be identified as the author of this work.
All rights reserved. Without limiting the rights under copyright reserved above,
no part of this publication may be reproduced, stored or introduced into
a retrieval system, or transmitted, in any form or by any means
(electronic, mechanical, photocopying, recording or otherwise),
without the prior written permission of both the copyright
owner and the above publisher of this book.

British Library Cataloguing-in-Publication Data
A catalogue record for this book is available from the British Library.

Library of Congress Cataloging-in-Publication Data
Goldsby, Robert.
Molière on stage : what's so funny? / Robert W. Goldsby.
p. cm.
Includes bibliographical references and index.
ISBN 978-0-85728-442-6 (hardback : alk. paper) – ISBN 978-0-85728-444-0 (pbk. : alk. paper)
1. Molière, 1622–1673–Stage history. 2. Molière, 1622–1673–Dramatic production. I. Title.
PQ1871.G65 2012
842'.4–dc23
2012001708

ISBN-13: 978 0 85728 442 6 (Hbk)
ISBN-10: 0 85728 442 8 (Hbk)

ISBN-13: 978 0 85728 444 0 (Pbk)
ISBN-10: 0 85728 444 4 (Pbk)

This title is also available as an eBook.

Dedicated to Angela Paton who has shared my life on stage, backstage, and in countless audiences as well as in every word and comma of this book.

CURTAIN RAISER

What happens when the dramatic art of Molière is unloosed on stages and Past and Present come together to create new life? My intention is to lead the reader to discover just that: what happens when Molière's silent lines of text are transformed into a noisy play in a three dimensional space. I write having been, like Molière, an actor, director and theater manager. A director and a playwright both know the conventions of theater craft; both know the spaces in which actor and audience meet. But above all, the originating playwright and his subsequent interpreters desire to create communal life through an ecstatic experience shared with other human beings. Theater is a form of communion. It answers a need for union that is deep and universal. It was what held the aboriginal motionless in the circle as he watched his shaman enact the lion's bloody death and they both became that lion. That union was once evoked with pity and terror before the altars of Dionysus. The French loved to suffer through it to the hot alexandrines of *le feu* and it made Englishmen's hearts beat as one as they gloried in the freedom of their iambic pentameter. It was eagerly sought by enthusiastic hippies in LSD; it is often felt in the deep-throated *ohms* of the nirvana seekers; many hope for it in the loneliness of their Facebook. It has been analyzed endlessly by psychiatrists in the *id* and at the moment it is being pinpointed by excited neuroscientists in a dopamine site in the *caudate nucleus*. Union is the endorphin rush granted us by Molière as his words are given voice and his characters made flesh by a living actor before an audience and all individuals involved merge together in the joyous blessedness of shared laughter.

> *The healthier people always prefer Comedy to Tragedy …*
> *ah … one is never tired of laughter.*
> *One can tire of gambling, rich food, women, but of laughter, no.*
> *Have you ever heard anyone say,*
> *"We've been laughing for a week; I beg you, let us weep today."*
> *… The gods never weep. Their portion is laughter.*
> *… Blessedness consists of laughter.*

Molière to La Fontaine

TABLE OF CONTENTS

Acknowledgments   xi

Chronology of Plays Discussed   xiii

List of Illustrations   xv

Act One: The Back Story

I.   "'Allo, Molière"   3

II.   The First Stages   7

III.   Finding His Light   15

IV.   The Actor Unmasked   23

Act Two: The Agon

V.   Into the Mouth of the Wolf   33

VI.   "Go Saddle Yon Braying Ass!"   47

VII.   Entrances…   53

VIII.   …And Exits   69

IX.   She Loves Me… She Loves Me…   87

X.   …Not!   93

Act Three: The Comic Relief

XI.   Blessèd Laughter   111

XII.   Classic Routines   119

XIII.   Musical Comedy   127

XIV.   The Bones of Farce   137

Act Four: And Leave 'em Laughin'

XV.   The Dancing Skeleton   157

XVI.   The Imaginary Invalid   167

XVII.   Full Circle   179

Notes   181

Works Cited and Consulted   191

Index   197

INTERPRETERS

Molière in all plays
Madeleine Béjart in *Les Précieuses Ridicules*
Catherine de Brie in *L'École des Femmes*
Armande in *Le Misanthrope*

Jacques Copeau, Louis Jouvet, Jean-Louis Barrault in *Les Fourberies de Scapin*
Louis Jouvet and Dominique Blanchar in *L'École des Femmes*
Ariane Mnouchkine versus Ron Leibman in *Tartuffe*
Andrzej Seweryn and the Comédie-Française in *Dom Juan*
California Variations on *Don Juan* and *The Miser*
Molière and Lully for Louis XIV, King of France
Richard Wilbur and *The Learned Ladies*
Jean-Baptiste Poquelin in *Le Malade Imaginaire*

ACKNOWLEDGMENTS

Those who read and helped in earlier drafts:

Family: Wendy Goldsby, Robert E. Goldsby, Matthew Goldsby, Cynthia Wong, Gigi Bermingham, Maryse Bermingham.

Friends: Allen Weiss, Ariel Parkinson, Warren Travis, Jim Kerans, Kitty Winn, Adam Leipzig, Alvia Golden.

Colleagues: Eric Bentley, Robert Belnap, Carl Hovde, Dunbar Ogden, Grant Barnes, Travis Bogard, Lissa Renaud, Herb Blau, David Littlejohn, Mary Kay Martin.

Actors: René Auberjonois, John Apicella, Ron Leibman, Nadine Marziano, Ruth Maleczech.

Like anyone in the theater I am a product of people I felt close to in the profession:

Scholars like W. G. Moore, Ramon Fernandez, Virginia Scott, Henri Bergson, Sylvie Chevalley, Roger Herzel.

Teachers like Joseph Wood Krutch, Mark Van Doren, Andrew Chiappe, Constance Welch.

Directors like Elia Kazan, Jean-Louis Barrault, Louis Jouvet, William Ball, Michael Langham, Ariane Mnouchkine.

Translators like Richard Wilbur, Neil Bartlett, Morris Bishop, Albert Bermel.

Actors like Jacques Charon, Robert Hirsch, Jean Meyer, Louis Seigner and others at the Comédie-Française as well as all those at the Berkeley Stage Company, San Francisco's American Conservatory Theater, and Los Angeles' Antaeus.

Very important over the decades were the perceptive and imaginative students at Columbia University and at the University of California,

Berkeley where I spent most of my professional life, and at places like the Schools of Drama at the University of Washington, UCLA and USC, where I visited.

And finally, those who helped immeasurably through the publishing process:

Janka Romero at Anthem Press, Leslie Lowe in Los Angeles, Barbara Ann Sapp in Paris, Mélanie Petetin at the Comédie-Française.

CHRONOLOGY OF PLAYS DISCUSSED

Chapter III: FINDING HIS LIGHT
Les Précieuses Ridicules (1659 at the Petit-Bourbon, Paris)

Chapter IV: THE ACTOR UNMASKED
Sganarelle; ou, le Cocu Imaginaire (1660 at the Petit-Bourbon, Paris)
L'École des Maris (1661 at the Palais-Royal, Paris)

Chapter V: INTO THE MOUTH OF THE WOLF
L'École des Femmes (1662 at the Palais-Royal, Paris)

Chapter VI: "GO SADDLE YON BRAYING ASS!"
La Critique de L'École des Femmes (1663 at the Palais-Royal, Paris)
L'Impromptu de Versailles (1663 at Versailles)

Chapter VII: ENTRANCES...
Le Tartuffe; ou, l'Imposteur, in three acts (1664 at Versailles)
Le Tartuffe, in five acts (1669 at the Palais-Royal)

Chapters VIII and IX: ...AND EXITS and
SHE LOVES ME... SHE LOVES ME...
Dom Juan; ou, le Festin de Pierre (1665 at the Palais-Royal, Paris)

Chapter X: ...NOT!
Le Misanthrope (1666 at the Palais-Royal, Paris)

Chapter XI: BLESSÈD LAUGHTER
Le Médecin Malgré Lui (1666 at the Palais-Royal, Paris)

Chapter XII: CLASSIC ROUTINES
Amphitryon (1668 at the Palais-Royal, Paris)
L'Avare (1668 at the Palais-Royal, Paris)

Chapter XIII: MUSICAL COMEDY
George Dandin; ou, le Mari Confondu (1668 at Versailles)
Le Bourgeois Gentilhomme (1670 at Chambord for the King)

Chapter XIV: THE BONES OF FARCE
Les Fourberies de Scapin (1671 at the Palais-Royal, Paris)

Chapter XV: THE DANCING SKELETON
Les Femmes Savantes (1672 at the Palais-Royal, Paris)

Chapter XVI: THE IMAGINARY INVALID
Le Malade Imaginaire (1673 at the Palais-Royal, Paris)

LIST OF ILLUSTRATIONS

Cover   Argante and Scapin in *Les Fourberies de Scapin* (1920)
            by Jacques Copeau. Artist: Jean Dulac. Rights reserved.

Figure 1   Detail from "Molière en costume de tragédie" attributed
            to Sébastien Bourbon (1616–1671). There has been some
            question as to the correctness of the title, some saying it is
            not Molière but another actor in Molière's company.
            However, it is obviously a young man and Molière was the
            youngest actor in his company at the time of this painting
            when both Bourdon and Molière were in the provinces
            during the 1640s and Molière was still trying to conquer
            the tragic style. Musée Cantini, Marseilles.
            Photo © Jean Bernard.   5

Figure 2   *Les Précieuses Ridicules* at the Comédie-Française
            (1993) with Thierry Hancisse as Mascarille and
            Yves Gasc as Jodelet on stage in aristocratic finery.
            Photo © Laurencine Lot.   20

Figure 3   Detail from a painting by Molière's friend, Nicolas
            Mignard (1606–1695), seen at the Musée Granet, Aix-
            en-Provence. There seems to be some question as to the
            accuracy in the identification of Molière in this painting,
            but Madeleine's image is unquestioned. Mignard was located
            mainly in Avignon, which was part of the Béjart-Molière
            circuit in 1641–42, so the 1657–58 date given for the painting
            of the duo is either inaccurate or offers Mignard's aging
            memory as the reason for the lapse of accuracy in the
            likeness of the pair, or invalidates their inclusion altogether.   20

Figure 4   Jillian Boyd as Magdelon and Hilda Guitormsen as Cathos
            in *Girls with Ridiculous Airs* (*Les Précieuses Ridicules*) (2000)
            at the University of Washington School of Drama, Seattle,
            Washington. Photo © Adam Kaplan.   20

Figure 5   Detail from "Trapolino and Beltrame" (early sixteenth-
            century *Commedia* figures) from the Feather Book at
            McGill University Library, Toronto, Canada. The picture
            was evidently executed entirely in feathers in 1618 by
            Dionisio Minaggio, gardener to the governor of Milan.   25

Figure 6   Flautino in a seventeenth-century drawing by N. Bonnard.
            Bibliothèque Nationale de France.   25

Figure 7   Scapin as seen in the feather drawing of "Schapin and
            Spinetta" by Dionisio Minaggio in 1618. Also in the
            Feather Book at McGill University Library in Toronto.   25

Figure 8   Frontispiece for *L'École des Maris* showing
            Molière and Catherine de Brie. F. Chauveau, 1661.
            Comédie-Française Archives.   25

Figure 9   Portrait of Madeleine Béjart. French School. Private
            collection: Rights reserved.   27

Figure 10   Unquestioned portrait of Molière. Seventeenth century, by
            Pierre Mignard (1612–1695). Comédie-Française Archives.   27

Figure 11   An anonymous portrait of a young Armande, titled simply
            "Armande." Private collection: Rights reserved.   27

Figure 12   A picture seen in the program copy of the 1951 production
            of *L'École des Femmes* that Louis Jouvet brought to
            Broadway in New York. Rights reserved.   36

Figure 13   Detail from a large painting of French and Italian
            comedians and clowns of the sixty years or so prior to 1670.
            Molière is seen down stage right in that painting, with Jodelet
            standing behind him. Comédie-Française Archives.   36

Figure 14   Catherine de Brie with a knowing look in a sketch
            by Fr. Hillemacher in 1857, copied from a portrait
            painted in her time whose present location is unknown.
            Comédie-Française Archives.   36

Figure 15   Dominique Blanchard as Agnès and Louis Jouvet
            as Arnolphe in the 1940 Paris production of *L'École
            des Femmes* at the Théâtre Athénée, a production
            he later took to New York. Rights reserved.   36

Figure 16   A watercolor sketch of Du Croisy as Tartuffe – before
             the king in 1664 and at the Palais-Royal in 1669.
             Private collection: Rights reserved.   66

Figure 17   Shahrokh Meshkin as Tartuffe in Ariane Mnouchkine's
             production of *Tartuffe* for Le Théâtre du Soleil in Paris
             at the Cartoucherie in the Bois de Vincennes in 1995.
             Photo © Martine Franck.   66

Figure 18   Shahrokh Meshkin kneeling as Tartuffe and Brontis
             Jodowsky as Orgon in Ariane Mnouchkine's production
             of *Tartuffe* for Le Théâtre du Soleil in the Cartoucherie
             in the Bois de Vincennes in 1995.
             Photo © Martine Franck.   66

Figure 19   Ron Leibman as Tartuffe and Jessica Walters as
             Elmire in the Los Angeles Theater Center production
             of *Tartuffe* directed by the author in 1985.
             Photo © Chris Gulker.   66

Figure 20   Andrzej Seweryn as Don Juan and Françoise
             Gillard as Donna Elvire in the Comédie-Française
             production of *Dom Juan* (1993).
             Photo © Laurencine Lot.   82

Figure 21   Two peasant girls, Emmanuelle Wron as Charlotte
             and Florence Vialla as Mathurine, succumbing to the
             seductions of Andrzej Seweryn as Don Juan in the
             Comédie-Française production of *Dom Juan* (1993).
             Photo © Laurencine Lot.   82

Figure 22   Thomas Lynch as Sganarelle in the Marin Shakespeare
             Festival production of *Don Juan* in 2003.
             Photo © Morgan Corwin.   82

Figure 23   LeAnne Rumbel as Charlotte and Darren Bridgett
             as Pierrot in the Marin Shakespeare Festival production
             of *Don Juan* in 2003. Photo © Morgan Corwin.   90

Figure 24   Frontispiece for *The Misanthrope* by P. Brissard in
             1682 showing Molière as Alceste and La Grange
             as Philinte in hot discussion on the stage of the
             Palais-Royal. Comédie-Française Archives.   98

Figure 25   Michel Aumont as Alceste and Simon Eine as Philinte
            facing off on the stage of the Salle Richelieu at the
            Comédie-Française in 1984. Photo © Laurencine Lot.   98

Figure 26   A famous Célimène of the early 1800s, Mlle Mars,
            in a portrait by Girard. The illegitimate child
            of a would-be actress, she achieved great fame and
            was evidently charming and delightful on stage and
            a termagant off. She even picked a fight with Napoleon;
            he lost, according to the *New York Times* on 25 June 1876.
            Comédie-Française Archives.   105

Figure 27   Marie Bell, a great French actress, as Célimène,
            with Aimé Clariond, the French Resistance hero
            figuring in the first chapter of this book, as Alceste
            in the production of *The Misanthrope* presented
            at the Comédie-Française in 1937.   105

Figure 28   Kim Cattrall as Célimène and David Darlow
            as Alceste in the 1989 production of *The Misanthrope*
            at California's La Jolla Playhouse directed
            by Robert Falls. Photo © Micha Langer.   105

Figure 29   The very famous "Le vrai portrait de M. Molière
            en habit de Sganarelle" by Simonin. Bibliothèque
            Nationale de France.   115

Figure 30   Richard Fontana as Sganarelle and Catherine Heigel
            as Martine in the Comédie-Française production
            of *Le Médecin Malgré Lui* directed by Dario Fo
            in 1990. Photo © Laurencine Lot.   115

Figure 31   Madeleine Renaud in Armande's role as La Nuit
            in the New York production of *Amphitryon*
            at the Ziegfeld Theatre by the Renaud-Barrault
            Company in 1953. Armande must have preferred
            the prettier costume. Barrault Archives: Rights reserved.   121

Figure 32   Stephen Epp as Harpagon and Vincent Gracieux
            as Master Jacques in the Théâtre de la Jeune Lune's
            production of *The Miser (L'Avare)* directed
            by Dominique Serrand at La Jolla Playhouse
            in 2004. Photo © Michal Daniel.   121

Figure 33   The 1669 frontispiece for *George Dandin* by P. Brissard
showing Molière as Dandin, kneeling in his final
humiliation by Armande as Angélique before her
parents, the Sotenvilles, played by André Hubert
as M. and Louis Béjart as Mme. Comédie-
Française Archives.   133

Figure 34   Muriel Mayette as Angélique and Alain Pralon
as the title character in *Georges Dandin* as it was
produced at the Comédie-Française in 1992. Mlle
Mayette is the current administrator of the
Comédie-Française. Photo © Laurencine Lot.   133

Figure 35   Jacques Charon as M. Jourdain with Geneviève
Casile in the production of *Le Bourgeois Gentilhomme*
directed by Jean Louis Barrault in 1972 for performance
in a huge tent at the Gare D'Orsay before it became
a museum. Comédie-Française Archives.
Photo by François Darras. Rights reserved.   133

Figure 36   Louis Seigner as M. Jourdain learning to fence
in the 1948 Comédie-Française production of *Le
Bourgeois Gentilhomme*. Comédie-Française Archives.
Agence Roget-Viollet: Rights reserved.   133

Figure 37   The publication by Louis Jouvet of Jacques Copeau's
prompt script for Copeau's 1920 production of Les
Fourberies de Scapin at the Vieux-Colombier in Paris,
which premiered in New York in 1917.
©1950 Éditions du Seuil: Rights reserved.   151

Figure 38   A drawing by Jean Dulac for the 1917 program
of Copeau's production of *Les Fourberies de Scapin*.
©1950 Éditions du Seuil: Rights reserved.   151

Figure 39   Jean Louis Barrault in the 1948 Louis Jouvet production
at the Marigny in Paris that was brought to New York's
Broadway in 1951 under the aegis of Sol Hurok.
Barrault Archives: Rights reserved.   151

Figure 40   Jean Louis Barrault as Scapin with Pierre Bertin
as Géronte in the famous sack scene of *Les Fourberies
de Scapin*. Barrault Archives: Rights reserved.   151

Figure 41   Thierry Hancisse (shown as Mascarille in Figure 2)
            as Chrysale in the Comédie-Française production
            of *Les Femmes Savantes* at the Vieux-Colombier
            in 2010. Photo © Brigitte Enguérand.   164

Figure 42   Clotilde de Bayser as Philaminte in the Comédie-
            Française production of *Les Femmes Savantes*
            at the Vieux-Colombier in 2010.
            Photo © Brigitte Enguérand.   164

Figure 43   Angela Paton as Philaminte in a workshop production
            of *The Learned Ladies* (*Les Femmes Savantes*)
            with the Antaeus Theater Group in Hollywood
            in 2010. Photo © Alyson Aliano.   164

Figure 44   Barry Creyton as Chrysale in a workshop production
            of *The Learned Ladies* (*Les Femmes Savantes*) with
            the Antaeus Theater Group in Hollywood in 2010.
            Photo © Alyson Aliano.   164

Figure 45   René Auberjonois as Argan in the Shakespeare
            Theatre Company's 2008 production of *The Imaginary
            Invalid* (*Le Malade Imaginaire*). While I did not have
            the pleasure of seeing this production, having worked
            with René for years, I know he is an actor well suited
            to bringing the joy of life to the works of Molière.
            Photo © Carol Rosegg.   175

Figure 46   An old and sick Molière (age 51) by Charles Le Brun
            now at the Pushkin Museum in Moscow. Le Brun
            (1619–1690) was first painter of Louis XIV as well
            as a favorite of Nicolas Fouquet until that gentleman's
            fall from favor contributed to Le Brun's loss of
            credibility with many in the court except for the king.
            Photo © akg-images.   175

Diligent effort has been made to identify the copyright holders of the images contained herein. If the lawful owner of any unaccredited image in this book will contact the author and publisher, an acknowledgment of ownership and permission will be incorporated into all future editions of this work.

Act One

THE BACK STORY

I

"'ALLO, MOLIÈRE"

La Comédie-Française

My introduction to Molière came through an ecstatic experience as a member of an audience. Since it was the beginning of my long obsession with Jean-Baptiste Poquelin *dit* Molière, I share it as a springboard into my subject.[1]

In the late forties I was in Paris on the GI Bill. By a great stroke of luck I had rented a room in Montmartre behind the Sacré Coeur. It was owned by an actress, Mademoiselle Nadine Marziano, a *pensionnaire* at the Comédie-Française,[2] who became my friend and mentor. She told me that a famous actor she greatly admired was making his return to the theater after his absence during the war. She, a Swiss citizen, had played in the repertory during the German occupation, while many French actors had left the public view for various personal and political reasons. Monsieur Aimé Clariond,[3] who had left the company to work heroically in the World War II French underground Resistance, was returning that night for the first time to perform his pre-war role as Alceste in Molière's *Le Misanthrope*, a role for which he had been highly acclaimed. I accepted her invitation to join her at the theater.

The square in front of the Comédie-Française was swarming with people; the lobby was packed; throngs crowded around *le contrôle* – a high counter that served as a VIP box office, behind which sat three black-suited officials presiding like minor Brechtian gods over everyone's fate. Mlle Marziano managed, with much fervent discussion, to obtain two green slips that allowed us to enter the theater. I found myself sitting in the center aisle on a little *strapontin* – a fold-down seat attached to the permanent aisle seat in the first row where Mlle Marziano was installed. The place was buzzing with rapidly spoken French discussions and much moving about. Looking around, I saw the boxes surrounding the orchestra all overflowing with eager spectators awaiting the curtain's rise on the stage of what is familiarly known as "The House of Molière."

At that time I knew little of Molière and had hardly any real knowledge of either the theater or the language around me; yet I experienced an unusual heightened excitement of waiting for something very special to begin. I heard for the first time the famous rapid pounding on the floor and the final three heavy, slow blows – *les trois coups*. The curtain rose, and a figure burst out of the up-center door of a faded old-fashioned set and stormed downstage shouting a French phrase that even a beginner like me could understand: "*Laissez-moi je vous prie!*" ("Let me alone, please!") He was standing right above me as he finished this explosive entrance. At that moment, the entire audience stood up as one person and yelled. I got up slowly, looking around in shock. Never had I heard such a sound, such a roar. He stood there on stage; they stood there in the audience. He started weeping; they did too. What the hell was going on? This exuberant welcome went on and on. The sound was overwhelming. I found myself weeping with the others without quite knowing why. Finally, finally the noise subsided into intense quiet and he began the scene, struggling against his emotion-wracked voice.

At the intermission, we went backstage – in this theater granted to Molière's company by Louis XIV in 1680 – where actors receive friends in their comfortably appointed dressing rooms. The sweating actor, still reeling from the reverberations of his ecstatic welcome, was hoarsely regaling his friends with details of the scene he had just gone through. Obviously, my cursory reading of Molière in a humanities course at Columbia in an old Everyman translation had not prepared me for this kind of experience. This was museum theater?

Later that night I asked Mlle Marziano about that evening's extraordinary event and she told me the story of Molière's death. As she was telling the story she began to weep as if describing the death of a parent or a lover. She sobbed as if she had been in the small torch-lit procession of friends that took his body out in the middle of the night and lowered it into unhallowed ground, without the rites of the Catholic Church.

These two emotional events – one of joy and one of grief – made a profound impression on a twenty-year-old beginning to have yearnings toward the theater. Who was this long-dead playwright? How is it he is so alive in performance for a modern audience? Why does his work have such an emotional hold on people of today? What made those actors last night weep: one for joy; the other for grief?

Figure 1. A young Molière. Photo © Jean Bernard.

II

THE FIRST STAGES

Molière
a film by Ariane Mnouchkine

In writing this book, I want to bring Molière back to the place he loved – the stage – by using the language and theories, the written and unwritten laws and trade secrets of his chosen craft to better understand this complex artisan of the theater, and in so doing to evoke through the comic spirit of Molière the miracle of the theater as a whole: a unique, deep and ongoing experience as it is born in the coming together of writer, actor and audience.

In 1947, when I saw my first Molière performance, the man inside the character of Alceste, transforming the actor standing in front of me and that ecstatic audience, was Molière. That ecstatic experience in the public grew out of feelings of joy for the ending of the Nazi Occupation; pride in the return of their national theater to French hands; admiration for the actor who had played an heroic role in the Resistance – all coalescing in their great love for Molière. The people in the audience who were standing and yelling – as well as the actor standing weeping right above my little *strapontin* in the front row center – all had some knowledge of the "given circumstances," to use Stanislavski's later words, surrounding Molière's work. Everyone knew, at the very least, some details about his life while the actor on stage knew him as if he were his brother.

Some research will make a director, actor or audience member appreciative of the atmosphere of Molière's time. Three fine books in English tell the reader almost everything one needs to know about his life. Their authors are Virginia Scott,[1] W. G. Moore[2] and Ramon Fernandez.[3] But with an eye to his obsessions, his passions and his comic instincts, my mission in this brief chapter is to point to key developments in the boy's life which are indicators of how the man became a master at firing the raw clay of his worldly fixations – the stuff of all comedy – into some of humanity's greatest comic masterpieces.

His name was, in the beginning, Jean-Baptiste Poquelin. The first of six children he was born in 1622, six years after the death of Shakespeare.

He died in 1673 in Paris not far from his birthplace. He grew up as the son of
a well-to-do bourgeois craftsman whose title was *Tapissier du Roi* (Upholsterer
to the King) and whose work was, among other things, furnishing bed covers
to the king and tents to the military. The father, Jean Poquelin, was even called
upon to make up the foot of the king's bed from time to time when the king
traveled. Someone else made up the head! His mother, Marie Cressé, bore six
children in six years and died when Jean-Baptiste was only ten years old. It was
a terrible loss to the family. Ariane Mnouchkine, in her film entitled *Molière*,
which is in essence her book on Molière,[1] captured that loss beautifully. She
shows the beloved mother in an imaginary scene in which she sits cooing a
song while picking lice from the head of her little daughter. Jean-Baptiste, a
stalwart nine-year-old son, then pushes the sister away and smiles beatifically
as the crooning mother put her hands lovingly on his head; then the father
appears, pushes aside the son and sits down between her knees to have his
head caressed. It may seem obvious to say that Marie Cressé's early death
created an almost inconsolable yearning in Molière's heart for the touch of
love, but such a fact in the life of a ten-year-old is hard to ignore. And the
fact that his mother was bled to death by misinformed doctors may well have
created an unforgiving animosity to the entire medical profession. Thus out of
one death, two great emotional themes for his later plays were born.

Molière grew up playing in the markets and streets around the Pont Neuf,
not far from the charnel house where his mother's corpse would have been
taken. The broad and cobblestoned bridge – the only bridge over the Seine
without houses – was an oasis between the muddy Parisian streets on either
side, a little suspended world peopled with masked "medicine" sellers, farceurs,
hussies, varlets, strumpets and showmen of one sort or another. A short
distance from the family home was the theater in the Hôtel de Bourgogne[3]
where famous comic actors held forth when they were not replaced by the
more important tragedians. Molière's grandfather was reportedly a theater-
goer, and in another scene from Mnouchkine's film, he takes Jean-Baptiste
out of the home while the doctors are bleeding his mother to death, to watch
a street farce featuring Death as a grimacing, white-skull-masked giggling
actor making fun of a black-masked grunting old man – surely a Pantalone
character from the *Commedia dell'Arte*[5] – sitting noisily on a chamber pot.
He was learning the delight and joy of laughter even in the face of death.
It was a hands-on schooling in the all-too-human, non-intellectual, unbound
world of farce.

Molière would have crossed the Pont Neuf in order to get to his school, the
Collège de Clermont, one of the best schools in Paris. The Jesuits, who ran
the school for both aristocratic and wealthy middle-class sons, had as a goal
"a perfect knowledge of Greek and Latin." There was dawn-to-dusk study

six days a week featuring fierce, competitive struggles to recite – perfectly – passages from Latin works and from time to time, to enact Roman comedies or tragedies. Notably, this sounds much like Shakespeare's education as described by Stephen Greenblatt in his book, *Will In The World*.[7] Rhetorical skills were seen as essential if one was to have power and influence over others. These skills included analyzing the great speeches from the orators of Greece and Rome, as well as vigorous work in how to win arguments and persuade others to your point of view. Debate structures are seen throughout the plays of Molière and this is where he began his understanding of rhetoric. He may also have studied philosophy with Gassendi – a follower of Epicurean atomism and materialism which was at variance with both Descartes' teachings and the absolute faith promulgated by Jesuitical Christianity – in after-school meetings organized by the father of his school friend, Chapelle, for a small group of boys (one of whom was the real-life Cyrano de Bergerac). The Collège was a school handling several thousand students and so required a program of intense discipline, often demanding vicious competition among the boys who were seated in the classroom on benches arranged to separate the best from the worst students, thus making manifest their successes and failures. What better instruction and preparation for the rigors of a theatrical life: the rejections, the inspiration, the burning determination to succeed.

Reportedly, to distract him from a burgeoning interest in the theater, Molière's father sent him off to Orléans to study "law" in 1640. This may have meant a bit of tutoring and the money to buy a degree. This foray may have deepened his rhetorical skills of debate and argument, but it did nothing to dampen his growing love for the theater. In a last-gasp effort to distract him, Père Poquelin sent his son to Avignon to serve Louis XIII in an apprenticeship as *tapissier du roi* where, as fate would have it, Poquelin *fils* met the ravishing Madeleine Béjart, the famous tragedienne he had often seen on stage in Paris. When he came back to Paris he uttered the famous words that so many parents dread to hear their nineteen-year-old son say: "I want to be an actor." Three years earlier he had been granted the rights of succession to his father's business and was pronounced ready to practice the trade, but the record confirms his giving up his "office" as *Tapissier du Roi* in January of 1643; another record shows his starting a theater six months later in July of 1643 with nine other actors, most of whom were in the Béjart family, a family that had been active in the Parisian theater for some time. It was not, however, this well-known theatrical family that mesmerized the young Jean-Baptiste. It was their leading lady.

The famous Madeleine Béjart had flaming red hair and a magnetic personality on stage. He was nineteen; she was twenty-six. She was a *femme d'esprit* oozing charisma. She had been the mistress of Esprit de Remond,

Comte de Modène, and in 1638 bore him a daughter named Françoise.[8] She had a second illegitimate daughter by the name of Armande born somewhere in the mists of late 1642 – or early 1643! The precise identity of Armande's father has always remained in question. The Comte de Modène acknowledged paternity for the first illegitimate daughter but no one ever did for Armande, though Molière raised her as his daughter. Over the next thirty years, both mother and daughter became the most important people in Molière's life: he played opposite them on stage and in life he was the passionate lover of each at different times. In the beginning he joined Madeleine on stage and in her bed, and Armande was elsewhere. Maybe in a cradle in the corner? Fifteen years later he was sleeping with Armande and Madeleine was rocking in another room.

The theater the two lovers founded together in 1643 in a converted tennis court they named Le Théâtre Illustre.[9] It was at this time that he took the name of Molière. This "illustrious" theater was one of the more famous flops in theater history. It lasted two years, at the end of which the young co-founder was hauled off to jail for the company's debt. After being bailed out with a little help from Madeleine's mother, twenty-one-year-old Molière and Madeleine led their troupe out of Paris and headed to southern France, where they traveled in the provinces for the next thirteen years. During those long years of apprenticeship, Molière set about to learn his craft and to shape his company in his own image. He learned that though he loves tragedy and tragediennes his true talent is making people laugh, even, unfortunately, in the tragedies.

Among the actors the lusty young theater manager added to his roster were two young women who would eventually become stars in his plays. The first one to join the company in its travels was nineteen-year-old Catherine Leclerc, the daughter of two actors. She became a member of Molière's troupe by marrying one of his character actors, named Edme Villequin de Brie, a man twice her age. By the time they all arrived in Paris in 1658, she was a major actress along with Madeleine. She was known as Catherine de Brie or Mlle de Brie; she created thirty of Molière's characters. Many of her roles were romantic ingénues that she continued to perform for years, even after Molière's death in 1673. She also played countless other roles in the comedies and tragedies of the time. She was an actress of formidable talents, able to transform herself into a great variety of complex characters. She was a woman of soft grace and beauty who could play with delicious delicacy or surprising force. Many think she and Molière had become lovers by the time they returned to Paris.

The second woman to join with them on their stage as a company member came into sight as an acrobat huckstering for her father who ran a carnival show from Italy. Here is how Ramon Fernandez describes the arrival of Molière's third "goddess," Marquise-Thérèse de Gorla:

> She executed some remarkable acrobatics. Her legs and part of her thighs were visible, because her skirt was slit at either side, and her hose was modestly fastened at the top to short underpants. She was destined to wreak havoc on the susceptibilities of our great men, for, if we must trust the record, those who fell in love with her were Molière, both Corneilles, La Fontaine, and Jean Racine.[10]

In other words, she came to share the bed of the most successful playwrights of the day – and probably some unsuccessful ones, too. This gorgeous creature married the fat character man, René Berthelot Du Parc, who was already a popular member of Molière's company under the name Gros-René (Fat-René). She gained considerable fame as an actress – more in tragedy than in comedy – and was billed as Mlle Du Parc.

The troupe had a large complement of competent male supporting actors, mostly older, mostly strong physical types that the provincial audiences loved because they were much like them. The men had vibrant comedic talents, learned as they intermingled with the Italian troupes sharing their nomadic paths. But it was the women who took the lead, co-starring opposite Molière who always took the best male parts. They added their own strong sense of charming feminine wiles and gracious unbending female determination to the roles they were assigned. It was not long before the troupe became noted for its beautiful women, a roster that now included three seductive women and one nymphette daughter named Armande who first appeared in the performance records at age ten under the name of Mlle Menou – which may be some playful form of "little kitten" or "pussycat" – in a big production of Corneille's *Andromède* in Lyon. During these years of one-night stands, most scholars believe that Madeleine was Molière's chief partner, although he never married her. Others think that towards the end of their time in the provinces, he had Catherine as his mistress. It also seems quite likely that Molière would have exercised his *droit de seigneur* with the glamorous Mlle Du Parc. No one really knows how they arranged their bedtimes, or how Molière could have kept the three competitive ladies in the troupe happy as well as staying on good terms with their husbands. But he did. And one also has to keep in mind that little Armande, who will become a devastating obsession for the playwright, was growing up watching some highly entertaining performances – on stage and off. Having begun her life as the child cared for by Madeleine and Molière as parents, she was also one of the children in the larger familial melting-pot of the troupe. She would have helped with the work of the theater: taking care of props and costumes, cueing actors, fixing hair, pulling wagons, making offstage sounds, playing small roles, and being, as needed, a little "go-fer" for the director. The records show her to be about fifteen when the troupe had a stunning change in its bookings.

After thirteen years of performing countless tragedies and old farces, and after Molière had succeeded in writing two popular plays, *L'Étourdi* (*The Blunderer*) and *Le Dépit Amoureux* (*The Lovers' Quarrel*), he and Madeleine, through much effort and string-pulling, secured an invitation from the king's brother to come to Paris and perform for the king. Their long trek through the meadows of southern France and the chateaux of important nobility in Bordeaux and Lyon ended with their going back to Paris and into the Salle des Gardes of the Louvre Palace, where the absolute monarch – King Louis XIV – was waiting to be amused.

Mnouchkine's film portrays Molière, after the flat reception by Louis XIV to his troupe's rendition of a Corneille tragedy, putting on his comic mask and playing a little farce in which he busily sweeps the stage, the props, and finally, in a moment of sublime inspiration, dusts off the bosom of a voluptuous lady statue. In the silence, the king, only twenty years old at the time, smiles, then chuckles. The entire court cautiously begins to giggle and then at last roars – aristocratically – with laughter. When Louis cracks a smile in the film, Molière's eyes, behind the blackness of the hard leather mask, dance and beseech and grovel, as he relishes the promise of divine acceptance by the only public that really mattered – the king. Not only do his eyes betray his ambition but in Mnouchkine's interpretation his tongue flops out as well and he pants like a starving dog – an ecstatic moment, to be sure. Indeed, it can also be said that we have here a historic moment of transformation, a breakthrough that encouraged and sustained Molière as a maker of comedy and farce. And through his comedy and farce, as through the fixed mask of his characters, some of his deepest personal agonies and yearnings will be revealed on stage in public. All three of his "goddesses" were on view this fateful day as well as Armande in the wings, and at the end of the performance all the close-knit troupe must have been ecstatic, for the king granted to the company the right to perform on the stage of Le Petit-Bourbon, a vast space inhabited by a group of relocated Italian actors under the leadership of the great Scaramouche. A fortuitous development all around, for Molière surely had much to learn from sharing time and space with those inheritors of the *Commedia dell'Arte*.[11]

It was 1658 when he began to perform in Paris, his birthplace and the city where his plays would be seen on stage continually for the next three hundred and fifty years. He had only fifteen years left to live and work. He would go on to write thirty-four plays and the same loyal troupe of actors will play in all of them. He was thirty six when he stepped through a masking curtain onto his temporary stage in the Louvre, enduring the horrible silence of rejection before the Sun King smiled. Some think that the winning little farce he played as a desperate afterthought that day was another medical lampoon called *Le Docteur Amoureux* (*The Love Doctor*). He was fifty-one when he died playing an imaginary invalid seeking an imaginary doctor's degree. One does tend to believe the irony of such bookends to a life.

III

FINDING HIS LIGHT

Les Précieuses Ridicules

as conceived by Molière
as acted by Madeleine Béjart
as acted by Catherine de Brie
as translated by Robert W. Goldsby

That first year in Paris, they did poorly. Playing tragedies, these comedians may have looked like the proverbial image of a herd of deer caught in the headlights. They were no competition for the well-known tragedians at the Hôtel de Bourgogne. Molière was pilloried when he played tragedy. A rival actor of the time, Montfleury,[1] maliciously described Molière's talents as a tragedian:

He enters ... nose in the air,
Feet in parentheses, shoulder in the lead,
His wig, that swings from side to side as he walks,
Is more covered with laurel leaves than a spiced ham.
Hands at his sides, with a negligent air,
His head down like an overloaded mule,
His eyes rolling, he speaks his lines
With that eternal little "uh" separating his words.[2]

The plays that had the best attendance were the two comedies he had written while in the provinces: *L'Étourdi* (*The Blunderer*) and *Le Dépit Amoureux* (*The Lovers' Quarrel*).

One can imagine Molière, remembering that people had flocked to his comedies in the provinces, coming to recognize that comedy was his special talent; it's also easy to imagine him, as he walked around the familiar haunts of Paris, "a grave, deliberate, somber man,"[3] coming to realize that Paris was now to be his subject. He must have watched the passers-by with their secret dreams and foibles hidden beneath their coats and wondered how he could exaggerate those dreams and foibles for laughter's sake as he had done in his farces about country doctors, provincial lawyers and peasant pedants. Thus we can see the genesis of his first great play about a family from the country coming to the city and trying to become citified just as his family of actors was trying to do. In a one-act play he exposes the "deep superficiality"[1] of the phony Parisian intellectual who wants to rigidify and strangle with rules the marvelous pleasures of love and literature. Some scholars have seen *Les Précieuses Ridicules* (*Girls with Ridiculous Airs*) as little more than a sketch, but to theater people it is an absolute masterpiece of comedy. He has a huge hit in this outrageous, one-act rambunctious romp filled with pheromones and testosterone. The youthful spirit of exuberant omnipotence bursts from the seams of this brilliant short play satirizing intellectual pretensions.

Molière cast himself in this play as Mascarille (Little Mask), the servant of one of two aristocrats who are each interested in two girls newly arrived from the country with lots and lots of money. Both these aristocrats bear the names of the actors playing them: La Grange and de Brie. This casting marks a significant event. Monsieur Charles Varlet *dit* La Grange had recently been hired as the company's young leading man. This passionate and very handsome twenty-year old actor not only goes on to play most of the lovers in Molière's plays, but as his finest actor plays these roles until 1685. What keeps him alive in our memory is not his lost fame as a performer of young lovers with a splendid and elegant collection of costumes at his disposal – a collection even more extensive than Molière's – but the fact that he took on the role of the chief accountant for the troupe, keeping records of all the financial matters of the company in his famous book, *Le Registre*.[5] He also assumed a leadership position in the troupe after Molière's death and – most importantly – he put together the first edition of the complete works of his friend and mentor. But here we have him in one of his first roles with the company, bossing his boss around, sending him off to woo the two girls who are too uppity for the would-be lovers.

The choices are extreme. Look at how Molière enters as Mascarille. He is dumped unceremoniously on stage from the filthy sedan chair carried by the two complaining louts he hired to transport him through the muddy streets of Paris. When he rises to his full dignified height we see the clothes he wore to go a-wooing in his master's stead as a joke to humiliate the snooty and naïve girls. There is a famous description by Mlle Desjardins on what he looked like:

> His peruke was so big that it swept the floor every time he bowed, and his hat was so tiny you guessed that the marquis carried it oftener in his hand than on his head. His bands could pass for a respectable dressing gown and the trimming on

his breeches looked as if it were made only to serve as a hiding place for children playing hide and seek; and really, Madam, I don't believe a young Scythian's tent was more roomy than that superb lace trimming on his breeches. A bunch of tassels stuck out of his pocket as if from a horn of plenty and his shoes were so embellished with ribbons that it was impossible to tell whether they were Russian leather or English cowhide; anyway I am sure they were a good six inches high and I was at a loss to imagine how heels so high and slender could possibly hold up the marquis' ribbons, breeches, trimming, powder and body.[6]

We know Molière's body was powerful, with thick legs and a large, heavy head, and if we imagine such a body teetering on six-inch heels, we are introduced – on the simplest physical level – to a comedic technique of contrast.

Magdelon, played by the flaming-haired Madeleine in an equally flaming red dress, is a starry-eyed provincial with great delusions about romantic love that have come entirely from novels by those oh-so-precious writers of multi-volume romances, an addiction that echoes the quixotic dreams in Cervantes. Molière has her give a long soliloquy about this kind of love in the early pages of the play, before Mascarille comes on to woo her. Only a great actress, who can "sing" a role, can do justice to this speech to her bone-headed father about the many rules of romantic love and how it must move through agreed-upon phases. This aria aspires to the frequencies of music, and in our production of the play at the University of Washington we had faint and delicate violins under the speech which goes, in part, like this:

> ... After the first fateful meeting the lover is to leave in a daze, a dream, a kind of melancholy. Later when he visits her he will hide his passion behind some edifying discussion on some wonderfully witty subject. A lover, if he is to be agreeable, must know how to recite beautiful thoughts with a sweet and tender turn of phrase. When he finally makes his declaration of love, it must take place in the intimacy of a leafy bower in some moonlit garden ...[7]

If we imagine the scene of Molière talking the married Catherine into sex as they untangle the laces of their sweaty costumes in the dusty dressing room, it surely bears no resemblance to some moonlit garden; if we picture the acrobatic Mlle Du Parc and Molière entangling ardently in the prop room amidst the tangle of swords and candelabra, there certainly was not much need for a sweet and tender turn of phrase; and if we think of his long years of sharing love squeezed in with Madeleine during their frantically busy days and nights doing theater – surely one of the most labor-intensive professions in the world – we can get a strong feeling for Molière's satiric point of view about such highfalutin sentimentality. Magdelon ends this long silly aria, rendered by the great tragedienne Madeleine Béjart, by talking about the difference between "precious love" and marriage:

> Father, to come out point-blank for marriage, is like beginning a four volume novel at the end. To substitute marriage for love is something only a shopkeeper would do and the very thought of it is enough to make me sick at my stomach.

An actress who had been living on perpetual tour and who never succumbed to marriage, Madeleine must have gotten the giggles in rehearsal playing this idiot who goes on every day, as her father describes her, "pomading herself with nothing but the whites of eggs, virgins' milk, creamy cheese and fiddle-faddles of all sorts." He wails that since the family has moved to the city "she's used up the grease from a dozen pigs; four servants could live for days on the pigs' feet she's used up."

If we look at *Les Précieuses Ridicules* by focusing on Madeleine and Molière as actors and as long-time lovers, one cannot help but feel the intense physicality of their relationship. The wooing scenes between these two veterans of many difficult times are filled with howling departures from common sense. In roles written expressly for each of them, Molière depicts a love where the two participants are equals. It is a joyous, exuberant, boisterous love, filled with laughter, openly fun in an earthy Rabelaisian way rather than as a salon comedy of manners. Magdelon commands with electrifying energy her bewildered servant to "run and convey to us some commodities of conversation" and after chairs are brought, the heavy set male and his two sensual and graceful female "stars" – Madeleine and Catherine – install themselves for the courtship ritual in which three fools each pretend he or she is something they are not. Of course, the topic has to be literary – they are "intellectuals" after all – and the conversation leads up to Mascarille's recitation of an ad-libbed *impromptu* to the two squealing sisters. The kind of mind both actresses are playing is far, far beneath that demanded by Corneille's ringing tragic verse. And Molière is facing Madeleine as Magdelon and Catherine de Brie as Cathos, both of whom he knows intimately.

MASCARILLE. (*Reciting his impromptu*)
           Oh! Oh! You've caught me off guard!
           While all innocent, I threw you a regard.
           You stole my heart away;
           Stop thief! Stop thief! Stop thief! Stop thief!
           .... I say!!
           (*He runs around the stage as if chasing the thief and collapses in exhaustion.*)
CATHOS.   Oh Heavens! That is the most very avant-garde.
MASCARILLE. My tongue is the tongue of a knight; you cannot say my tongue's passé.

MAGDELON.   Oh, no! You are most definitely beyond passé.
MASCARILLE. Did you pick up on the opening "Oh, Oh." That's what's
            extraordinary.
MAGDELON.   Oh yes, yes, I find that "Oh, Oh" so, so delicious!
MASCARILLE. Yet it seems like nothing at all.
MAGDELON.   I'd rather have written that "Oh, Oh" than an epic poem.
MASCARILLE. Zounds, but you have good taste.
MAGDELON.   Oh, you noticed.

One could use W. G. Moore's entire wonderful chapter on "Speech" to dissect this little scene, but here I'm simply pointing to the onstage relationship of the three great professional actors who lived together offstage. For Madeleine – a writer herself as well as a highly sophisticated tragic actress used to playing queens before royalty – to put herself in the mind of a sublime idiot who thinks that two empty vowel sounds ("Oh, Oh") put meaninglessly together are the substance of great literary value, shows us the transmutability inherent in the nature of the professional actress and demonstrates for us the combination of self-delusion and irony that is the very essence of comedy. And Mlle de Brie, who only nine days before this opening performance for King Louis gave birth to her second child, shows us the immutability of the demand that "the show must go on" and demonstrates the pride of discipline in the heart of a great professional actress.

If we think of the subtext in the scene as sexual seduction in its early stages, we can appreciate what Stanislavski called "the fluid exchange of emotion"[8] between actors. The Lunts, leading Broadway actors of the early twentieth century, on hearing this phrase, exclaimed "Oh, you mean 'Playing together!'" Molière and his two "goddesses" played together during the long twenty minute scene that followed and they used many comedic mechanisms. The heart of the comedy, however, and the energy of the scene remain sexual and physical.

Mascarille renders his poem again, this time singing it in operatic style and running around in circles hitting the Wagnerian high notes on "Stop thief!" Meanwhile Catherine swoons over his tickling plumes and Madeleine faints as she describes the lacy underwear she is wearing. The climax of the play comes when the white-faced Jodelet, masquerading as a wounded war veteran, makes his entrance in his idea of military clothes and vies with Mascarille over who has the most-worst-war-wound gotten by the most-bravest-bravery. He puts the make on Catherine/Cathos, who has been flirting around the edges of the two leading players. She finally gets a partner, even if it's only this white-faced clown. The spirit of male competition – remember those Jesuits – leads to having the girls feel the men's various war wounds and Mascarille finally wins the bout by offering to show Magdelon his wounded crotch. After this

Figure 2. Mascarille and Jodelet dressed to kill at the Comédie-Française. Photo © Laurencine Lot.

Figure 3. Madeleine and Molière portrayed as Mars and Venus by his friend Mignard. Musée Granet.

Figure 4. Magdelon and Cathos delighted with life. University of Washington, School of Drama. Photo © Adam Kaplan.

excitement, the four actors/characters, to keep themselves from fornicating on the spot, have to do something with their hyperventilating bodies and all that sexual energy goes into a thumping dance, which begins with these would-be aristocrats trying to do a proper minuet and then explodes into a stomping, whooping country whirligig. This is abruptly interrupted by the return of the real aristocrats, La Grange and de Brie, who come back onstage and force Mascarille and Jodelet to take off their outrageous disguises, revealing their dirty underwear and their all-too-human bodies.

All this sexual life is play-acting, extremely physical and joyful. When Mascarille is defeated by the societal power and position of the two masters and doesn't have his way with Magdelon, he is in no way diminished as a man or as an actor. When she shrieks at him that she will have her revenge, his exit lines reveal that he thinks of himself as if he really were a marquis:

> A fine way to talk to a Marquis. That's the way of the world. A slight turn in events and we are thrown away by those who love us. (*To Jodelet*) Come my friend, we shall seek our fortune elsewhere. I see clearly that it is only the outside show that society cares for and the inner worth is neglected.

In this world of theatrical comedy there is absolutely no doubt that offstage Mascarille will find a willing female, and that such relationships are simply a fact of life, by no means life-threatening.

Meanwhile, in the deepening real-life drama, a young girl waits wide-eyed offstage. Armande would have been in her teens and we can imagine the adolescent girl, watching from the wings, seeing these two "parents" act out this raucously physical play about the naked body and its colorful plumage. As she stood in the shadows she couldn't have had any idea she was to become the object of a sexual desire that would almost destroy Molière's life, a passion that caused intense suffering both in the man and the characters he acted. In the man the feelings were agony; happily in the characters the result was a laugh.

What created this obsession? A scholar would look to the documents, the letters and the records to discover the answer or the fact that would satisfy him or her. A director, such as Ariane Mnouchkine, would look beyond that, to her imagination to satisfy the questions asked of her by the actor chosen to play Molière, trying to help him discover the core that would ignite his performance. My wife looked to the portraits of Armande and Molière and said, "Look! The noses are the same," and her feminine common sense was satisfied – for her that said it all. He wanted to claim her as his own.

During this first great "hit" for the company Armande was still in her teens, still in the wings of the theater, but there is every indication that she may have been gearing up to say to the leader of the troupe, "I'm ready for my close-up,

Papa Molière." While Mascarille assures us he will find another willing female, to Molière's misfortune, the young girl in the wings did not seem to have her heart set on him; she was, according to Mnouchkine, focused cool-headedly on her own ambition. In her film, she creates a scene where the fifteen-year-old Armande crawls into Molière's bed to comfort him for the loss of Mlle Du Parc who had left the company to try her hand at tragedy. Armande was, indeed, ready for her close-up.

IV

THE ACTOR UNMASKED

Sganarelle; ou, le Cocu Imaginaire
as translated by Albert Bermel
L'École des Maris
as translated by Donald Frame

In the spring of 1660, following the winter opening of *Les Précieuses Ridicules* of 1659, Chapelle – one of Molière's closest friends who had been a fellow student with him at the Collège de Clermont – sent Molière the following verse which we need to read remembering Molière's place as the powerful head of the leading theater company in France. Obviously the tone of these verses indicates that his role as a surrogate father was being transformed into a different kind of love. Chapelle's little poem reads:

> The moss creeps o'er the meadow floor too young yet
> To wrap round the beckoning arms of the sighing willow
> That enviously eyes her new-born tempting charms.
> He stands tall, jealous of the dusty soil that holds her.
> She slowly weaves her way far below. Surely soon
> She will be his, held in his strong loving limbs.[1]

In the next few years Molière fell deeper and deeper under the spell of his teenaged ward. It was during this time he wrote and acted in three plays: *Sganarelle; ou, le Cocu Imaginaire* (*Sganarelle; or, The Imaginary Cuckold*), *Dom Garcie de Navarre*, and *L'École des Maris* (*The School for Husbands*). The primary emotion in all three is sexual jealousy. Gone is the free-for-all romp of sexual joy. New directions emerge in both his writing and his acting.

In *Sganarelle*, he introduced the terror of cuckoldry – even when it is imaginary. *Sganarelle* is designed to function, like *Les Précieuses Ridicules*, as an afterpiece to longer plays in the company's repertory. Molière again played the *Commedia*-inspired Sganarelle – now his signature role much like Charlie Chaplin's tramp – but the role underwent a major transformation and the play exhibited some significant new ideas for his life on stage. Scenically, Molière had already thought of removing the footlights in an effort to come closer to his audience by removing a barrier between the actors and the public, but now more radically, he put aside the traditional hard leather mask of the farceur in favor of the virtual mask of real-life character. He had a strong face, which Fernandez described as one that at first

> … would be seen as immobile, not to say frozen. But this same countenance would instantaneously unfreeze; its features would twist, lose composition, quickly regain it – a visage of flexible masks of flesh that emerged one from another at will. Then the face would regain its impassiveness and become again withdrawn.[2]

In other words, this face was too valuable a tool to hide behind an unchanging, rigid half-mask that revealed only his eyes and below that his mouth.

He needed to make this important change because Sganarelle, with others in the play, would be portrayed as a middle-class citizen, a bourgeois dressed as in real life and not in the usual *Commedia* servant costume. In this significant shift we see the first signs of his self-revelatory journey. Even more surprisingly, these characters, unmasked and part of the bourgeoisie, speak verse, the traditional language of tragedy, and not prose, the language of comedy and farce. These changes speak wonders about the elevation, the mainstreaming as it were, of the comedy of Molière and his troupe. This sparkling comedy in verse turned out to be his most performed play during his lifetime.

Molière next rehearsed and produced a "serious" attempt at tragedy with Madeleine playing Elvire, the Princesse de Léon in *Dom Garcie de Navarre*, and Monsieur de Molière playing the suicidally jealous Dom Garcie, Prince de Navarre. Maybe he needed to give Madeleine a starring role to make up for her playing a servant in *Sganarelle*, but there is no sense in this play of any real fire, of any passion underneath the lofty diction. He never could act tragedy; now he knew without a doubt he couldn't write it either. It's his last attempt at the genre, and Madeleine's last leading-lady role in his plays. After this failure, she moved into delightful soubrette roles, such as Dorine in *Le Tartuffe*, and it seems clear that his mind and heart were elsewhere.

With his company safely installed in the Palais Royale, Molière next turned to "School," perhaps in hopes of schooling the fevered passion he felt for Armande.[3] She was to be the unspoken but obvious subject of his next five plays: *L'École des Maris* and *L'École des Femmes*, followed by the three masterpieces – *Le Tartuffe*, *Dom Juan*, and *Le Misanthrope*.

Figure 5. Trapolino. McGill University.

Figure 6. Flautino. Bibliothèque Nationale de France.

Figure 7. Scapin. McGill University.

Figure 8. Molière as Sganarelle. Comédie-Française Archives.

In this series of plays we see the full flowering of his ability to fuse primal personal emotion with startlingly alive comedic character.

The beginning play in this upcoming cycle is *L'École des Maris* (*The School for Husbands*), which opened for the king in 1661. Molière played a middle-aged man of forty – again unmasked and costumed from contemporary bourgeois life – who is guardian to a young girl. He named him Sganarelle again and gave him a brother, Ariste, aged sixty. In this verse play about aging men marrying young girls, the dramatist divides himself into two characters who express two sides in an argument about such a May–December marriage. The men are brothers: one the kind, reasonable, sensible sixty-year-old Ariste, and the other a choleric, intemperate, selfish, forty-year-old prig. Of course, Molière plays the better role: the comic one – the illogical, unreasonable Sganarelle. It's all too easy to imagine his using these two male characters to argue the best course for himself, so in love with his young ward. It's almost as if he put himself on trial in front of the king and the rest of Paris.

Six months after opening this play – full of debates and intrigues about the pros and cons of marriage between the old and the young – he married Armande, twenty years his junior, in January of 1662 in, of all places, Madeleine's apartment. In February they married again in Molière's home church, St. Eustache. Madeleine was listed as Armande's sister, and Marie Hervé, a character woman with the company and Madeleine's mother, listed herself as the mother of Armande. Documents do not always tell the truth. Virginia Scott points out that Mlle Hervé would have been sixty at the time of Armande's birth. We don't know much about the motivations for such obvious misstatements, but we can surmise the need for propriety, and when it came to the church, actors needed all the help they could get. How intimate he was with Armande before their marriage is unknown, but he had taken a room for himself in October of that year while Madeleine had four rooms elsewhere. One can easily presume that the moss had joined with the willow tree.

There is a heartbreaking scene in Ariane Mnouchkine's film that takes place at a huge dinner table with the whole company feasting. Molière stops the laughing actors in mid-mouthful, telling them that he and Armande will be married and he wants her to have a full share in the company. There is an appalled silence. The actors have known Molière and Madeleine day and night, for decades in most cases. They each slowly rise and silently exit. Molière is left at one end of the table and Madeleine at the other. She says that he owes her for her costumes. He says they are all too old. Then slowly he walks down to her and touches her hair. At this she freezes; then she reaches up and takes his hand with infinite tenderness. Society was not so tender with them. Incest was not only rumored but written down in pamphlets, and by the time of *George Dandin* six years later, Armande was widely rumored to be the mistress

Figure 9. Madeleine Béjart. Private collection: Rights reserved.

Figure 10. Molière in mid-life. Comédie-Française Archives.

Figure 11. Armande. Private collection: Rights reserved.

of this or that powerful aristocrat. Audiences in France knew this story. They still know it. His plays kept it alive.

In the second scene of *The School for Husbands*, Molière as Sganarelle faced the entrance of his three goddesses: Mlle de Brie, who played Isabelle, his ward and the young girl he intended to marry; Mlle Du Parc – having returned to the company after a brief foray into tragedy with Corneille – who played her sister, the ward of Ariste and his intended bride; and Mlle Béjart, now cast as the earthy, tough minded companion with no sexual partner in the play. The scene is carried by Mlles Béjart and Du Parc while the main character, Isabelle, played by Mlle de Brie, is mostly silent. It is rather extraordinary to think of the three of them on stage playing against the head of the troupe, facing down this man with whom all three had been intimate. Mlle Béjart, in her role, characterizes him in the following speech – which we can certainly imagine resonating as a warning to Armande watching the play from the wings – about the perils of marriage to a man of such a possessive and jealous character. The playwright, himself, seemed to recognize this as he set down the following words for Madeleine to speak in act 1, scene 2:

> Come, do you really think all these precautions
> Are any obstacle to our intentions,
> And that when we've a mind, we can't prevail
> And make a fool out of the smartest male?
> You act like mad men when you spy on us.
> The surest thing is to rely on us.[1]

Such a man is primed for cuckoldry, is the message. And it might have had special weight since it was spoken by Mlle Béjart who had had years of experience living with just that man, especially if the man was thinking of winning a very young girl much like Isabelle played by Mlle de Brie, the real star of the piece, who knew Molière almost as well. She surely held the focus even while moving silently around the stage during these opening arguments for this is the younger up-and-coming star, Catherine de Brie, and in the following acts she drives the play with her cleverness, her energy, and her determination to satisfy her own best interests. Molière contrasts her to the three male characters who have no real imagination and who are unable to think in terms of strategy and intrigue to get what they want. She is clearly the superior creature, controlling her dumb young lover in an act 2 game of shuttle-cock messages, using Sganarelle himself as the bone-headed cock. In Molière the ladies always win. Sganarelle doesn't have a clue and his gloomy "phlegm" is roused to choking proportions when Isabelle emerges at the end of the play happily married to the young buck. His selfish idea of love is undone by the young girl's more appropriate attraction to youth. Ah grief! His final speech is excessive but does not yet have the primal emotional quality we will find in the final speeches of Arnolphe in *L'École des Femmes* (*The School For Wives*) and Alceste in *Le Misanthrope* (*The Misanthrope*). Here is what Sganarelle declaims with all the energy of a comic fool:

> I can't get over it; I am astonished;
> Such treachery leaves all my wits confounded;
> And I do not believe even the devil
> Can match this wench's aptitude for evil.
> For her I would have put my hand in fire;
> Who can trust womankind, since she's a liar?
> The best of them excels at machination;
> Their sex was born to be the world's damnation.
> To that deceitful sex, I say farewell,
> And heartily consign them all to hell.

Despite his prophetic vision, Molière lost all the arguments with his better self when he married Armande.

Act Two

THE AGON

V

INTO THE MOUTH OF THE WOLF

L'École des Femmes

as conceived by Molière
as acted by Catherine de Brie
as directed by Louis Jouvet
as acted by Dominique Blanchar
as translated by Richard Wilbur

Molière's sexual-romantic passion is at the heart of the next four major plays and his heart was solely possessed by Armande. She was the object of his yearning; she was the beloved; she occupied the center of his being. She was the one who drove him into despair with her disinterest and reputed lack of sexual response but, after all, he was the man who had lived in a parental mode with her almost from her birth. This ongoing tension created the life force in the four masterpieces he wrote in the middle of his life, a dangerous time for any man. It was this ferocity of feeling that engendered the mature voice of a poet in the theater by impressing primal and personal emotion into the mechanisms of comedy. It is said an actor uses as much adrenalin as a test pilot when he steps out onto the stage which is why they must wish each other "good luck" or "break a leg." The Italian actor, always more emotional, says *"in bocca al lupo"* and that certainly seemed where Molière was heading – into the mouth of the wolf.[1]

Leaving his home church, St. Eustache, as a married man in late February of 1662, the writer-producer-director-actor faced a busy year. The company made many guest appearances; the Italians were actively sharing the theater with them in Paris; and while living with his new ambitious young wife, Molière began writing the perfect role – for Catherine de Brie! Mlle de Brie opened Molière's first great poetic play, *L'École des Femmes (The School for Wives)* in December 1662. She created Agnès, a delightful character and her major starring role for the next twenty-three years. While at the time – and indeed, all through time – Agnès was associated with Armande and the subject is obviously about her relationship with Molière, Agnès was not Armande's role on stage. Catherine had paid her dues, as they say, and when Armande had entered the company she was barely twenty and relatively inexperienced. She had to wait a bit for him to write her a starring role comparable to the starring role she played in his life.

To play opposite Catherine de Brie's Agnès, Molière wrote for himself the role of Arnolphe, the would-be husband. This was the first in a series of "heroic" major roles and was a significant departure from the less complex Sganarelle his audience had come to love. The play is dense and "serious" as a work of comic art. To approach this work as it plays on stage I will turn to an artist in another century, Louis Jouvet, who received international praise for his brilliant interpretation of this play. I had the good fortune to meet this man backstage in Paris where I saw him starring in three of his productions: *Dr. Knock, Madwoman of Chaillot* and *Don Juan*. I am not alone in my admiration for this man's talents: Richard Wilbur, who has delighted us all with his brilliant translations of Molière's work, dedicated his book titled *Molière: Four Comedies* to Jouvet. This renowned French actor and director of the twentieth century proved that time does not weaken the emotional core in the work of a great author and does not dim the laughter of true comedy.

Louis Jouvet spent years of study on this play. Beginning in 1909, he performed the play 675 times until 1951. His final version of the play began in 1936 with an astonishing design by Christian Bérard. This was the production he brought to New York in 1951 where I was fortunate to see Jouvet find again the living essence of Molière and recreate Arnolphe as a vividly alive character more than three centuries after Molière; a feat he was acclaimed for in Paris and which thrilled me nearly twenty years later in New York – two performances that were separated not only by the years of World War II but also by an ocean. Jouvet also left a recording of the role – as well as searing memories for me of being in the presence of a powerful and dedicated actor.

Ramon Fernandez comments that "one of the considerations that differentiate a dramatic masterpiece from a mediocre work in the same form is its *vital* importance to the artist who creates it." (The emphasis is mine.)[2] Remember that between 1659 and 1661, while agonizing over whether to marry Armande or wait for her to grow up – and whether, in a sense, to replace his older goddesses with a new one – he wrote the three plays we looked at briefly in the previous chapter. All three plays deal with frustration and sexual jealousy. But none of them has the personal tone and emotion of *L'École des Femmes* which Molière wrote during his first year of marriage to Armande. Now, after ten months of married life he walks onstage in the middle-class splendor of Arnolphe to answer the question put to him by his friend, Chrysalde:

CHRYSALDE. So, you're resolved to give this girl your hand?
ARNOLPHE. Tomorrow I shall marry her, as planned.[3]

In bocca al lupo!

This dialogue in the opening scene sounds much like a conversation that might have occurred between Molière and his real-life friend, Chapelle, after his little poem about the moss climbing up on the tree. After all, Arnolphe has given himself the title of "Monsieur de la Souche," which translates as "Sir Stump." This is a multi-colored detail that not only links Arnolphe to the willow tree, but shows social ambitions akin to those of Jean-Baptiste Poquelin with his addition of "de Molière" to his name.[4] I'm sure it was the playwright's little in-joke on himself. And on all the similar pretensions of his fellow actors, who tried to raise themselves above the status in which actors were held.

The act 1, scene 1 debate is like *The School for Husbands* in form, but the zest and full-bloodedness Arnolphe radiates comes from another private and far more sexual world. Jouvet, like Molière, feeling this play's message was one of "vital importance," played an Arnolphe convulsed with laughter at the simplemindedness of his ward. He gloats over his success at bringing her up in a "perfect void." The poor dear thinks "children are begotten through the ear." Jouvet used a bawdy Rabelaisian wheeze to indicate being overcome by emotion at the thought, and his thought undeniably included images of possessing such a delicious virgin. One got the overwhelming impression from Jouvet that he knew whereof Arnolphe speaks when he mocks those poor husbands who are cuckolded by clever wives. Jouvet, like Molière, was a famous lover of women. And here we can see how the circles build one upon the other, like a tree's concentric rings: both actors' audiences were well aware of their stars' amorous reputation but Jouvet's audience enjoyed the double joke of knowing about Molière as well.

In his interpretation, Jouvet illuminated the *hubris* of the character with great energy and absolute clarity when insisting that his wife should be dumb, too simple to sin, and should always "say her prayers, love me, spin and sew." His selfishness, his stupidity about human nature and his misjudgment of the intelligence of others, all were vividly presented in the honesty of Jouvet's acting and in the complex understanding he had of rhetorical series and end-stops. Arnolphe goes from self-assured prolixity to speechlessness. Molière's clear intention in the writing is to show us a fool riding for a fall. Both actors, we can be sure, did so with wonderful stage energy and complete belief in the character's own infallibility. Set up as a controlling figure, such

Figure 12. Louis Jouvet as Arnolphe. Rights reserved.

Figure 13. Molière as Arnolphe. Comédie-Française Archives.

Figure 14. Catherine de Brie, the first Agnès. Comédie-Française Archives.

Figure 15. A modern Agnès with Arnolphe. Rights reserved.

a character fuels a mechanism of comedy which is known as the Controller Controlled.

Following a bravura exposition scene of self-congratulation, Arnolphe bangs on the door to his house. Jouvet staged this as an almost balletic scene, with percussive drumming on the doors, with second-story windows banging open and shut, with his recalcitrant servants' heads popping in and out like Henri Bergson's Jack-in-the-box comic technique as it was used on TV's *Laugh-In* years ago, and finishing with burlesque turns which brought blows down on the heads of the wrong people. Then, not only did the door to the house open, but the walls of Christian Bérard's set pivoted outward, opening like a book to disclose an immaculate inner garden with an espaliered vine growing along the garden walls as rigorously trained as the hapless ward enclosed within. Even the flowers were primly standing at attention. Two delicate chandeliers dangled over the space, which was backed by a tall narrow house with a second story window and balcony overlooking Agnès sitting – knitting – in the absolute center of the formal prison yard.

The clamorous chaos of the previous scene is silenced into a pacific quietude as the third scene of act 1 begins:

ARNOLPHE. Are you glad to see me?

AGNÈS.   Oh, yes, Sir; thank the Lord.

ARNOLPHE. I'm glad to see you too, my little ward.
                I take it everything has been all right?

AGNÈS.   Except for the fleas, which bothered me last night.

ARNOLPHE. Well, there'll be someone soon to drive them away.

This was followed by Arnolphe's wheeze or whinny of satisfaction, completely missed by Agnès but not by the public, with whom Jouvet shared his lustful needs. He was sure everyone knew exactly what he was waiting for – and everyone did.

A word here about voice and speech in comedy presented as a reminder that words alone don't get the laughs. We need the intonation and color that are elicited by some emotional sub-strata. Woody Allen is quoted in an interview on the BBC in London about his experience with Diane Keaton, one of the finest of screen comediennes:

It's in her intonation; you can't quantify it easily. When Groucho or Fields or Holliday say something, it's in the ring of their voices, and Diane has that. She's also an interesting woman, savvy about politics, art, culture, and I'm sure this contributes in some unquantifiable way. For the kind of humor the sophisticated

public appreciates you do have to have intelligence. It's never line comedy with
her. It's all character comedy.[5]

When the Parisian audience at the Palais-Royal heard the little scene
between the middle-aged Arnolphe and the innocent Agnès for the first
time, we can assume they heard immediately that Catherine de Brie, as
the sophisticated leading lady for the King's Company, knew how to play
the voice of a girl brought up to be the "perfect void." Onstage, she was
not the same woman she was in life: wife, mother, mistress, actress, etc.
Transformation! As for Dominique Blanchar, Louis Jouvet's Agnès, we
know her choice of a verbal style, made surely at the suggestion of the
director. She pitched her voice to its highest falsetto; her tempo-rhythm
was even and staccato, like the stitches in her knitting. In these first few
lines, the public may have felt that it was a voice so stripped of "sense and
sensibility" she would not be able to maintain it, but character triumphed.
Agnès has a teeny voice because she has a teeny life. This idea allows for
her to drop the pitch later in the play as she turns into a sexual woman,
before Arnolphe and all the rest of us who desire her. Jouvet's voice, in
extreme contrast, was a marvel for its range – from deep and "thrilling"
tones to certain hysterical high pitches when greatly excited. He used an
exaggerated vocal range to parody the "tragic" style and skewer "serious"
drama. He used his voice like a finely-tuned instrument to plumb the
depths of a man absolutely berserk with sexual passion, and at the same
time, murdering comic pretentiousness.

That little tease of a scene – just half a page – concludes with Arnolphe's
short monologue directed at those who are women-of-the-world, bragging
that they "can't match this good and modest ignorance" which he treasures
in his ward. Played by Jouvet in his deepest and most superior tone, it sets
his character up as if he were a pompous banker ready to step on Chaplin's
banana peel. And what trips him up is youth. In the very next scene of this act,
he meets the young lover Horace who confides to Arnolphe, without realizing
who Arnolphe really is, that he, Horace, has fallen in love with:

This girl whose beauty is past telling,
And yonder red-walled mansion is her dwelling.
She's utterly naïve, because a blind
Fool has sequestered her from humankind,
And yet, despite the ignorance in which
He keeps her, she has charms that can bewitch;
She's most engaging, and conveys a sense
Of sweetness against which there is no defense.

But you, perhaps, have seen this star of love
Whose many graces I'm enamored of.
Her name's Agnès.
ARNOLPHE. (*Aside*) Oh, death!

This aside, like many throughout the play, interjects a comedic counterpoint
to the scenic situation with a stab of private emotion. The ringing tenor
voice of a young juvenile – played, of course, by La Grange for Molière –
spins swiftly through the speech end-stopping only with the name "Agnès."
Jouvet, after listening in superior contentment to the description of love by the
young fool, spun front and in a deep melodramatic bell-tolling voice gasped
out, "Oh, death!" This moment, if taken out of this comedy and put into
Corneille, would fit like a glove. It was the dramatic parody and over-the-
top weightiness of moments like this that enraged Molière's enemies in the
"serious art" movement.

The rest of this scene follows turns and variations with the youthful Horace
expressing his ecstatic love for Agnès, interlaced with a barrage of withering
contempt for her keeper. Both subjects are greeted with apoplectic reactions
and wheezing from Arnolphe, who has the actor's tricky job of hiding his
identity from Horace while revealing his true feelings to us. The scene ends
with Arnolphe's decision to question Agnès, to see how far his rival has
proceeded in advancing his love affair.

Before that confrontation, the second scene in act 2 presents us with a
confrontation between Arnolphe and his two bemused servants, who
editorialize hilariously, like a chorus, throughout the play. The master, in a
state of near panic, tries hard to make sure they will keep this young buck
away from his precious Agnès, but it is all to no avail. Don't they speak
French? He bullies them and gets too emotionally entangled and involved in
his explanations. He finally moans an asthmatic aside: "I'm sweating, and
I need some air. / I must calm down: I'll walk around the square." He storms
off to get control of his jealousy but the two peasants continue this farcical
interlude by explicating the difference between what is their understanding
of bourgeois jealousy and their hands-on knowledge of farmyard sex, all
eloquently and scandalously put forth by boy peasant for the education of girl
peasant:

Then grasp this, if you can.
Womankind is, in fact, the soup of man,
And when a man perceives that others wish
To dip their dirty fingers into his dish,
His temper flares, and bursts into a flame.

This Rabelaisian flavor is followed by a soliloquy delivered by Arnolphe whose voice quivers with deep-pitched tragic resonance as he shares with the public a *tirade* about striving hard to control one's emotions – in a not-so-subtle put-down of Corneille:

> A certain Greek presumed once to advise
> The great Augustus, and his words were wise:
> When you are vexed, he said, do not forget,
> Before you act, to say the alphabet …

Jouvet played these lines very slowly, very much as if he were Epictetus himself, trying to wipe off his sweaty discomfort in a large handkerchief as he readied himself to face his fifteen-year old prospective wife. To begin, his low-pitched voice resonated with dignity and logic. His pitch then kept rising on each line until a brief caesura before the final "say the alphabet," which he took plunging to an absolute end-stop on the final syllable. The full audience caught that final "bet" with its reverberating period and instantaneously exploded into a huge laugh. In the French "*dire notre alphabet*," the beginning hard "d" sound, combined with the pushed out "b" and the clickety-clack of the intervening "t" adds an aggressiveness not quite possible in the English.

Emotion seemingly in control, he is ready for the infamous second act tête-à-tête in scene five. Jouvet moved in proud and geometrical patterns around Agnès, her blankness of expression pitted against his infinite, almost uncontrollable, fluidity of facial and bodily gestures.

ARNOLPHE.   The weather's mild.
AGNÈS.   Oh, yes.
ARNOLPHE.   Most pleasant.
AGNÈS.   Indeed!
ARNOLPHE.   What news, my child?
AGNÈS.   The kitten died.
ARNOLPHE.   Too bad, but what of that?
                    All men are mortal, my dear, and so's a cat.

He brings up Horace. Agnès quite innocently tells him the whole story in what is her first long speech in the play, featuring a repetition over and over of how she and Horace bowed to each other, both in the grip of mutual admiration. She says that had night not fallen they might have gone on bowing forever. All this is in the teeny voice. The energy creeps into the high pitches but does not bring them down. It is a virtuoso performance.

As she becomes more and more alive in telling the story about this young man, Arnolphe becomes more and more agitated, until in the middle of the scene, with lyric sweetness but still in those falsetto girlish tones, she says:

> He swore he loved me with a matchless passion,
> And said to me, in the most charming fashion,
> Things which I found incomparably sweet,
> And never tire of hearing him repeat,
> So much do they delight my ear, and start
> I know not what commotion in my heart.

These are among the most famous lines in French poetry, and they once echoed around the mirrored halls of Versailles, where lips puckered into kisses around all the wonderful "ooh" sounds of the French version: "La douceur me chatouille et là-dedans remue / Certain je ne sais quoi dont je suis toute émue."

The "*je ne sais quoi*" ("I know not what") is the hook into the most famous part of the scene as Arnolphe, who knows just what that "I know not what" really is, tries to find out if Horace has been "dipping his dirty fingers in his bowl of soup." After she admits he took her hand to kiss, he presses her to find out what else he might have taken in a scene played by Jouvet with lecherous connotations of maidenheads as did, most likely, Molière as well.

AGNÈS.   I fear that you'll be furious with me.
ARNOLPHE.   No.
AGNÈS.   Yes.
ARNOLPHE.   No, no.
AGNÈS.   Then promise not to be.
ARNOLPHE.   I promise.
AGNÈS.   He took my – oh, you'll have a fit.
ARNOLPHE.   No.
AGNÈS.   Yes.
ARNOLPHE.   No, no. The devil! Out with it!
            What did he take from you?
AGNÈS.   He took …
ARNOLPHE. (*Aside*)   God save me!
AGNÈS.   He took the pretty ribbon that you gave me.
            Indeed, he begged so that I couldn't resist.
ARNOLPHE. (*Taking a deep breath*) Forget the ribbon.

For Agnès' faltering lines, Wilbur substitutes "my" for the French word "*le*" meaning simply "the" but the tempo-rhythm of the scene is similar.

And so Molière (translated by Wilbur) built the scene around the pursuit of that little liquid "*le*" (or that melting "my") with staccato speech and agonizing pauses leading toward the major reversal when she confesses that this infamous "*le*" is not her virginity but her ribbon, whereupon Arnolphe's suffering of the damned recedes into his muttered "Forget the ribbon." In French or English, with the drops of "*le*" dripping into Arnolphe's brain, or the yummy "my" with its close-mouthed *m* opening wide into the diphthong formed by *y*, we are given a comedy of character floating on sexual passion and dipping into silliness. It is wonderful theater, as alive today as in 1662 or 1936 or 1951 or, for that matter, as it will be for years to come.

The teenage tickle in her "I know not what" is counterpointed in the excruciatingly comic second scene in act 3, when Arnolphe berates Agnès with an outrageous two-page lecture on the extreme beneficence of his taking her hand in marriage on this very night, done only to save her from falling into eternal sin. This speech starts by reminding her of the many reasons she has to be grateful:

> In raising you, a humble peasant lass,
> To be a matron of the middle class
> To share the bed and the connubial bliss
> Of one who's shunned the married state till this,
> Withholding from a charming score or two
> The honor which he now bestows on you.

The long peroration veers into comedic superiority when it culminates with Arnolphe trumpeting "Yours is the weaker sex, please realize; / It is the beard in which all power lies …" He then rants, in a thunderous rage filled with fire and brimstone, dire warnings that:

> … all misbehaving wives shall dwell
> In ever-boiling cauldrons down in Hell.
> These are no idle lessons which I impart,
> And you'll do well to get them all by heart.
> Your soul, if you observe them, and abjure
> Flirtation, will be lily-white and pure;
> But deviate from honor, and your soul
> Will forthwith grow as vile and black as coal;
> All will abhor you as a thing of evil,
> Till one day you'll be taken by the Devil,
> And Hell's eternal fire is where he'll send you—

One can just imagine the trio who might be watching in the wings as Catherine sat on stage listening to her stage partner expatiate on fidelity: Madeleine, listening to her lover of twenty years; the mysterious Mlle Du Parc, smiling like the *Mona Lisa*; the new bride, Armande, watching a fictional character obviously making fun of her own upbringing and courtship. "How will this fadge?" as Viola says about the complications of love's entanglements in *Twelfth Night*. It seemed to have "fadged" very well because the women all stayed happily with the company and the play has been a living work of dramatic art in many countries and many languages for over three centuries.

After Arnolphe gives his hell-fire sermon, he demands that his much desired pretty ward, Agnès, recite from the little book, *Maximes de Marriage* (*Duties of a Married Woman*), which are surely the silliest lines ever included in a major work of dramatic art. Dominique Blanchar, Jouvet's Agnès, recited all ten maxims – six lines apiece – in her completely lifeless, teeny-tiny squeak of a voice, with the scenic energy maintained by the physical reactions of Jouvet prowling around the convent-dressed little girl. A very daring theatrical decision to take away from the actress her natural desire to express herself in every line and word she speaks, but she, like Agnès, complied with the "beard" at this point in the play. Judy Holliday, famous for her portrayal of Billie Dawn in *Born Yesterday*, used a similar technique to equal success in her immortal line "Why don't you take your mind off, and give something else a chance to work?" Agnès, chanting like a comic Sarah Bernhardt, says over and over refrains like this:

It is not good for wives
To go on gay excursions,
Picnics, or country drives.
In all such light diversions
No matter who's the host,
The husbands pay the most.

Even the mighty "beard" cannot stand any more of this drivel. He cuts her off and leaves her to recite the rest of the book to herself as she waits obediently for the notary that is coming to marry them. In contrast with these rigid rules and regulations satirizing marriage, the "I know not what" of act 2 hinted at the tickle of "love" for the adolescent girl. In act 5, the tickle becomes love with a capital *L*, waxing full in the body and voice of a liberated and disobedient woman.

Act 5 contains the first great dramatic scene in Molière, the first brutal expression of the devil in the flesh. And the ending for the hero is wrenchingly far from marriage. It is brought about by the girl's absolute will to be married to a virile young male, and to have nothing to do with this wretched old man possessed by desire. The climactic scene takes place at night, when Arnolphe, having learned of his ward's plot to elope, swathes himself melodramatically in a black cloak hiding his face, and fools the girl into coming away with him. In a reversal from *The School for Husbands* when it is the young ward cloaked in disguise, this time it is the young ward who is deceived. She thinks the mysterious visitor is Horace's trusted confidant. Triumphant, he foolishly whips back his cloak and changes back to his real voice. Agnès sees it is Arnolphe – and screams in horror!! The sexual woman of passion emerging from within the coolly honest and innocent girl will not give up her young man. She declares that all she wants is to marry Horace. She cannot understand why Arnolphe is cross with her. Hasn't he, her loving guardian, told her often that marriage was absolutely necessary to avoid the fires of hell?

The great misunderstanding between them is the confusion between the Father/Caretaker and the Father/Lover. They cannot be the same, and she is deeply shocked when he doesn't accept the fact that she loves the other man and not him:

> ARNOLPHE. You don't, I take it, love me.
> AGNÈS.   Love you?
> ARNOLPHE.   Yes.
> AGNÈS.   Alas, I don't.
> ARNOLPHE.   You *don't?*
> AGNÈS.   Would you have me lie?
> ARNOLPHE. Why don't you love me, hussy? Tell me why!

He reminds her again of his nurturing care of her from infancy. She admits she is obligated for that, but as her voice drops toward womanhood she confronts him directly:

> Do you fancy that I'm blind to what you've done,
> And cannot see that I'm a simpleton?
> Oh, it humiliates me; I revolt
> Against the shame of being such a dolt.

The paradox of Arnolphe is painfully illuminated in this scene. He says he loves her, but his concern is only for himself and his loss. He sees the girl as the robber of his happiness and her words protesting injustice done to her only rouse a fury in him. In a state of barely controlled rage, he protests he wants to "beat her soundly," "to box her ears." She calmly says "go ahead and beat me if you desire." The shock of her unflinching courage startles him, and brings him first to the bewildered introspection of self-questioning, erupting finally into an ecstatic Q.E.D. of accusation.

> ARNOLPHE. (*Aside*) How strange love is! How strange that men, from such
> Perfidious beings will endure so much!
> Women, as all men know, are frailly wrought:
> They're foolish and illogical in thought,
> Their souls are weak, their characters bad,
> There's nothing quite so silly, quite so mad,
> So faithless; yet, despite these sorry features,
> What won't we do to please the wretched creatures?

Jouvet played the first lines of the preceding speech with each word in a long sustained vowel, very much to himself, as if overwhelmed by the discovery of a deep truth. Then he slowly built each succeeding line with sustained and rising intonations until he stuns us with the last words, "*ces animaux-là*" ("those animals there"). Wilbur has turned the last words to "creatures," which seems a little tamer, a little more fairy-tale-like, in the mind – but those two "tch" sounds in "wretched creatures," offer a wonderful chewing, chomping sound to mash down on – like a guillotine.

Molière's rhetorical structure is the same as in his earlier speech about the alphabet. He pulls us into his deeply felt chauvinistic point of view, then reverses it completely as he speaks of all the qualities of femaleness being summed up in the unexpected phrase, "*ces animaux-là*" ("those wretched creatures"). This final summary, his crowning compulsion, which overturns his litany of feminine weaknesses, triggers his own real feelings of sexual vulnerability, and he launches into a final desperate appeal:

> You can, my little beauty, if you'll but try. (*That is, you could love me if you tried.*)

Molière writes, "Il fait un soupir" ("He sighs"), and Jouvet uses his wheeze before proceeding with the final appeal for love:

> Just listen to that deep and yearning sigh!
> Look at my haggard face! See how it suffers!
> Reject that puppy, and the love he offers:
> He must have cast a spell on you; with me,
> You'll be far happier, I guarantee.
> I know that clothes and jewels are your passion;
> Don't worry: you shall always be in fashion.
> I'll pet you night and day; you shall be showered

> With kisses; you'll be hugged, caressed, devoured.
> And you shall have your wish in every way.
> I'll say no more; what further could I say?
> (*Aside*) Lord, what extremes desire will drive us to!

Molière's text in French is more explicitly sexual:

> Sans cesse, nuit et jour, je te caresserai,
> Je te bouchonnerai, baiserai, mangerai.

The literal sense, then, is that "night and day" he will "caress her, rub her down like a horse, kiss her, eat her."[6] Not only are the verbs stronger in the French, but their sounds occupy the full mouth, moving from front to back, with the guttural *r* scraping passion up from the gut, as it rolls the words out in classic French hauteur. The hissing *s*, the hard *k*, the dammed-up *b*, all give the actor a wonderful palette of expression, ending with the chomping down felt in saying the word "*mangerai*." But the *coup de grâce* is the repeated growl of the Gallic rolled *r* – seeming almost to come from the groin – that is generated by the future tense in French but not rendered in the more genteel English. Then, knowing that he has nothing else to say, he goes on anyway and completely falls apart, asking her if she wants him to cry, to beat himself, to tear out half his hair, to kill himself. He declares he will do it all to prove his love for her.

By this time Jouvet is on his knees sobbing. But is he tragically persuasive? After all, he did just speak about tearing out "half his hair." Evidently Talma, the great nineteenth-century actor, was told he could not make Arnolphe a noble tragic hero so long as he had this line which created an image of Arnolphe with half a head of hair competing against the thick blond curls of Horace. In a submissive posture, Arnolphe hears her cool retort:

> Somehow, your lengthy speeches fail to move me.
> Horace, in two words, could be more engaging.

Ice water freezes the scene, and Arnolphe instantly recovers to resume his role as a blustery tyrant who is soon totally defeated not only by Agnès' indifference but by the playwright who finishes him off with the miraculous return of her real father. This appearance finally leaves the protagonist speechless, his lust denied by real fatherhood, with nothing to say for himself but "Ouf!" Jouvet/ Arnolphe spun around and, using his wheeze planted throughout the play to get laughs, he exited to great applause. Which, for any actor, be he Molière or Jouvet, may somewhat ease the pain of unrequited love. The actor escapes that wolf.

VI

"GO SADDLE YON BRAYING ASS!"

La Critique de l'École des Femmes
as translated by Morris Bishop

L'Impromptu de Versailles
as translated and adapted by Angela Paton
as translated by Albert Bermel

The critic is a part of every artist's life that cannot be ignored. Most actors memorize their best reviews; some memorize their worst reviews and will recite them with blood vessels swelling and much editorial comment. The desire to answer back is maddeningly strong. For Molière the nasty criticism grew louder and more personal as references to his marriage mounted and even charges of incest were openly discussed. Molière answered with fighting words in the most public way at his disposal: by writing the two short plays discussed in this chapter. His first attack is indirect.

After the production of *L'École des Femmes*, which may have been the greatest success of the seventeenth century, controversies over the play swirled around the city and the court. After the run of performances in theaters and in the homes of the aristocracy during the winter season, Molière decided to bring back the play accompanied with a one-act called *La Critique de l'École des Femmes* (*The Critique of the School for Wives*), which was performed following the five-act play starting in June of 1663.[1]

For this piece he wrote his first role for Armande. She played the supporting role of Élise opposite Mlle Béjart and Mlle Du Parc. As a shrewd producer, Molière kept his star, Catherine de Brie, in the role of Agnès.[2] She did not appear in the play that parodied the critical comments on her role. Armande, who must have been pregnant by this time – she gave birth to their first child in January of 1664 – joined the famous company on stage for the first time as a full member. She played in the following little scene with Madeleine Béjart, her mother and former mistress of her husband. She did not have the voice or the character of Agnès; her Élise is of a more deliciously ironic and coquettish nature, who appears to have resembled Armande in real life:

URANIE (*Mlle Béjart*). How's this, my dear cousin. No one has come to call?
ÉLISE   (*Mlle Molière*). Not a soul.
URANIE. Really, it's surprising that we've both been alone all day.
ÉLISE. I'm surprised too, cousin Uranie. This is hardly our custom. Your house, thank God, is the accepted refuge of all loafers of the court.
URANIE. Well, cousin Élise, intellectuals love solitude.
ÉLISE. Thanks for the compliment but you know I'm hardly an intellectual.[3]

They proceed to bring up examples of all the "bores" they have to put up with, including hilarious descriptions of various snobbish ladies and foppish courtiers. Élise describes the character to be played by the glamorous and acrobatic Mlle Du Parc, who in a few minutes will enter trying to live up to this description:

… she's the most affected person on earth. Her whole body seems to be loose jointed; her hips and shoulders and head all seem to be moved by springs. She affects a languishing, simpering tone of voice and she pouts to make her mouth look littler and she rolls her eyes to make them look bigger.

Mlle Du Parc had an elegant demeanor and a dancer's body, but she was obviously well able to play opposite body types.

Later in the gossip session, Armande, as Élise, describes the character of her husband, Molière, who is the writer/subject hidden behind the character Dorante. When the two of them are alone on stage, Armande/Élise says to Mlle Béjart/Uranie:

You know what he is like, and how he is too lazy to keep a conversation going. She had invited him to supper to play the "wit" and he never seemed so dull, among half a dozen people whom she'd asked to hear him perform; they were staring at him wide-eyed as if he weren't an ordinary human being. They all thought he was there to amuse the company and every word he uttered was bound to be extraordinary … but he fooled them all by keeping silent.

Does this sound like the yearning green moss longing to cling to the heights of the willow tree? No, but it does sound like others who talked about Molière in society, and it also signals the beginnings of her future starring role, Célimène and her famous put-downs of everyone in *Le Misanthrope*. However, there's no sense yet of the cruelties of Célimène in *Le Misanthrope* and later of Angélique in *George Dandin*. Élise's voice and stage manner tend toward naturalness and intelligence. She is set against anyone who acts and speaks as if entrapped by rigid and mechanical ways of acting and thinking.

The three actresses have a hilarious time in pursuit of the infamous "*le*" which teeters and dances around the idea of sex. Uranie (Mlle Béjart) maintains, with heavy irony, that the "*le*" may actually just refer to the ribbon. Climène (Mlle Du Parc) is apoplectic and squeaks that that "*le*" is "furiously scandalizing" because she, and everyone else, recognizes that the "*le*" refers to a particular part of the female anatomy. Élise (Armande) smiles sweetly as she mischievously argues with the prude, but only in order to prolong the sexual imbroglio:

ÉLISE.   (*To Uranie*) You're quite wrong to defend that "*le*."
CLIMÈNE.   It has the most intolerable lubricity.
ÉLISE.   What was that word, Madame?
CLIMÈNE   Lubricity, Madame.
ÉLISE.   Oh, my God. Lubricity. I don't know what that means, but it sounds
              perfectly lovely.

No wonder Molière loved her. He had, I'm sure, a great time camping around in this little play as another Marquis, one flowing from his former gyrating "Marquis" de Mascarille, which reminds the public and the king about his past success in *Les Précieuses Ridicules*. His ardent and articulate spokesperson in the piece was Dorante, played by Brécourt.[1] His rivals would attack him at their peril!

But they did. The attacks offstage turned more mean-spirited and even more vicious. They became personal; songs were sung about his impotence and about his age in comparison to his wife's youth. I give two examples of the slurs directed against him. Racine wrote to an abbot (italics mine):

Montfleury (*the actor at the Hôtel de Bourgogne previously quoted as mocking Molière's tragic style*) has made a petition against Molière and sent it to the King. He accuses him of having married his daughter, having formerly slept with the mother.[5]

A second example came from the once friendly Prince de Conti, proclaiming that there was nothing more shocking than the language heard throughout *L'École des Femmes*.[6]

The church stirred ominously, and his own actors, in alarm, urged Molière to retaliate. And he did. While the two "School" plays were performing at the Palais-Royal in the spring and into the summer, he wrote a new piece to be presented in his own defense. In October 1663, when the king wanted a performance of *Dom Garcie de Navarre* brought out to Versailles, Molière had a play in hand called *L'Impromptu de Versailles* (*Rehearsal at Versailles*), a backstage play with all the company appearing as themselves. *L'Impromptu de Versailles* was shown before the king as he sat surrounded by his court, the birthplace of most of the sniping.

What the king was treated to, after the lifeless bombast of *Dom Garcie*, was a view of Molière and his four goddesses in rehearsal. The goddesses become highly competitive actresses, and each woman is given sharp one-liners that only add to Molière's directorial frustration. What follows is a brief slice of that backstage life as adapted by Angela Paton – a denizen of the backstage world for many uproarious years – as a prologue to our production of "Molière, With Love"[7] at the University of Washington:

MOLIÈRE.	Come, ladies and gentlemen! We're wasting time. Let's rehearse.
MLLE MOLIÈRE.	Rehearse what? We don't know any lines.
MLLE BÉJART.	Can't we just improvise? It's an impromptu, after all.
MOLIÈRE.	You know the situation. If you go up just …
MLLE DU PARC.	This impromptu is going to need a lot of prompting.
MLLE BÉJART.	Of course, you're not worried about going up. You wrote the damn thing.
MOLIÈRE.	For God's sake, the piece is in prose not verse.
ALL THE WOMEN.	Prose is worse than verse.
MLLE MOLIÈRE.	You know what I think? I think you should have written a one-man show for yourself.
MOLIÈRE.	Shut up, my little wifey-poo. You're about as useful as a bedbug.
MLLE MOLIÈRE.	Oh thanks, my great big chubby hubby. Eighteen months ago you wouldn't have talked to me like that.
MOLIÈRE.	Please be quiet.
MLLE DU PARC.	Be careful, dear. Remember, you've got understudies.
MLLE MOLIÈRE.	Isn't it strange how a little ceremony can erase all the good qualities in a man? A husband looks at you different than a lover.
MOLIÈRE.	Different-ly!
MLLE DU PARC.	That's why we never married him.
MLLE DE BRIE.	He's a great lover but my sweet de Brie is a nicer husband.
DE BRIE AND GROS-RENÉ.	Please, ladies. There are gentlemen present.
MLLE DU PARC.	Where?
MLLE DE BRIE.	All I see is a bunch of actors. (*Hilarious female laughter*)

MOLIÈRE.	People, people, let's get started. If you don't know the lines, just remember who you are. If you get lost, improvise! My dear, sweet, charming little wife ...
MLLE DE BRIE.	Oooh, you're making me jealous!
MOLIÈRE.	... just play the scene as charming-ly as you did in *School for Wives* and you'll be great.
MLLE MOLIÈRE.	I wasn't in that play. Remember?
MOLIÈRE.	Right. Big mistake. I mean as you did in *The Critique*. Well, let's take it from the opening with the entrance of the two marquises. Out of the way everybody. (*General dismay*) Marquises need lots of space. So enter like this, on "La, la, la, la, la, la."

Molière's work as a director centered on observation about character and type, about private ego and public roles in society and about intonations, rhetoric and "ways of walking." He gave line readings and made his actors imitate him. Horrors! But remember: His world was a monarchy; Democracy and the Bill of Rights had not given actors the creative voice they lay claim to now. Molière himself bowed to the aristocratic hierarchy by giving the king an important offstage presence as the motivator and director of the onstage action.

Obviously King Louis XIV did not agree with the critics. He became even more involved in the life of Armande and Jean-Baptiste as the godfather of their first son in February 1664. He chose to side with the man and the artist who wrote and spoke the following credo, near the end of *L'Impromptu de Versailles*. This short play is most famous for a speech Molière makes to his company about the spurious attacks he was suffering. Here is Albert Bermel's translation of Molière's speech, from Bermel's more complete version of the play:

They can say the very worst things about my plays; I don't mind. They can take my plays and turn them inside out like costumes for their stage; they can try and profit from whatever good things they find in them and from my modest success; I give my consent. They need the material, and I'm only too happy to contribute to their keep, provided they are happy with what I grant them. But courtesy has its limits; there are some things that don't amuse either spectators or the people being mocked. I willingly offer up my plays, my face, my gestures, my words, my tone of voice. I sacrifice my tricks of the trade for them to use as they will. I have no objections to whatever they take, as long as the audience likes it. But in yielding all this to them, I reserve the rest as my own property. They must be fair and not accuse me of moral or religious delinquency, as they have done in the past – and that is the only retaliation they shall have from me.[8]

It's a little wordier than John Barrymore's famous put-down when he shouted "go saddle yon braying ass" to a member in his audience who was disrupting the scene, but many a celebrity today would find these words useful. After this one-act about mounting a one-act, he finds more subtle ways of dealing with the gossip. He writes a series of great plays about liars, hypocrites and credulous fools. He never spoke of these matters directly again, even though the attacks never stopped. However, with Molière, nothing is ever as simple as it seems, and it's likely that he had already been working on *Tartuffe*, creating a monster of vanity, lust and hypocrisy, whose dark soul would release some of the anger in Molière's heart.

VII

ENTRANCES...

Le Tartuffe; ou, L'Imposteur

as conceived by Molière
as directed by Ariane Mnouchkine
as translated by Richard Wilbur
as directed by Robert W. Goldsby
as acted by Ron Leibman

Entrances are of extreme importance in the structure of a performance. The actor and the director join together to search for the right note to begin the stage life of a character. The Greeks and *Commedia* employed masks that left no doubt – when combined with gestural body language – as to the immediate impression their entrances would make upon an audience. In later theater, the means employed are more subtle, more subliminal, more suggestive. The entrance is the first note in the polarity of the whole play that will be remembered, perhaps subconsciously, when the character's journey is completed at the end of the play.

Le Tartuffe; ou, L'Imposteur, Molière's first psychological thriller, offers the possibility of several brilliant entrances, and we submit three "case studies" to illuminate "how" these moments became *coups de théâtre* in three different productions: Molière's own, as reported by contemporaries; my production at the Los Angeles Theater Center, in which Ron Leibman created an unforgettable portrait of the quintessential hypocrite; and Ariane Mnouchkine's prescient political interpretation for the stage as experienced by the audience in which I participated.

Here is how Ramon Fernandez, in his *La vie de Molière,* describes the first entrance in 1664 of the lusting religious imposter, Tartuffe. In the play that bears his name, he entered the enormous space designed to accommodate the hordes of singers and dancers in the huge festival for the king called *Les Plaisirs de l'Île Enchantée (The Pleasures of the Enchanted Island):*

> On May 12, in the midst of all this gold and splendor, by the blaze of torches and the blaze of jewels in this ambient atmosphere of artifice and eroticism, a black

clad man appeared on the stage and in a muffled voice delivered the lines that were to dumbfound the age.[1]

And here are the words as translated by Richard Wilbur, spoken by Tartuffe to his offstage servant, after he observes the voluptuous figure of Dorine, the maid servant of the house:

Hang up my hair shirt, put my scourge in place.[2]

If we imagine the stage of the festival – or look carefully at a drawing of the stage – we can see that the corpulent character actor Du Croisy, who played Tartuffe, had a long, long cross of at least 30 feet before getting to Dorine, who has just hidden the apoplectic son, Damis, in the out-of-place (in the king's gardens) middle-class clothes closet. The closet would most likely have been set in the middle of the vast Versailles festival stage. How Molière staged this long entrance we don't know, but the length of time it would have taken the rotund actor to reach Dorine would have been significant. The actor must have filled that time with some kind of compelling action – heavy breathing, physical discomfort? In the warp of time it might be useful to describe two other entrances to mark how differently one can interpret Molière but how much he remains, nevertheless, in control of both the situation and the character.

Ron Leibman made his entrance as Tartuffe in the Los Angeles Theater Center production of Richard Wilbur's translation that was directed by the author in 1986. The brilliant light on the parquet floor of the ramped stage dimmed, and the focus shifted from Dorine at the door of the isolated armoire upcenter – into which we had just watched an outraged Damis cram himself in order to overhear Tartuffe's lecherous pursuits. The audience's gaze was pulled to a black space downstage left where a section of the orchestra pit opened. Solemn, quasi-funereal music (composed specifically for the entrance) faded up. Tartuffe came up a stair in his dirty white monkish cloak, hunched over a chicken bone. Seeing nothing but his food and feeling nothing but the pleasure of gnawing at the bone, he slowly rose out of the darkness. Suddenly he saw Dorine in the shadows upstage and with the quickness of an animal, he crouched, turned, threw the bone back into the hole, grabbed the Bible he wore chained to his belt, and for Dorine's benefit, loudly spoke the famous first line of drama's most famous hypocrite, following it with instructions to his unseen servants under the stage to tell anyone who asks that he is going to prison to console the wretched. Dorine crossed directly downstage center to tell the audience, "Dear God, what affectation, what a fake." Leibman assumed a pious shuffle, and, head bowed as if in prayer, he demurely came toward her, eyes on the floor, muttering "You wished to see me?" The music ended; the lights restored, he lifted his head to look at her. The actor's upper body recoiled sharply; his arm held the Bible out as if warding off the devil; his face turned to the public with a horrible grimace. Then he spun round and his other hand held a huge white handkerchief which he patted in place to cover her substantial bosom. As he felt her breasts, he declaimed in horror that the sight of her bosom could undermine his soul. The contrast between the touch and the words provoked her laughing response:

> Your soul, it seems, has very little defenses,
> And flesh makes quite an impact on your senses.
> It's strange that you're so easily excited;
> My own desires are not so soon ignited,
> And if I saw you naked as a beast,
> Not all your hide would tempt me in the least.

Leibman's reaction was indescribable – and very funny.

Ten years later, Ariane Mnouchkine, the extraordinary director of Le Théâtre du Soleil, a world-renowned theater based in an old munitions warehouse in Vincennes near Paris, put a different world on stage, not Christian but Islamic, and not comedic but dramatic. When Tartuffe finally makes his first appearance in act 3, he came on, not alone, but with a sinister group of men, all dressed and coifed in the same beards and gowns, much like the ones we see today in countless stories about wars in the Middle East. The entrance made clear that this "cell" was here to take over the happy community of women and children, and that they were completely and literally terrifying all the people in the family compound. Their aim was apparent, as Olivier Schmitt explained in *Le Monde*:

> Tartuffe and his followers are all here to gain their paradise, Hell, and are playing
> as virtuosos of corruption, intrigue, plotting against this community's domestic
> tranquility.[3]

While these three "entrances" of Tartuffe in Versailles, Los Angeles and Vincennes were made in very different times and places, and each was very different in style, design and acting, they all occur almost half way through this famous play. The audience has been waiting to see Tartuffe from the opening lines of the first act; but the hypocrite only enters after we know all the other principals in the family. Highly unusual for a title character to be so delayed, but further inquiry into the core of the play and its productions accounts for the dramatic choice.

If we look at the given circumstances of each of the three productions here representing Molière's ongoing stage-life over the centuries, we find that they converge on the mask of religion over the lust of the male. In the "School" plays, the leading middle-aged male is openly lustful and desperately in love with the young girl. No such love in this play: the two young lovers, who take over act 2 in the full-length version of the play, are back in the grip of those silly infatuations that are characteristic of some hot-headed juveniles and simpering ingénues; and the leading character is a man who will try to get what he wants sexually if it takes deceit, theft or rape. An understanding of this play may well be found in the fury Molière felt when he was accused of incest by members of the church and supposed friends among rival actors and playwrights. They are the real sinners: hypocrites hiding their own human cravings behind self-righteous piety, and wreaking havoc on Molière's family as well as on the larger society.

Any production of *Le Tartuffe* opens – i.e., the play's "entrance" – with a domestic picture of a contented and happy family whose main problem is a puritanical grandmother and a stubborn father turning to religion to ease his mid-life crisis; it comes to an end with the whole family huddled together in terror, caught between a "clerical" figure and a glorious messenger from the Sun King himself. *Le Tartuffe* is really about a family in peril, not a play about an old comic type lusting after a luscious girl, even if the title role is played by Du Croisy, who played major comic support roles in Molière's troupe for thirty years, and the luscious young wife is played by Armande married to Orgon played by Armande's real-life husband Molière. Thus the family unit is the central and most important character – both offstage and on. The play establishes Tartuffe's effect on them in his absence, before he enters late in the play.

Molière, who acted the doting and duped husband opposite Armande, had at the time been a family man for only three months, since February 1664, when the king himself served as godfather to their first son, Louis, in the Church of St. Eustache. By this act the king clearly sided with Molière in the scandals surrounding Armande's birth and protected their first-born son's legitimacy. In May of this same year the recent mother played in her first starring roles for the company in the sensational festival, *The Pleasures of the Enchanted Island*. She appeared first as the Princess d'Élide with great success – in a lush gown of lace and silver – carrying on her slim shoulders an enormous spectacle-play described as a "gallant comedy mixed with music and balletic entrances." She sang and danced with grace and skill. Four days later she appeared in *Le Tartuffe* as Elmire: the new wife of an obsessive husband.

This time she was costumed, at the insistence of Molière, in a simple dress of his favorite color – green – instead of the glittery clothes in which the princess was costumed. Clothes were of great importance to this young actress. Still, silver or green, she was the leading actress in both plays and it is her slender and piquant beauty that arouses Tartuffe's lust. Apparently it did the same for many young lords of the court, who made no effort to hide their infatuation.

Our stage in Los Angeles was nothing like the one in Versailles. In Karl Eigsti's design we defined the stage as an interior with two period doorways downstage right and left, made of very strongly detailed and heavy pieces. The stage was raked and covered with parquet, making an acting space that rested on top of old theater stuff from ancient stages vaguely visible underneath the seventeenth-century polished floor. Downstage was a large beautifully painted period design, an oval scene of rococo splendor on a dimensionally molded flat used as a pre-show curtain to mask part of the upstage area.

To the accompaniment of bright and brilliant music composed by Robert MacDougall,[1] the players entered individually, circling below the screening flat, waving at the public and to each other. The stage was filled with long curving moves, brilliantly colored costumes and the happy salutations of the smiling, laughing actors who flowed upstage as the scenic curtain piece was pulled smoothly up and turned into the interior ceiling of the set, at which point in time the small family froze far up center for an instant "portrait of a Functional Family." The tight, formal pose in painterly lighting quickly broke up, and the group moved downstage to face the severely dressed grandmother, Madame Pernelle.

Elmire, as the new young wife of Madame Pernelle's son, Orgon, has only three lines in the ten-minute argument carried on by others in the family. Dorine, originally played by Madeleine Béjart, speaks out as the dominant voice opposing the grandmother, played by Madeleine's older brother, the venerable Louis Béjart, due to retire the following year. A close-knit theater family initiates this intense debate between Puritanism and Moderation. Safe to begin such a play with Madeleine Béjart, the troupe's most famous actress, controlling the scene, and of course it fits the circumstances of family protocol: a new wife is not likely to play a dominant role against her mother-in-law, especially if the mother-in-law is played by her real-life uncle. The subject of the heated argument and powerful rhetoric is of course Tartuffe, the newly adopted member of the family whom Orgon, the "head of the household," has taken into the home to instill Christian virtues by his presence and his teachings. By Christian, what is understood is the Christianity expounded by the "Society of the Holy Sacrament," a tyrannical, fundamentalist Catholic sect in Molière's time – who were probably the ones behind the scurrilous accusations of incest being directed at him. Their view of the world – a world constantly suffering the cruelty and strife of warring religious doctrines – was as absolute as the more current Taliban. The argument that divides the generations within the family is comprised of moderation opposing zealous Puritanism. The illuminating conclusion of this first scene comes when Mme Pernelle, who has been angrily preaching Christian virtue, turns suddenly on her mute servant, Flipote, and smacks her senseless:

> Wake up, don't stand there gaping into space.
> I'll slap some sense into that stupid face.
> Move, move, you slut.

One cannot but ask, what would Jesus say to this kind of virtue? Would he claim such people as his disciples? Neither Armande, nor her character, Elmire, would want to get into such a dispute, and the writer wisely kept his new star in the background during this first act.

With Ariane Mnouchkine's stage production, as with all her work, we were presented with a surprisingly opposite concept. Even before the performance the conventions were countered; the actors made up in a public space, members of the audience moving noisily in and around them as the performers all prepared for the opening scene. With our Mr. Leibman insisting on screening off his make-up space from the other actors by having curtains pulled around him in the men's dressing room – which itself was buried in the bowels of a former bank building replete with vaults – we had a solitary artist preparing in silence for his individual performance. At Vincennes, one would never have picked out Mnouchkine's Tartuffe because there were many men all dressed in black and all bearded in much the same way.

Mnouchkine's company opened their performance in a huge sunny communal courtyard enclosed by high walls and filled with the many women living in the compound. They were working at daily chores, laughing and singing. Behind them was a large iron gate – decorated with tufts of fresh flowers from the southern Mediterranean shore – in the center of a stucco wall, the sandy color of cities and deserts across North Africa. There was an atmosphere of feminine softness and sisterhood, all controlled by a truculent Dorine. Some reviewers thought it reminiscent of a feminist Eden. All the women were happy at the arrival of a peddler playing music and with many fruits for sale. Then Mme Pernelle arrived totally covered in black, her hair hidden, her eyes hostile. She was accompanied by two slumped and beaten female forms totally shrouded in black burkas, as if for burial. This vicious grandmother/crone promptly browbeat the community of women for their frivolity. The mood shifted; their daily tasks and joyful behavior had been tainted; and after her brutal treatment of her two followers, she left us with a sense that we were watching a vulture picking at her prey.

The next entrance in the play is that of the husband and head of the family, Orgon. How Molière would have staged his own first appearance as Orgon is not ours to know. We do know the play came almost at the end of the festival, and had been preceded by some astonishing events. The audience had watched the dazzling debut of Armande as a mythical princess in a play in which, ironically, Molière's stage lover was Madeleine; they had seen revivals of two other plays by Molière; they had watched teams of horses galloping; troops of dancers dancing; and on the third day just before *Tartuffe* opened, the audience was seated before an artificial lake where three huge artificial whales floated with Molière, Mlle Du Parc and Mlle de Brie sitting on top of them. A huge rock in the lake opened and out came a ballet with demons and dwarfs, and then everything blew up with fireworks. We can surmise that his audience, after so many hours of such hyped-up entertainment, would greet their favorite actor with good humor and settle down to watch him give them some good laughs playing another "fool." He probably went right to it. He surely didn't need any kind of preparation or spectacle. He probably just came in, sat down, and started. Bang!

In Los Angeles, our theater was in a depressed area of the city and we needed some spectacle to take us away from the rigors of downtown Spring Street. For our Orgon, we took almost a minute of stage time, accompanied by "processional music," for a magnanimous Tom Rosqui to enter upstage center and promenade to down center, saluting his servants, waving to invisible family offstage, flinging his hat to one flunky and his gloves to another, as he regally and blissfully arrived home after two days away in the country. Our Orgon, a healthy, self-satisfied baby like Argan in the later *Imaginary Invalid*, was happy to be back in his own home like a king in his castle. He came to rest down center, where he gave his remaining outdoor clothing to waiting servants. When the music then stopped, a scene of wildly criss-crossing purposes began in which a "fool" is so extremely foolish as to border on insanity. The dialog in all three productions shares the same concerns as written long ago by the actor who had originally played the character and just came on and started talking:

ORGON. Has all been well, these two days I've been gone?
　　　　How are the family? What's been going on?
DORINE. Your wife two days ago had a bad fever,
　　　　And a fierce headache which refused to leave her.
ORGON. Ah. And Tartuffe?
DORINE. 　　Tartuffe? Why, he's round and red,
　　　　Bursting with health, and excellently fed.

ORGON. Poor fellow!

DORINE. That night the mistress was unable
To take a single bite at the dinner table.
Her headache pains, she said, were simply hellish.

ORGON. Ah. And Tartuffe?

DORINE.   He ate his meal with relish,
And zealously devoured in her presence
A leg of mutton and a brace of pheasants.

ORGON. Poor fellow!

This same block of repetitive question and answer goes on *two more times*, which is very long indeed for a repetitive gag. It therefore has considerable weight. Indeed, it defines the illogic of a person who is rigid and absolutely fixed in his obsession. It is not easy to act because it seems mechanical, but it is the first action of a father who will later threaten to dismember his son when faced with a truth about his "religious" guide. Obviously in our work in Los Angeles the emphasis was on the individual actor, and the style and atmosphere were, in a word, theatrical. And this sunny, everyday theatricality was presented in vivid contrast to the later skulking entrance of Tartuffe, as well as to the magisterial entrance of the King's Messenger at the end of the play. All were directed to set off the presence of the individual actor in each of their roles.

Mnouchkine's Orgon, with black beard and fez, made his entrance swathed in a long black coat. We saw a man with his macho superiority absolutely established in the submissive female household. He lay down in oriental fashion as though he were a Pasha in his harem, while Dorine took off his shoes. He eased himself into his favorite obsession: the religious life and Tartuffe as its messenger. This was a serious person; this was the man of fundamentalism; this was a man who thought he loved God in the person of a man. Whether it is Christian or Jewish or Islamic is not the point. A fanatic is a fanatic. "Ha. Et Tartuffe? ... pauvre homme." Not a comic scene. This was a very dangerous place for human beings.

In France, Tartuffe – like Hamlet in English – has been played by all the great actors. A great play and a great role can be filled by very different presences. From the pictures of Louis Jouvet in the role, we can see that his was a magisterial figure, clearly from the world of the French Catholic Church. With Mnouchkine, he was a small ferret-like creature who was clearly murderous, and with Ron Leibman, far away on the west coast of the United States, Tartuffe was played by an actor of comic ferocity whose lust was real and uncontrollable – but whose technique was hard as nails. Ron Leibman was a kind of American wild man, a dissolute, huckster charlatan well-supplied with cheap snake oil and the spirit of capitalist greed, willing to suck on a woman's shoe laces to show how much he wanted her.

Plays that live on in time also have in common extraordinary scenes and speeches, pieces of dramatic writing that produce ecstatic moments for the actors who play them and for the audiences who share them. *Hamlet* has its soliloquies and the "closet scene." Racine's *Phèdre* has the astonishing scene where she confesses her lust for Hippolyte, and the great arc of her rage that follows her discovery of Ismène as his beloved. *The Tempest* has the final great poem of Prospero giving up the rough magic of art, Shakespeare's grand farewell. *Tartuffe* has the two great scenes between Tartuffe and Elmire, both highlighted by an unexpected entrance: one too soon; one too late. The first scene takes place with the son, Damis, hidden in the clothes closet; the second one is played with the husband, Orgon, hidden under the table.

The third scene in act 3 finds Elmire and Tartuffe alone. (Or so he thinks. We know that Dorine has allowed Damis, the son of Orgon, to eavesdrop while hidden in the upstage wardrobe.) Elmire's intention is to sound out Tartuffe about the horrible plan of her husband to marry his daughter to the revolting cleric instead of to her trim young lover, Valère. It may be worth remembering that Armande who is playing Elmire is younger than Catherine de Brie, the company's great ingénue, in the role of Mariane, the daughter.

Tartuffe is written in perfect double entendres and impeccable rhyming verse by both Molière and his translator, Wilbur, using a religious vocabulary to mask the subtext of physical desire. He inquires about her health with priestly unction and tells her that he longs "to serve you better" and that he has prayed to be alone with her in order to "bare my inmost heart and soul to you." The choice of the word "bare" in the diction moves him from politeness to touch as he takes her hand and speaks of his "great fervor." Then, after being chastised for pinching her, his big hand finds itself on her knee. While he is using words from religion about "zeal" and his eyes are rolling toward heaven, his quivering hand is moving up her leg. The "mask" slips and the soul is naked. A moment of shock for both of them. Silence. Her line "What can your hand be doing there?" is followed by her movement away from him, his movement toward her, and another sexual gesture with which he feels her breast as he admires the workmanship of the lace on her bodice. She smacks him with her fan and strongly changes the scene to talk "business." He sulks at the blow and mumbles that his heart "is not made of stone, you know."

The scene then moves into two long, defining speeches by Tartuffe as he first "woos" the young wife, Elmire/Armande, by teaching her about the nature of love. Using an argument from Dante and medieval religion, he speaks of God giving woman the beauty that causes a man to yearn for God through admiring His handiwork. Sure. The rhetoric remains gallant, but she reminds him that he might well have "done better to restrain your passion. / It ill becomes a pious man like you."

The scene thus explicitly dramatizes sexual desire and the use of language as a mask. So the uncontrollable yearning for a woman centers this play as it did, in another way, *L'École des Femmes*. It remains the vital core of the author at this point in his life, and on through *Le Misanthrope*. Acting the roles of Arnolphe and later Alceste, Molière confronted on stage his own passion for Armande directly in shaping the core of his characters from his own deepest feelings. The "mask" is the character; the feelings are his own. In *Le Tartuffe*, however, he writes from another point of view about the grossness of lust and invents another character who is sexually obsessed, but this one is a hypocritical fraud with nothing but sex and material greed on his mind. After all, Molière was by love possessed and a major artist of his time as well as a respectable newly married man and a recent father. He has created a scene-stealing character he chose not to play. Yet one feels that the violent seizures of longing are not just "let's pretend."

Tartuffe, aroused and sweating by now, throws the mask of religious devotion away and begins his astonishing confessional. If we think of the doting husband and new father saying these words, they disclose a moving tenderness. In these lines ring the voice not only of the writer, the actor, and the new husband of the young, young Armande, but these achingly sincere words are spoken in the craven voice of a liar in such a way that Molière's deepest feelings become the subject for laughter. It is the church turning his love into something evil! In this way Molière took his vivid deepest passions and wove them into richly layered inversions for his purposes, into revelations with startling resonances cutting in many directions:

> I may be pious, but I'm human too: …
> With your celestial charms before his eyes,
> A man has not the power to be wise.
> Your loveliness I had no sooner seen
> Than you became my soul's unrivaled queen;
> Before your seraph glance, divinely sweet,
> My heart's defenses crumbled in defeat,
> And nothing fasting, prayer, or tears might do
> Could stay my spirit from adoring you.

One can almost see the tear drop on the vellum. Not wise, but obviously entirely possessed by desire for this girl. Molière writes a passionate sincere speech to highlight the total insincerity of a despicable character who, throwing away reason, rushes on into the ecstatic expression of the great lie. It indeed feels blasphemous to put these beautiful heartfelt words into the mouth of a conniving imposter.

Primal emotion moves into the diction of a courtly lover as Tartuffe begs her to ease his pain and he will raise to her an infinite hosanna. He begins to believe himself safe enough to speak of his plan for them to become lovers protected from suspicion by his robe and saintly reputation. He offers her the ultimate: "Love without scandal; pleasure without fear." She, in her cool and superior way, uses his passion by telling him that she will not inform on him if he relinquishes his claim to marry the daughter, Mariane. She takes his desire no more seriously than did Agnès on discovering that Arnolphe wanted to be her husband.

In our Los Angeles production, the choleric son of a choleric man, Damis, played with hyperactive bravura by Danny Sheie, explodes in a rage from the armoire all entangled with the clothes in the closet. His appearance is so ridiculous that Elmire laughs to see his infantile condition. She pulls a shawl off his head and tells him to cool it. He behaves more and more like a teenaged pinwheel of firecrackers, and when her husband appears she leaves the three emotionally stupid men to sort themselves out.

After the son's violent accusations, after Elmire's cool sophisticated take on man's lust, after Orgon is told all about this lust, after all this hot dialogue, we realize that Tartuffe has been silent for pages. Finally, when asked by Orgon if it can be true, "this dreadful tale I hear," he replies:

Yes, brother, I'm a wicked man I fear
A wretched sinner, all depraved and twisted,
The greatest villain that has ever existed.

He tells the truth! And the truth converts Orgon once again into a believer. And not only a believer but even more of a fanatic – who threatens to tear his son limb from limb.

In an ultimate act of hypocrisy, Tartuffe kneels to Orgon and tells him that he, the Christian cleric, forgives Damis; to save himself Tartuffe uses the core message of Jesus: forgiveness. Orgon kneels with Tartuffe and tells him he believes in him. The son, looking down on the scene of religious fervor, pulls his feet up on the sofa as if there were crocodiles in a river before him. But he is too late. In a fatal fit of rage, the father chases the son out of the house after disinheriting him, and gives not only his daughter to Tartuffe but gives him all his possessions as well.

What's more, I'm going to drive them to despair
By making you my only son and heir;

This very day, I'll give to you alone
Clear deed and title to everything I own.

While all this has undeniable elements of melodrama, it also has reverberations of the true faith: "Give up all and follow me." All through these scenes Tartuffe never drops the perfect Christian tone of love and forgiveness intermingled with confessions of his sins. After all, such a tone and such words are the perfect disguise. With them, one has the enormous respectability of the ubiquitous church to mask the lechery and "the human stain." One is safe to be, as Don Juan will put it in the next play, "the worst man in the world."

The second great scene is in act 4. To set up this sexual encounter, Leibman began the act with Tartuffe going over huge account books, using his abacus with flamboyant skill. Various family members plead with him for mercy and understanding but he just quotes scripture and leaves the room. Elmire asks her husband to hide under the table. Since amorous men are easy for a woman to manipulate, she will get Tartuffe to drop his mask and reveal himself as the evil person that he is. Orgon scoffs but takes up the dare and gets under the table, hidden by a tablecloth reaching to the floor.

Tartuffe re-enters, greatly suspicious. Even though he now has the whole house under his dominion, he does not feel safe: he checks the doors, and then checks the armoire. Finding nothing in the room or behind the doors, he rechecks the armoire and violently throws the clothes about, then strides across the stage to recheck the doors. When Elmire sweetly croons that she can now be "alone with my Tartuffe" he begins to melt. Still, he wants reassurance. He says he is confused since not long ago she spoke in "quite a different style." He is finally captured when she moves into a long speech about her passion for him, and, in her best actress mode, says: "That what our lips deny, our pulse confesses / And that, in time, all noes will turn to yeses." He moves toward her on each of her loving declarations. By the time she gets to the end of her speech and is speaking against the marriage to Mariane as something that causes her unhappiness because she "Deplore(s) the thought that someone else might own / Part of a heart I wished for mine alone." She is faint from struggling to escape without giving away the pretense and yearns for her husband to appear and save her. No husband appears. She stares unbelievingly at the table.

Tartuffe moves in on her to advance his seduction:

Madam, no happiness is so complete
As when, from lips we love, come words so sweet;
Their nectar floods my every sense, and drains
In honeyed rivulets through all my veins.
To please you is my joy, my only goal;
Your love is the restorer of my soul …

From this point on, the scene lives in the physicality of sex. Leibman and his Elmire, Jessica Walters, orchestrated a language of gesture that began with hands mingling, knees opening, arms embracing, shoes being kissed, shoelaces being sucked, and all punctuated by a ballet of fleeing and pursuit around the table to the accompaniment of Elmire's many agonized moans and loud coughs and table poundings to wake up the non-appearing husband. Exhausted and trembling with shock, she finally agrees to "satisfy" him and he ecstatically goes offstage to make sure no one is about. Long pause. The husband crawls out in craven silence, dragging the tablecloth around him as if still trying to hide. She delivers her classic line:

> What, coming out so soon? How premature!
> Go back in hiding, and wait until you're sure.

After Tartuffe re-enters like a bull in heat, Orgon, in our production gathering his precious tablecloth around him, rises in rage against Tartuffe as he did earlier with his son, only to be put down this time not by Christian rhetoric about forgiveness, but by a vicious hard threat from Tartuffe that *he*, Tartuffe, now holds the deed to and the power over this house and that *they* – not he – will leave the house. We thus have the setting for the act 5 denouement.

Mnouchkine's take on these sexual scenes was, of course, very different. They presented no courtship, no gestural language moving from light caressing to embracing and sucking on shoelaces, but an actual rape scene. They presented no comedic point of view towards sexual desire; we witnessed a rape based on fear and power, with no vestige of any love or even sexual desire: just a brutal struggle in which the more powerful male smashed the despised woman in a sea of sweat and hostility. Stripping to his filthy long underwear, he threw her on the floor, forcing her legs apart and it was very clear that it was sheer terror that kept Orgon from reappearing. We next watched two defenseless people wait in terror for the perspiring Tartuffe's return. Such weakening fear was the core in the scene, as the prostrate husband tried to make a futile effort to throw Tartuffe out of the community. No chance at all in the face of a fanatic person, surrounded by a tribe of like-minded zealots, with absolutely no human vulnerabilities.

Another contrast in important entrances in *Le Tartuffe* could be seen between the brilliant individuality of a gifted actor in Los Angeles and the equally brilliant political statement of a director in Vincennes. The Notary, a Monsieur Loyal, was played in our production in Los Angeles by Basil Langton, a British actor of great experience. He made the Notary a sly, sweet character that, as an enabler for Tartuffe, slid on stage in polite fashion to throw the family out of their own home. He did it so nicely, so graciously, so lovingly! He even allowed them until tomorrow morning to get all their belongings – if they had

454. Du Croisy dans le rôle de Tartuffe

Figure 16. The original Tartuffe
at Versailles in 1664. Unknown owner.
Private collection: Rights reserved.

Figure 17. Tartuffe in Vincennes
in 1995. Photo © Martine Franck.

Figure 19. Tartuffe and Elmire in Los
Angeles in 1985. Photo © Chris Gulker.

Figure 18. Tartuffe and Orgon in
Vincennes. Photo © Martine Franck.

any – out of the house. He always got a hand on his exit. The audience loved and hated him.

In the Mnouchkine production, the entrance of this character hit too close to home. In this sun-baked middle-East environment, the individual who came on stage to evict the despairing family, was a tall figure in a beige suit with a cowboy hat and boots. His lanky, relaxed body gave him away, even before we heard the heavy, unmistakable American drawl. The American had arrived to consolidate the terrorist's power, and to dispossess the peaceful people of their warmly human community – with a friendly lopsided grin, of course. "Ah. And Tartuffe?" Touché, Ariane.[5]

The first version of the play presented originally at Versailles did not have a final ode to Louis' glory and good sense. That version was in three acts – probably 1, 3 and 4 – and was promptly banned from all public venues for the next five years. Tartuffe's religious posturing stepped on too many sensitive, high-ranking holy toes.[6] Someone close to the king must have felt the shoe fit too well and refused to wear it.[7] Molière continued to press the king for permission to do Le Tartuffe at his theater in Paris, where he knew the play would bring real financial profit for his company. He wrote letters. He did the three-act version for the king's brother at his palace, "Le Raincy," in September and then on November 29, 1667, he introduced a five-act version of the play for Prince Condé at "La Palatine."

After Tartuffe has won Orgon's house and property, and stolen the compromising strong box; after the breathtaking "notary" scene in which the "legal" expert comes in to the astounded family and politely tells them that they have to vacate the house no later than tomorrow morning; after Tartuffe himself reappears with armed men and tells Orgon that he has to leave for prison at once on orders from the king, Molière added a royal *deus ex machina*. In this extended version an officer of the police, who has entered with Tartuffe and has listened to Tartuffe threaten the family, suddenly completely reverses the scene and the whole movement of the play when he states it is the King's decision that it not be Orgon who is going to prison but Tartuffe. The open-mouthed imposter, in total unbelieving panic, cries out, "To prison, this can't be true!" The king had left the prince's palace the day before that performance. Mlle Dussane of the Comédie-Française, in her novel *An Actor Named Molière*,[8] wrote that, after the five-year ban of *Le Tartuffe*, King Louis finally did allow Molière to read for him the last monologue in which the king is glorified and he decided that, even if it was a bit exaggerated, it was good for the people in France to know that their king knew about everything that threatened them.

The added scene presents a final major entrance in this play which any production must consider. It comes at the very end of act 5. For Molière, just to have a character from the king's police say the king's final words on the subject was sufficient to make a great effect on the public. He didn't need any other signals to stage this reversal. For us, in the provinces of North America, we needed something else to finish this spectacular play. The stage froze at the threat of prison for Tartuffe; the lights changed; Tartuffe knelt downstage with his back to the audience; the family was all tightly gathered on and around the sofa; and entering from upstage to a glorious piece of music came the ancient *deus ex machina*. We had tried to engineer the ceiling piece opening up, so that the splendid figure coming from the king would have descended like a God from heaven, but, alas, it could not be done, so we put him on stilts and designed a magnificent golden costume and cast a handsome young man, who moved with stately and towering grace downstage to deliver the final long rhetorical wrap-up to music. His "aria" describes how Louis could see through charlatans and how the great king will always treat a good man like Orgon with forgiveness. So the family was saved and justice was done! Theater and the laws of comedy prevail; as for the world itself, one still has to face the ironies of justice, and all of us in all audiences, including Louis himself, know that this is an ending for the theater rather than a solution for life. Kings no longer have a hold on divinity; machines no longer can invoke our gods.

Mnouchkine, post-revolution, post-guillotine, used her pen to submit XIV to the fate of XVI: she cut him off. Mnouchkine, like Vladimir Mayakovsky,[9] believes that theater is not a mirror to reflect society but a hammer to shape it. For her there was no *deus ex machina* in the form of a messenger from a king. She returned to Molière's original text. The family was simply left, dumbfounded and bereft of all. She went even further. The lights went down and when they came up again for the curtain-call … the stage was empty. She deprived the audience as well. One of the reviewers we have cited, Olivier Schmitt, said that Mnouchkine "has never stopped taking hold of our times in order to render back to us our souls," souls sadly besmirched by those "black and grained spots" that so frighten Gertrude in *Hamlet*. Molière's character of Tartuffe is a highly individualized non-believer who wears the mask of faith over his human lust; Mnouchkine's title character is just one of a murderous group – true believers whose teachers believe in a god that gives them the right to destroy anyone they consider to be a non-believer by rape, misappropriation or assassination. With her stunning and controversial interpretation, she took a stand against Eastern extremism and Western greed, but in turning her production into a political drama she also took a stand against Molière's deep belief that comedy is the weapon of choice against totalitarianism in any form.

VIII

...AND EXITS

Dom Juan; ou, Le Festin de Pierre
as conceived by Molière
as directed by Stephen Wadsworth
as directed by Jacques La Salle
as acted by Andrzej Seweryn
as directed by Robert W. Goldsby
as acted by Thomas Lynch

Don Juan, unlike Tartuffe, has no problem with entrances, but he does have to figure out his getaways. This section begins with some observations about the physical choices for the play *Dom Juan*, and works backwards into the core of the two characters that dominate the play. In essence, this follows a director's path. A major reason for focusing on externals is the necessity for any production to solve the problem of the hero's – in this case, the bad guy's – last exit, which must be absolutely satisfying, breathtaking, spectacular, and, above all, climactic, final and blood-chilling, all brought about by the imaginative and synchronized use of "spectacle": space, lights, sound, music and what they call in movies *SFX* (special effects). So our focus this time is directed not to the entrances, as in *Le Tartuffe*, but to various interpretations of the final exits in *Dom Juan*, first scenically and then emotionally. And Molière, like most directors, first turned his attention to the ground plan and the scenery before he started rehearsing the play.

Molière must have known that *Le Tartuffe* would not be approved in time for production during the new season that was almost upon them. Facing a deadline for his next season, he decided that a box-office hit was essential for the life of his actors. Molière was facing financial catastrophe. He desperately needed another new play to put on so that he could sustain his family of actors and pay their salaries. He chose to go along with the current fad for "machine plays" – *sans deus* – and the fascination for works based on the famous seducer, Don Juan. As further proof of the constraint of time on Molière, the play is in prose, not in verse.

It was to be his only major multi-set play. We have descriptions of the scenery he ordered for six set changes on December 3, 1664. Time to build and paint scenery is different from time to write dialog and he knew he would have to get the scenery ordered before writing the text. *Dom Juan; ou, Le Festin de Pierre (Don Juan; or, Invitation to Dinner)* opened on February 15, 1665, a little over two months after he ordered the scenery. It seems likely, therefore, that he must have decided on the physical order of the play before he wrote and rehearsed the text. One might even hazard the thought that he planned the action of this production as a director before he set it down as a writer. Molière spent a lot more hours as an actor and director than he did as a writer, and he knew whereof he spoke when he wrote in his note to the reader of *L'Amour Médecin*, written, rehearsed, and performed in five days:

> It is not necessary to tell you that life depends on Action. Everyone knows that comedies are made to be acted, and my advice is that only readers who have the eyes to discover the play behind the text should read this work.[1]

So he begins *Don Juan* – to use the English spelling from now on – with a clear idea of the Action as understood from the plot taken from the legends and from the Italian and Spanish plays about his hero. The Action (or intention or what Stanislavski called the objective)[2] for the character is to seduce women; the über-Action (or what Stanislavski called the super-objective) is for his new secular hero to challenge God and his Absolute Representatives on Earth.

The Don has bedded a thousand women in many different locations: to have sex outside of legitimate marriage is a damnable sin against God and His Church; to promise marriage to get sex and then desert the woman is to break the laws of human society. This immediately suggests two facets controlling a scenic metaphor: many romantic places for the conquest of his ladies on this earth, and a heavenly or hellish place to end his struggle with the supernatural world because, naturally, God must win. A director staging this play, while he may have different ideas about sin and punishment, ultimately has to solve the story's scenic demands: five or six different places for the various seductions, and a way to stage a cataclysmic ending involving heavenly – or hellish – retribution. There is also the small matter of a statue that walks, talks – and sits down to dinner. *Quels SFX*. All this has to happen without stopping too long for scene changes. Because of the pressure of time, before Molière could even address how his leading character would challenge God and confront various metaphysical problems, he had to put in an order to the scene shop to start building and painting the scenery.

His choices for a production idea had an intriguing history. He didn't have Shakespeare's Globe Theatre, so ideal for multi-scene plays, however his theater in Paris, the Palais-Royal, was able to house scenery built on the model developed by Giacomo Torelli. In France, Molière had worked with Torelli on his play, *Les Fâcheux* (*The Bores*) in 1661. Jean Loret, describing another Torelli production, wrote in his gazette, *La Muse Historique*, that:

> ... one saw so many rarities, ranging from Paris to China, made possible by amazing machines; one never saw things so majestic and so surprising; in four ballets there were twelve changes of scenery; there were hydras, dragons, and demons; there were oceans, forests, and mountains; decors so, so brilliant ...[3]

It seems that it wasn't only the bourgeoisie in town who loved theatrical transformations but the aristocracy favored them, too.

In Venice Torelli had rigged his theater so that all the units were connected to a drum under the stage and, by a counterweight system, he could change scenic elements simultaneously. There was no such stage in Vaux-le-Vicomte, the chateau of Louis XIV's finance minister Monsieur Fouquet, but when Molière and Torelli put together the *comédie-ballet* of *Les Fâcheux* for the six thousand guests of Monsieur Fouquet, there were sumptuous scenic inventions: for example, Madeleine Béjart hidden inside a realistic rock that changed into a seashell, out of which she emerged as a naiad; trees that spoke and marble statues that turned into living fauns and bacchantes. Even La Fontaine spoke about the wonders of seeing statues giving birth. The famous conclusion to this dazzling display was that the king, seeing all these riches, was not amused and had his finance minister thrown in prison for the grand crime of embezzlement.

While the Palais-Royal was limited, the theater space could accommodate a wing and border set, and Molière had learned enough from Torelli as well as from other productions of Don Juan plays to have developed his own ideas on how to make a statue walk and talk, and how to send his protagonist to Hell. His order contracted two scenic painters, Jean Simon and Pierre Prat, to create six different locations, each consisting of five wing flats arranged in parallel series on either side of the stage, plus a series of appropriate backdrops. The key was – appropriately enough – deception. The wing flats were painted to give the lie to their flatness and distance was created by using the Italian discoveries about perspective drawing. Not a bad "scenic metaphor" for a play about hiding the criminal face behind the mask of aristocratic correctness.

In my old variorum edition on great French writers, there is a production description of the play sent to the city of Grenoble stipulating a list of what they would need if they booked the play – not quite the scenic machines of Torelli but expensive for Molière at the Palais-Royal, and probably too much for Grenoble since there is no record that they ever did the play there. Here is part of that production plan sent from Molière's theater that discouraged poor Grenoble (the italicized interjections are the author's and indicate Molière's directorial modifications of his original contract with the scene shop):[4]

Act 1: During the overture, the audience will gaze at a palace with a magnificent garden. They will have time to appreciate the beauties of the decor before the character of Gusman enters. (*I can add that the ground plan of the garden was to be framed by 18-foot flats in diminished perspective which were part of the original contract, and that Molière later changed the opening of the play by writing a direct speech to the public for himself as Sganarelle.*)

Act 2: The scene is made of rocks and a backdrop of the sea. (*The original order included a country hamlet, which was in no way necessary to Molière's final performance text, and so was cut. In Tirso de Molina's early Spanish Don Juan play there is a long, long speech by a fisher girl, Tisbea, who is so, so proud of her virginity and very, very determined to keep it. The Spanish play places this scene outside her little hut. By the end of the scene Don Juan, obviously, gets into her little hut. This scene was completely re-imagined by Molière, who created a fisher girl, Charlotte, played by Armande as an engagingly comedic and totally anti-romantic character, who very quickly consents to marriage, but only if her Auntie will agree.*)

Act 3: The scene with rocks and sea transforms itself into a forest with Don Juan and Sganarelle in disguise. In the background is the exterior of a temple. Later in the act the temple opens to reveal white marble statues, and far upstage is a statue of more than six feet on top of a pedestal representing the Commander whom Don Juan had formerly killed. (*This is the statue that will appear later to eat dinner with the Don.*)

Act 4: This act takes place in a splendid interior room which includes a special scene with Monsieur Dimanche (*a bourgeois business man seeking payment for his services*) in a "painting of our time" (*or what was later called "a slice of life"*). At the end of the act the Stone Statue appears and invites Don Juan to supper.

Act 5: This final act takes place in a scene with stone statues stretching into infinity. (*The original contract was for a city with a port visible behind. The idea of scenic infinity for this act is much more appropriate for the finished play than the earlier request for a view of a port city. What follows is the full description detailing Don Juan's final exit at the end of act 5 from the old text sent from Paris to Grenoble describing the events at the end of the play as directed by Molière.*) Time flies in, *un vol merveilleux* (a breathtaking flight), and warns Don Juan to repent because he only has a moment to live. Don Juan laughs at the warning. The Ghost of Elvire enters and repeats the warning. After the Statue warns him as the final voice in the chorus of warnings, the Statue throws him into the pit preceded by a display of lightning and thunder. The whole theater appears to be in flames. The Statue appears to fly away and Sganarelle finishes the play. (*We should note that the actions are descriptive of theatrical illusions – "appears to be" – while Sganarelle "finishes the play" is a "finding of fact," not make-believe.*)

Now, we skip over three hundred years in time to 2004 and move from the 500 seats of the Palais-Royal in Paris to the larger Old Globe in San Diego on the West Coast of California, where we can revisit a period version of the play as directed by Stephen Wadsworth.[5] Mr. Wadsworth and his designers, Kevin Rupnik and Anna R. Oliver, mounted a richly layered "period" interpretation of Molière's notes to his painters. At the Old Globe Theatre in San Diego, the audience faced a beautifully painted false proscenium which looked something like etchings for theater in the seventeenth century. Here the space was framed by modified Corinthian columns; it was cornered by draped flags and centered by a gold crown supported by fleurs-de-lys. Inside the frame was a red velvet curtain in front of which were handsome black footlights. When the red curtain parted, we saw a drop-curtain on which was depicted an ancient ruined wall – the kind you see bordering a thousand pathways all over France – which would be used in the act breaks throughout the play.

The set for act 1 was a wing-and-border ground plan with a fountain upstage centering the design. At the end of the act, the rebuffed Dona Elvire left the stage moving slowly along the old ruined wall depicted on the lowered front curtain, in a move that covered the scene change going on behind it before it was raised to reveal act 2 at the seashore. Here we enjoyed a machine effect of waves in the upstage plane. Made out of two long low panels, curved and painted like waves and moving in opposite directions, this design clearly situated the action in a different place from act 1. The forest scene in act 3 featured another mechanical invention: a tread-mill across the upstage plane kept the two actors moving all during the scene. As they walked along, the two close companions – as master and servant can sometimes be, each needing the other in their own way – were telling each other their opposing beliefs about medicine and morality. At the end of the act, a towering and realistic renaissance statue of a man on horseback moved on stage with stately magnificence from offstage left. It was true to historical art and created an eerie effect. Acts 4 and 5 featured a very handsome grey vaulted interior, complete with ceiling and an infinite receding perspective to an upstage exit. This gave an extraordinary sense of scale and wealth. Both acts 4 and 5 played in the same room; such an elaborate set could not be moved quickly and the lumbering noise coming through the curtain would spoil the magic of transformation. This stunning interior took an intermission to put its solidity in place and so replaced Molière's orders for either a port city or an infinity of statues.

Wadsworth's staging of the final exit of Don Juan was surprisingly simple. After a very successful series of ghostly apparitions – Dona Elvire was particularly impressive as she floated high above the stage floor – a trap door opened downstage and the Don went down into a flickering red light. We will look at other choices for this final exit in a moment.

Within the Wadsworth production, we can also see how the costume designer, Anna Oliver, looked to the text and historical sources to structure her costumes. At his first entrance, we saw him change, piece by piece, from a formal traveling ensemble to an outfit more congenial to being at home with the occasional help of Sganarelle. We all know how layered and luxuriant the clothes were of that period, and Anna Oliver took nice advantage of it. However, the best description of the layers of material needed to cover the naked beast – and proclaim his status – may be the one given by Pierrot in act 2 when, with awe and disbelief, he describes to Charlotte the clothes of the men he has rescued from the sea (the following translation by Angela Paton and Robert W. Goldsby – with thanks to a combination of American backwoods dialect with a soupçon of inspiration from an anonymous eighteenth-century version – was staged by the Marin Shakespeare Company in 2003):[6]

We took'em home to the fireplace and they stripped stark-nekid to dry off, and then in coom Mathurine and one of them made sheep's eyes at her all nekid-like. He must be some great, great man, cause he had gold on his clothes from top to bottom, and even his servants was swells themselves. What a mess of fiddle-faddle doohickeys these gentlemen wear. You know, Charlotte, they got hair that ain't stuck in their heads and they put it on last like a great hunk a hat. They got shirts and sleeves so big you an' me could crawl inside – if we wanted, yuh boy, together. 'Stead of pants they wear a skirt thing as big as from here to Easter. They wear little teeny vesty things that don't reach down to their ass. They got great lace bandanas with four huge hunks of linen which is hanging down their fronts. They got itty bitty frilly things round their waists, great globs of stuff round their legs, and all over the place they got ribbons, ribbons, hunks of ribbons, so many ribbons it adds up to a sort of mish-mash of ribbons. Even they shoes be stuffed with'em from one end to the other. I'd break my neck in'em that's for sure.

Charlotte replies, breathlessly, that she'd "best go have a look-see at that." Her tone of curiosity does not tell us whether she wants to see them naked or clothed, but it does tell us she's a pushover. The original actress playing Charlotte was no pushover as far as comedic brilliance goes. She was Armande!

In order to see another way this curiously great play has been brought to life in our time, we move on to a famous production by the Comédie-Française when a Polish actor in that company, Andrzej Seweryn, created his memorable Don Juan. Directed by a fifteen-year veteran director for the theater, Jacques Lasalle, at the 1993 Festival of Avignon, the production played outdoors in

July, and then returned to their home at the Salle Richelieu in Paris where it has been in the repertory ever since. I saw the production in Paris in 1996. The following section is comprised of my memories of it, helped along by reviews of the production in France.

The curtain in Paris rose on an enclosed wooden space, elegant and hotly lit, accented by huge swaths of heavy cherry-colored velvet drapery. The first image was Don Juan's powerfully muscled, naked back. Turning front, he stretched his black silken-hosed legs out in front of him to await the ministrations of his attendant, Sganarelle. Olivier Schmitt in *Le Monde* describes this stage business in some detail:

> Sganarelle approaches him with a make-up box. Cream for the skin, powder for the face, a black make-up pencil for the eyes, red rouge to define the lips; then the clothes: black and heavy velvets with ribbons of scarlet and gold.[7]

Obviously we have here a far different scenic metaphor from either Molière's or Wadsworth's. During the "dressing" scene, Don Juan used the heavy drapes as if in a seduction and the whole impression, as another critic noted, was of an "environment more like the house of the Marquis de Sade than a set for a comedy." Another reviewer, Michel Cournot, who saw the performance at Avignon, wrote that when Sganarelle says to Gusman that:

> "You don't know, believe me, what sort of man is Don Juan" he is telling the truth. If such a man were, in our time, guilty of sins like Don Juan's in the seventeenth century – murder, seduction of the innocent, blasphemy, even debt – he would have to be presented on stage today as if he were someone who had attacked twenty children, tortured old people, blown up synagogues, and at the end is punished by the man he had killed six months ago who comes back to life, throws gasoline all over him, and a match ... poof. In the seventeenth century if one was guilty of blasphemy he might have had his lips and tongue cut out, bigamy sent one to the galleys, debts sent one to prison; even duels were a capital crime against the King.[8]

While Lasalle did not overtly buy into such painful criminality, his production was suitable for the "black diamond" of Mr. Seweryn's Don Juan, whose bitter voice and swift movements defined a truly dangerous personality. When Dona Elvire came in dressed in riding clothes complete with whip, he seized her physically, embraced her, dragged her around the stage, and although she tried to resist by tearing off his peruke, she was no match for him and ended the scene as a defeated, humiliated woman. In act 2, he shamelessly caressed two peasant girls at the same time "as they had never been caressed before, reducing both of them to quivering with '*la jouissance physique*' and had them on the floor rolling about." *La jouissance physique* is a French term for orgasm. Mr. Seweryn's great predecessor, Louis Jouvet, played this same act 2 scene standing upstage center motionless as the two women – one way downstage left and the other way downstage right – reacted to the words of the scene. All three characters were facing front; the connection between them was mental. With Jouvet, sexual conquest was about will and power – no physical touch was necessary for seduction. Jouvet treated us to an interpretation at the Théâtre Athénée that was miles away from the *sociétaires* of the Comédie-Française playing at being peasants and submitting to a *mise-en-scène* that had them on their backs on a stage covered with cherry-colored drapes. Mr. Seweryn's power was in his loins, not his frontal lobe. After his act 2 sexual scene which had little to do with a seashore and colorful peasants, the two leading male characters moved away into the forest on their journey toward the final exit.

In the dark forest of act 3, Seweryn's Don Juan cleaned his weapons in the light of a campfire as Sganarelle and he held their dialog about the meaning of life. In this production, neither of them cared much about what they were talking about and the play moved swiftly toward the pivotal scene with the Poor Man. Seweryn viciously humiliated the Poor Man by sarcastically forcing him to curse God in order to get a much-needed gold coin.

Next, he proved himself as professional a killer as he was a lover. Having cruelly dismissed an all-protecting God with ironic contempt, he raced off to protect the life of a fellow nobleman, whom he later discovered was searching the woods with his brother for the cad who had dishonored their sister, Dona Elvire. There follows a hilarious debate with Dona Elvire's two demented Spanish brothers on the subject of "Honor." While it may have had echoes of Corneille at the beginning of the scene, it is clear by the end of the scene that "Honor" is an even more ridiculous concept in the rhetoric of these Spaniards than it was to Falstaff. After the two brothers exited without killing Don Juan – one of them had had his life saved by the Don therefore it would be *dis*honorable to kill his rescuer too quickly – the two companions turned upstage where they are surprised to see the Tomb of the Commander. When the tomb opened we were greeted with a large gilded metal statue of the Commander Don Juan had murdered, now on horseback and resplendent in armor as though ready for battle. A reviewer in 2002, for *Les Échos*, described it as a "statue of gilt somewhere between the Renaissance and 'Star Wars.'"[9]

The great moment in this production came at the end of the play, which was brilliantly summarized by Olivier Schmitt in *Le Monde*:

> Sound of a deep bell. An indistinct form appears. Don Juan goes up to it and removes the somber veil covering the figure. What is revealed is a skeleton

covered with velvet and jewels. The Commander appears and takes Don Juan by the hand. The Don's whole body shrivels up and shrinks to the floor. As the Commander disappears, the entire upstage wall moves forward and rolls the body into a pit. He disappears. Sganarelle weeps. The play by Molière is a dark work by a poet frightened and bewildered by the world he lives in. Molière chose a foreigner to say things to the world around him, and to invoke the brutalities of seventeenth-century France. Jacques Lasalle picks up the glove thrown down by Molière and adds his own convictions about his own century, and when the body of Don Juan rolls into the pit, pushed by a heavy wall advancing toward the public, one remembers Auschwitz and bulldozing corpses into huge graves.[10]

One may protest that the comparison is not well taken, since the bodies in our century were innocents and the body of Don Juan is one of a man capable of evil, but he is still considered by some as a kind of secular hero, an individual who is crushed by a force greater than himself, an anti-hero whose heroism is extraordinary.

Deeper, perhaps, than directorial choices lie those of the actor. Molière not only used Torelli for directorial ideas, but his actor's body remembered the comfortable fit of Sancho Panza's everyman physique, and his actor's mind called out to Sancho to help him find a sure success by transforming the great squire of the noble Don Quixote de la Mancha to his own signature role, Sganarelle. While he may have known the novel by Cervantes, he unquestionably knew the play based on that novel by de Guerin du Bouscal. His company, according to La Grange's *Registre*, opened this play in 1659 and had recently revived it in November 1664 in Madeleine Béjart's adaptation. It is pleasing to know that in the midst of the struggles with huge institutions and poisonous critics, and the battle of trying to get approval from the king for a public production of *Tartuffe*, Molière was playing the parable-speaking Sancho Panza and he was playing him just a month before he started writing *Don Juan*. Grimarest writes that Molière, as Sancho, waited one night in the wings to play the scene in which he is installed as Governor, seated astride a donkey. The donkey, apparently, did not know his cue, and wanted to go on stage right away. Molière struggled to keep him out of sight and whispered loudly for help. The other actors were so convulsed with laughter at the sight of Molière sliding off the ass of an ass and clinging to its tail, they couldn't – or wouldn't – move to help. Finally the human actor gave up and let the bestial actor go out and play the scene the way he wanted. Great story, and if it didn't happen it should have.[11]

Working as a writer, Molière took two major ideas from his Spanish models: the sexual predator in the master, and the servile fear in the servant. This time his hypocrite was not mired in the faith-based fire and brimstone of the church but is securely ensconced in the safety of aristocratic authority. Arnolphe and Tartuffe are defeated, in part, by their inability to control or even understand the nature of their passion. In this play Molière wrote a character, Don Juan, for whom sex is easy and controllable, and who sleeps with many women never obsessing about a single one. La Grange is cast in his usual role of the successful lover. For himself, Molière wrote another variation on the role of Sganarelle, the quintessential age-old Uncle Tom of a servant, who watches in fear and disbelief as his master overrules emotion and morality with cool reason and ironic intelligence. This is a play where the aristocratic male goes through life observing the emotional vulnerabilities of others as if he were a demigod with little sympathy for his victims. The passion is not his. Don Juan, as the latest in the ancient line of a great family in Spain – or really in France, but Molière can't say so – dismisses God and all morality, replacing religious fervor with the terribly cold and simple credo that "two and two makes four," while Molière's Sganarelle is quivering emotion itself, his feelings wedded to survival, not sex.

When Molière wrote and played Arnolphe, the great passion was lust for a girl-child (Armande). In *Tartuffe* he created and played Orgon, a misguided family man seeking virtue and pious rectitude through the ministry of Tartuffe while ignoring the lust the phony prelate felt for his beautiful young wife – a lust which would prove to be a danger to the well-being of his family just as the Catholic Church was attempting to undermine Molière as the leader of his troupe. For Sganarelle, in *Don Juan*, the primary emotion was the fear of punishment by God, lord, master – or king. The subtext was Molière's private struggles between his strong desires and his fearful emotions toward Louis XIV, who had unexpectedly withheld his approval for public performances of *Le Tartuffe*, thus threatening the very survival of the company of actors.

The fear in Sganarelle is primary to his character. Bulgakov, in his book on the life of Molière, which was the source of the Royal Shakespeare film, says outright that Sganarelle's relationship to Don Juan is akin to Molière's own fear of the king.[12] Molière hits very close to the hypocrisy of the court's morality in *Le Tartuffe* but always backs away, deferentially hiding behind the mask of comedy. But Louis was like God – absolute in his power. Neither servant nor actor playing servant has any thought whatsoever of challenging that authority. This was over a hundred years before the Revolution. Sganarelle's pattern throughout the play is to speak up passionately and then fall apart emotionally. Molière's pattern is to write lines of deep conviction that confront injustice and then to give the speaker an escape with a pratfall. He can then always maintain that he is writing comedy and not attacking the men in power. One can see this subtlety in the playwriting when Molière turns the matter of sexual seduction into a mask over the real obstacle to the game: God. Women fall easily; God is yet to be reached. No one, however, would think that Molière actually meant Louis XIV – and he didn't – did he? Aren't those the king's colors that his Don Juan is wearing?

In act 1, he gives his scarlet-and-gold-clad hero, Don Juan, a long speech about conquering beauty wherever he finds it, and how pleasant it is to overcome virginal shyness by using marriage as bait, winning sex, and then moving on to the next battle to be won. He claims he is like Alexander the Great, who conquers one world after another. Sganarelle, as he dresses his master's body in the aristocratic layers of clothing, begins to speak his point of view about how to live in society (the italics are my stage directions):

SGANARELLE. But sir, would it be included in the permission you have given me to speak freely, if I told you that I am a little ashamed of the life you lead.

DON JUAN. And what kind of life do I lead?

SGANARELLE. A very good one, to be sure. But to marry every month as you do.

DON JUAN. Is there anything more delightful?

SGANARELLE. True. I'm sure it's very delightful and most amusing. I might put up with it myself but Sir, you know it's against God's law and to make sport of a holy sacrament, which …

DON JUAN. Come, come. That's just my little joke on God. He and I will unsnarl ourselves without you butting in.

SGANARELLE. Well, Sir, I've always heard that it's wicked to joke around with God...and that free thinking libertines come to no good end.

DON JUAN. (*Suddenly out of nowhere a dagger is at Sganarelle's throat.*) Hold on, Sir Idiot! I don't like to be preached at.

SGANARELLE. (*Seized by trembling*) Oh, I'm not talking about you, God forbid!

In his terror he goes into a long speech as if talking to an imaginary master in an imaginary wig at the same time that he is putting a real wig onto a real person, and the Don, knowing Sganarelle is just acting, doesn't mind, and is in fact amused by the performance. And so was the king. After all, so what if the king also had a different mistress every month; everyone knew he didn't marry them. Besides, he made the rules, not God.

In act 3 the conversation moves well away from sex and women as the two carelessly disguised men walk through a forest. In our 2003 production in Marin, we had Don Juan in an oriental robe he had picked up along the way somewhere – but actually picked up by our costume designer, Julie Weiss,[13] in a Hollywood costume rental house – and Sganarelle in a doctor's gown that with more logic, he had picked up from Dr. Marphurius, a clown we used from an earlier version of the play who is not usually included in modern editions. They are fleeing at a leisurely pace from the pursuing Spanish brothers – and some oar-brandishing fishermen also derived from that earlier version. This scene has no parallels in the earlier Don plays and is indicative of the close relationship between the characters as well as between the long acting partnership of Molière the comedian and La Grange the lover and straight man. Short vignettes on the grand themes of medicinal fraud, religious hypocrisy, and epistemology are woven together in a series of mini-scenes – subjects that could (and did) furnish fodder for full-length plays.

The given circumstance of the scene has the two characters pausing in the woods to rest a moment. They begin by talking about medicine and how Sganarelle believes in emetic wine even when it kills you. The atmosphere of the scene feels to me so much like those wonderful times in *Don Quixote* when the Knight and the Squire decide to stop looking for adventures and take a needed break. They sit and talk to each other to pass the time. In Cervantes, the scenes are long and full of wisdom and parables. In Molière, the scenes are short; the diction is simple; the subject is one in which a humanist would take delight. As a writer Molière, in his brevity, is often much closer to Chekhov than to Cervantes. Here is part of the scene with some of my comments in italics:

SGANARELLE. But enough of medicine which you don't believe in. Let's talk about other things. This costume inspires me with wit (*He's wearing the comic doctor's outfit.*) and I feel in the mood to debate you. I promise not to preach. (*He remembers a dagger at his throat.*)

DON JUAN. Begin. (*They sit on a rock in the center of the stage.*)

SGANARELLE. I'd like to get to the bottom of what you really think. Is it possible that you don't believe in God?

DON JUAN. God?

SGANARELLE. That means no. What about Hell?

DON JUAN. Oh, come now.

SGANARELLE. No again. And what of the Devil, if you please.

DON JUAN. Get on with it.

SGANARELLE. Mmm. Maybe a little teeny bit. Do you believe in life after death?

DON JUAN. Ha, ha, ha!

SGANARELLE. You are beyond converting! Tell me now, what about the Bogey Man? What do you think about him?

DON JUAN. An ass.

SGANARELLE. Now that's more that I can take because there's nothing truer than the Bogey Man. I'd go to the galleys for the Bogey Man.

A note here about acting the scene. Sganarelle begins the scene seriously and as a conversational equal with a question about belief in God. As he warms up to the action of questioning the Don's beliefs, Molière moves his comic character toward the extreme and finishes the beat by bringing in the Bogey Man. After the laugh – or several – our Sganarelle took a moment of silence before he moved back into the scene, looking around at the night and the forest, and in a new tone of voice he asked with simplicity and a real desire to know the answer:

SGANARELLE. Now look, Master, a man must believe in something in this world. What do you believe in?
DON JUAN. (*After a moment*) What do I believe in?
SGANARELLE. Yes.
DON JUAN. (*Another pause*) I believe that two and two are four, Sganarelle, and that four and four are eight
SGANARELLE. (*Pauses to consider; maybe repeats the formula*) What an inspiring Credo; what a beautiful faith. So ... your religion is arithmetic.

One of those primary moments in which an actor finds a personal touchstone that cracks open the play also occurred in this scene in our production, when Thomas Lynch as Sganarelle sat down with Don Juan in the middle of the forest to rest and talk philosophy. During this scene there were no moves. It was very quiet. Many nights there was the added magic of the moon over our outdoor festival space. They had begun by jesting about medicine and how wine enemas kill people, then moved on to God and the Bogey Man, and when Don Juan says his only faith is that "two and two is four, and four and four is eight," Tom's Sganarelle got up and moved out into the dark starlit space of the outdoor theater surrounded by tall rustling trees, to share with us all the "credo" that his common sense had taught him. "I can see things better than the books and I know for sure this world we see is not a mushroom that sprang up overnight. I ask you: who made these trees, this earth, that sky way up above or did these make themselves?" Whether Molière himself wonders out loud through his character, or whether Tom Lynch was taking us up into the stars over Marin – or whether it was the ghost of Sancho Panza – it was a moment when time stood still, and as Jean-Louis Barrault said of such moments: they don't come too often in the theater – or in life – when a thousand hearts come together and a group becomes one with nature and with each other and we come in touch with that god stuff of eternity.

The great mystery leaves him ultimately speechless and inarticulate and he begs the Don to interrupt him so he can stop talking. The Don

Figure 20. Don Juan and Donna Elvire at the Comédie-Française in 1993. Photo © Laurencine Lot.

Figure 21. Don Juan seducing two peasant girls at the Comédie-Française in 1993. Photo © Laurencine Lot.

Figure 22. Sganarelle in California 2003. Photo © Morgan Corwin. M.S.F./L. Currier.

refuses and says he is waiting for the end of his argument (again with my parenthetical notes).

SGANARELLE. The end of the argument is that no matter what you say, there is something marvelous in man, and all the learned men can't explain it. (*There is a breath in the audience that agrees with the actor here.*) Isn't it wonderful that I am here and you are there and that we have something in our heads which can think one hundred different things in a minute and make our bodies do whatever it wants? (*The public begins to doubt.*) I want to clap my hands, (*The actor is now on his feet feeling wonderful as he moves freely about the seated Don.*) lift my arms, raise my eyes to Heaven, bow my head, move my feet, go to the right, go to the left, forward, backward, turn around ....
(*He spins around and falls down in an undignified pratfall, and the audience who is so superior to what they now see is a fool, releases their doubt into a laugh.*)

DON JUAN. (*Joins the laughter*) Good, your argument ends with a broken nose.

The scene with the Poor Man follows, which moves us into a more ethical world as the aristocrat tries to force a poverty-stricken, religious hermit to curse God. Here is a clear "sin," not an opinion. Even in this secular age it is a moment that chills the stage as the Don offers a bribe of a gold coin to the pious man in need on the condition that he curse God. After the suspense that precedes the man's refusal, the Don flips him a gold piece for *l'amour de l'humanité*, (for the love of humanity, a clear parody of "for the love of God") and goes off leaving the new world of nihilism to join the old in a fight for Honor. Of course the bribe of gold is offered by the skeptic to the believer, and symbolizes the intellectual's scorn at the illogic of praying to God and getting nothing in return for his prayer, not even the gold coin that a man will give him.

Thus to continue our deepening spiral into the central core of this play and its place in Molière's work, we move past the choices about scenery, costumes, props, and acting to find the writer. While questions of ground plans and scenic devices may have occupied the man of the theater as he worked on *Don Juan*, questions of right and wrong ways to live seemed to occupy his soul. After the attacks over *L'École des Femmes* and the "trivial pursuit" of sexual innuendoes in such phrases as "cream tarts" and "bowls of soup," and the time spent on the short plays that followed in answer to the many pamphlets of hostility, Molière had decided, La Grange reported, to write plays from then on about what matters in human behavior. The three great works at the center of his œuvre – *Le Tartuffe*, *Dom Juan* and *Le Misanthrope* – all ask big questions about religion, hypocrisy and truth itself, and try to show how they affect individual behavior moving in or against society.

The great argument of this play between right and wrong is in the final act. This act, changed from "a port city" to a place "filled with stone statues moving into infinity" is astonishing. We transformed those statues into a mood-setting mummer's parade of all the characters intoning their way through the audience led by a skeleton who juggled bones. The parade of torch-bearers exited on the stage as act 5 began and Don Juan, dressed as a filthy penitent/flagellant, entered bent under the weight of a heavy, thick, wooden cross, the great symbol of passion. He dragged the huge burden slowly across the grey stage, knelt under it, and muttered prayers as Sganarelle brought in the Don's disbelieving father. Don Juan spoke in sincere tones of repentance, convincing both the father and the audience that he was, indeed, born again. The father went off joyfully to tell the poor unseen and probably despairing mother; Sganarelle was ecstatic at the conversion. Then the Don stood up and pushed the black cross away, which fell to the floor with a deafening crash of wood against wood. He then sits on it as he laughs and scolds Sganarelle for being such a fool.

Then to the deeply shocked servant and the astounded public, Don Juan gives the long summary speech about his cynical view of the world of power. He, who believes in nothing, will pass into society as a man of Faith. Hypocrisy means wearing the mask of respectability over the face of lust and greed, and doing whatever one chooses to do to have pleasure and power over others. He speaks with intensity and purpose as he describes how no one can tell the difference between true piety and false:

> How many men do I know that by this strategy have covered over the lies of their youth? How many have made a shield out of the respected cloak of sincerity and under venerated robes are free to be the worst men in the world.

He goes on to speak of the legion of hypocrites in the world – the fellowship of Tartuffes – who will fight to protect him against discovery. He tells how he will profit by man's weaknesses. He concludes by saying directly to the public, "This is the way a successful politician adapts himself to the evils of his time."

The dramatic form of this speech is similar to a major aria in an opera or a revelatory soliloquy in Shakespeare. In our production the actor moved out on the forestage jutting into the audience where he talked directly to them as if he were one of them and he knew that deep down they shared his opinion of human nature. And almost unfailingly, in the Marin production, there was a gasp at the end of the speech and, of all things, applause. However, all is not ceded by the writer, who is playing Sganarelle, not Don Juan. He stares at his master and at the public:

> My God! What do I hear? Being a hypocrite was all you needed to finish you off. This is the final abomination. This is more than I can stand, and I have to speak out. Do what you please to me, beat me, break my bones, murder me if you will, but I must open my heart and, as a faithful servant, tell you what I think. You should know, Sir, that a pitcher that goes too often to the well, breaks, and, as that author, whose name I forget, says so well, man in this world is like a bird on a branch; the branch is attached to a tree; he who is attached to a tree follows family values; family values are better than fine words; fine words are found at Court; at Court there are Courtiers; Courtiers follow the fashion; fashion comes from the Imagination; Imagination comes from the Soul; the Soul is what gives us Life; Life ends in Death; Death makes us think of God; God is in Heaven; Heaven is above the Earth; the Earth is not the Sea; there are storms at Sea; storms toss ships; ships need captains; captains need wisdom; young people have no wisdom; they should obey the old; old people love money; rich people are not poor people; poor people lack necessities; necessity knows no law; without law men live like animals and therefore you will be damned for all Eternity.

To this speech the public roared approval, and the applause was not only for this character, who was beloved in spite of his series of maxims drawn from Sancho Panza and in spite of his familiar pattern of going out of control. It was also respect and admiration for an actor totally in control. It was delight in his use of a comic rhetoric which would begin in absolute realism and emotional shock at Don Juan's betrayal and build inexorably, through a wildly illogical series, to the harrowing climax of damning him to all Eternity. Sganarelle speaks with the voice of a comedic prophet on behalf of the people and for justice. He speaks against the man who is acting as if he were God. He receives a rousing applause and Sganarelle wins the debate. The final exit is not far off.

After the two great personal manifestos from the two protagonists, each arguing for the audience's approval, we knew, like our more distinguished predecessors, we had to keep the idea of hell-fire alive. In addition we wanted the finale of our production to provide a total contrast with the human comedy at the end of act 2 with Pierrot and Charlotte, which ended our first half of the evening.

Our stage had no scenic units left; grey floor; large and empty space; cold and diffuse lighting. An ominously armored Commander appeared upcenter, surrounded by the black-clad monks who had been changing the scenic elements for the five different sets that were the background for

Don Juan's adventures. In front of the Commander, Dona Elvire – in the ghostly remnants of her white nun's habit in act 4 – appeared on stage calling for the sinner to repent. Don Juan shook his fist at God and cried, "Never!" and then fearlessly approached the Commander and accepted his invitation to dinner. A spectacular thunderous streak of lightning crashed into the scene as their hands met. The figures of the black-clad monks contorted and writhed about the Don as they forced him into the center of the stage. The stage opened under him, emitting flickering red light and smoke. He screamed; he tore off his penitent robes as if they were burning his beautiful flesh. Then naked, in front of the monstrous statue of the Commander and surrounded by the gibbering monks, he was drawn down, down, down into the fire's mouth. The monks circled around him tighter and tighter as he disappeared. Firelight and sound faded as the monks and the Commander seemed to vanish into thin air. Sganarelle, far downstage left, knelt trembling until all was silent. He slowly crossed to where Don Juan used to be. Everything had vanished. He looked down and saw Don Juan's penitential rags, picked them up, looked at the remnants, and said, "WOW!" Not in the French text, needless to say, but it did return the play to comedy. As he spoke about the loss of his master, thunder was heard again, now from a great distance – as if some god were tossing off a few self-satisfied thunderbolts as he returned to his Olympian Circle. The stage was cooled further by a slight flurry of snow as Sganarelle bewailed his bleak future without a master and, even worse, with his back pay lost: "My wages, my wages, my wages." Behind the comedy is a mystery – or an irony, depending on your choice, because this time for Molière, the *deus* exiting in the *machina* was more like Zeus than Louis.

But you can be sure that the final words of Sganarelle, bewildered by the unfairness of being cheated of his wages, "finishes the play" with an ending that is comedic not religious. And his cry is not that of an aristocrat or of a Church Father, but of Everyman.

IX

SHE LOVES ME... SHE LOVES ME...

Dom Juan; ou, Le Festin de Pierre
act 2 as precursor to
Le Misanthrope; ou, L'Atrabilaire Amoureux

In the midst of the moral dilemmas of Don Juan and Sganarelle, Molière brings on another clown: pale, white-faced Pierrot, with the eternal tear on his cheek. Pierrot is a distant *Commedia* cousin of Sganarelle (possibly derived from the Italian *sgannare*, to undeceive, and the name Pierrot has a faint echo of *pierre* or stone.) Pierrot is often a sufferer of unrequited love – later in the eighteenth century he wears soft white clothes and carries a flower. His modern incarnation was as Baptiste in Jean-Louis Barrault's *Les Enfants du Paradis (Children of Paradise)*. Through Pierrot we glimpse the deepest part of Molière's heart. We go beyond the man of the theater and his choices about the production; beyond the actor's sense of the stage and his audience; beyond the writer's sense of literary precedent and topical thematic material, to his wrenching feelings about Armande. We know he was already working on *Le Misanthrope,* and we can also venture the opinion that ever since falling in love with the girl-child of fifteen, he had been waiting to write that play. He also had in his memory the little scene he wrote for the servants in *L'École des Femmes* about women being the "soup of man." Grinning at his own obsession, he writes in Don Juan a comic version of the love between an obsessed male and a disinterested female and he gives it to his fisher-folk in act 2, not in poetry but in the rough dialect of the peasant. Just as Sganarelle need not be dressed traditionally, so Pierrot can be costumed as Julie Weiss did it, straight out of a Brueghel painting. It was not the externals that drew Molière to this lovely character but his spirit of unfailing love, so the writer put quill to paper and scratched out this wonderful scene for us in which Armande was cast as Charlotte, the object of Pierrot's frustrated agony of love, giving us a farce version of the dramatic situation which will be the center of his next masterpiece, *Le Misanthrope*. I find Molière's heart in this scene in Don Juan more than in the cold ironies of his title character, therefore I chose, in this book as in my production, to give it a clearer voice. The italics are some stage directions from the Marin production and the dialect, as mentioned, is a compilation of an old eighteenth-century English translation and good-old-boy Appalachian syntax. Remember: Charlotte was played by Armande.

PIERROT. Charlotte, I have a need to talk to you 'bout other things.

CHARLOTTE. So coom then. Spout it out.

PIERROT. You see, Charlotte, I've got to, as the sayin' goes, open the sluices of my heart. I love you. You know it. And we be fenced to be married. But, by God, I'm not, well, I'm not happy with you.

CHARLOTTE. You're not happy with me?

PIERROT. Frankly, you be vexin' my spirit.

CHARLOTTE. I be vexin' your spirit?

PIERROT. Gadzooks, Charlotte, you don't love me.

CHARLOTTE. (*Laughing*) Is that all?

PIERROT. That's all and that be plenty.

CHARLOTTE. Lordy me, Pierrot. You always be sayin' the same thing.

PIERROT. I always be sayin' the same thing, because it always be the same thing. If it wasn't the same thing I wouldn't be always sayin' the same thing!

CHARLOTTE. (*Annoyed, and challenging*) Lordy-me what do you want? What do you want me to do?

PIERROT. My little pea hen .... I want you to love me.

CHARLOTTE. Well, I do. I love you.

PIERROT. No, you don't love me and I do all I can to make it coom to be. Don't I break my neck climbin' after birds' nests for you; don't I make the old fiddler play for your birthday; don't I buy you purty ribbons for your purty hair? (*He touches her hair with great tenderness.*) I might better bang my head against a wall. You know it's not nice to not love people who love you.

CHARLOTTE. But I tell you, I do love you.

PIERROT. (*Exasperated*) But you be so polite!

CHARLOTTE. (*Even more exasperated*) How do you be wantin' me to love you?

PIERROT. (*Shouting*) I want you to love me like one loves when one loves how one ought to love!

CHARLOTTE. (*Shouting back*) Don't I love like one ought?

PIERROT. NO!! (*With great energy and pounding on the floor as he explains love.*) When one loves like one ought to love, everyone sees it. And one does a thousand little monkey tricks to those one loves when one loves with a good heart. Look at Fat Thomasina, she's wild about Robin. She always be tormentin' him, and never lets him be. She's always playin' around, bumpin' and slappin' when he coom by. Why the other day he's sittin' on a three-legged stool and she whips it right out from under him and sprawls him flat on the ground. That's how folks that loves behaves. But you!!! You don't wrassle me at all...you're just there...like a great sack of flour an' I could go by twenty times and you wouldn't give me the least little...the least little thump. Now that's not a good thing and besides... (*He runs out of energy and flops on his belly in front of her, exhausted.*) ...and besides you be just too cold for anybody.

CHARLOTTE. Well I'm not the thumpin' type. That's not my way. Can't change that.

PIERROT. Change or not change, when someone loves a body someone always gives the body some sign or other that a body loves a body.

CHARLOTTE. Well, I love you the best I can, and if that don't suit you, go love some other body somewhere else.

PIERROT. (*Rises, and they play the last lines warmly and lovingly very close to each other*) See? That proves it! I said right! If you loved me, would you talk like that?

CHARLOTTE. Why do you always be botherin' me so?

PIERROT. What bother do I do you? All I want is a friendly little tap or two, coom all of a sudden, all by itself, without thinkin' 'bout it.

CHARLOTTE. So don't bollix me so. Maybe it'll coom all of a sudden, all by itself, without thinkin' 'bout it.

PIERROT. Give me your hand then, Charlotte.

CHARLOTTE. Well ... there be my hand.

PIERROT. Promise me you'll love me more.

CHARLOTTE. I'll do what I can, but love must coom by itself.

In our production at Marin Shakespeare, we developed a play-within-a-play format. We framed the scene with draped and colorful fishing nets, placed the action on a platform down center around an open orchestra pit surrounded by a burlesque-inspired walk-around. This placed the scene right in the laps of the audience and tended to increase the warmth of this charming dialogue played by two equally charming, beautiful young comic actors, LeAnne Rumbel and Darren Bridget.

We also added to the end of the act a Dr. Marphurius – a character found in another published version of the play – who tells the Don that the fishermen who rescued him from the sea are coming to kill him with their oars for non-payment of the reward money. The actor playing Dr. Marphurius

Figure 23. Charlotte responding to Pierrot's passion. Photo © Morgan Corwin. M.S.F./L.Currier.

was skilled in the art of clowning: juggling, balancing on stilts, riding on unicycles, fire-eating and various gymnastics. We heightened the theatricality of our production by using these various skills during the scene changes with the assistance of an incompetent but undaunted lady partner.[1] Act 2 came to an end with a chase scene with all the characters of the scene – including the fishermen – providing a raucous exeunt into intermission. This offered a comedic polarity to the lonely cold spaces that marked the end of the play.

Fourteen months after the last performance of Molière's production of *Don Juan*, *Le Misanthrope* opened, and we can see another polarity: a single action, classical verse play, taking place in two hours of real time in a single set, about a hero's inability to understand his hopeless love for his beloved. Armande was to be the sophisticated Célimène and Molière would face her onstage as the noble Alceste. As an actor, Molière leaves the servant class and the rustic landscape to enter the world of the nobility for the first time.

X

...NOT!

Le Misanthrope; ou, L'Atrabilaire Amoureux
as conceived by Molière
as translated by Richard Wilbur
as translated by Neil Bartlett
as directed by Robert Falls
as directed by Pierre Dux

Le Misanthrope stands at the exact center of Molière's life's work. He was in the middle of his journey – "in a dark wood where the straightway was lost."[1] This chapter will deal with that dark wood, that lost straightway, that is the subtext behind this magnificent play.

In March 1665, *Don Juan* closed at the Palais-Royal after only fifteen performances, in spite of a very strong box office. No reason has ever been given as "the" reason. There are many guesses, among them that Molière was ill or that La Grange had an uncontrollable cough. Some more likely reasons are: pressure put upon the king by the French nobility who didn't like seeing even a Spanish aristocrat going down in flames; or by the clergy who were outraged by the blasphemy in the Poor Man scene; or quite probably, both. A clue may have been given a few months after the second forced closure in a year of a major play: Molière was summoned by the king to Versailles and was told a new title had been created for the company, "La Troupe du Roi," which would bring with it a handsome stipend and the king's protection. Maybe that was the "deal" the king made to compensate for the closing of two controversial plays in a row because they roused the indignation of highly placed members of the church and the nobility. Surely Molière would not have closed a major play before they had paid off the scenery, so this must have been an "offer he couldn't refuse." Molière and his family of actors were firmly established in the Palais-Royal.

Whatever the reason, Molière abruptly canceled a successful performance and, according to most biographers, removed himself by water taxi to a retreat in suburban Auteuil. He had been forced to abandon two major plays about significant themes; he was ill from tuberculosis and had been put on a milk diet; he was in despair over Armande, who was paying too much attention to the aristocratic stage-door Johnnies paying her court. Stardom, it seems, was turning her beautiful head. While isolating himself from the company and his wife, he worked on a new play about two people in love. The days had grown darker and the grin over a love quarrel between Charlotte and Pierrot was meeting up with a real life grimace of pain. He worked and reworked each line of his new play as he wrestled with a major artistic and personal dilemma. He struggled to put down on paper his anguish over loving a woman he felt was indifferent to him. His words seem to bleed on the page.

As he fashioned these thoughts into rhymed couplets, he also had to face the necessity of fashioning a role he could act that would not violate his contract with his audience. He had been seeking and achieving his public's love as an actor for twenty years. He knew that, above all, to be self pitying or to whine does not create sympathy for an onstage character. Raw sexual yearning cannot appear naked on stage. The outrageous greed of the hot Tartuffe and the cruel nihilism of the cold Don Juan had not offered comedic protection to him; he had played supporting roles to them. For his next play, he was seeking a theatrical mask through which his own obsession could be expressed. He was always two spirits: man and actor. His first title for the play was *Le Misanthrope; ou, L'Atrabilaire Amoureux*. *Atrabilaire*, as defined by the Littré's *Dictionnaire de la langue française*, goes back to a word used by the doctors of classical times meaning a person with "a thick or dense humor, a black bile, causing melancholy."[2] He had used the familiar choleric fool as a mask in many roles but this "dense, black-biled" persona was new to him and would be new to his public. If he could put this over his own personal agony he could be sure that his play would stay in the world of comedy. Behind the mask of black bile, the man would be there, wearing a costume bedecked with green ribbons.

In Pirandello's play, *Traversi*, a young actress says about her search for her "self":

> It is true only that one must create oneself, create! And only then does one find oneself.

Robert Brustein, artistic director of the American Repertory Theater at Harvard, says that this young actress was:

> ... seeking her essential but illusive personality. She discovers that it lies not in herself but in her art, in the various roles she has played and the theatrical

disguises she has assumed in front of her audiences. These are what constitute her real identity ... actors are not only the sum of their own actions, but *they are the sum of the roles they play.*[3]

Molière, like any great professional actor, knew his type; knew what he could do best on stage; knew that what he did had to be funny as well as true to his inner "self." The melancholic "black-biled" soul had to live on stage in the body of a choleric fool. The solitary writer, cloistered in the suburbs of Auteuil, worked out this duality by constructing a classic play in verse in which, as a playwright, he was moving in a totally different direction from *Don Juan*. He had to present the battle between himself and Armande in a way that was winning for both of them before their public, and to do so he needed the concentration of time and place.

Thus immersed in solitude, he was interrupted by an abrupt summons from the king for the newly baptized "Troupe du Roi" to appear in Versailles with a new play in September of 1665. Molière left Auteuil and wrote, rehearsed, and performed *L'Amour Médecin* (*The Love Doctor*) in five days. In this little formula *comédie-ballet*, Molière played a tyrannical father with his wife, Armande, acting the role of his listless, melancholic – but non-choleric – daughter, Lucinde. In the first act he talks baby-talk to her but that all changes when she confesses she wants to marry a handsome young man she has met. A fatherly explosion results! Sound familiar? In the second act, five doctors appear. For these five doctors Molière turned again to masks but ones that he had modeled and painted to resemble well-known physicians at court. They each treat her "illness" and after their examination they each give the father their final diagnosis that she is "ill" – in Latin. In the third short act, the young lover appears disguised as a doctor and, of course, the wedding is approved. Shades of the more complex *Imaginary Invalid* to come. The play moved to the Palais-Royal and was a success in most of 1665 and 1666. *Le Misanthrope* did not open until June 4th of 1666, and we can assume that, after this hasty visit to Versailles, Molière returned to his task of developing his new character, Alceste.

The man behind the *Atrabilaire* role is someone passionately in love with one woman. Gone is the infatuated guardian with his girl-child; gone is the hypocrite in lust; gone is the womanizer with multiple sexual partners; gone are the liars and pretenders. This character was to be one who is an absolute truth-teller, one who wants an idyllic union with his true love. Alceste, however, unlike his author's other choleric fools, is a man of great intelligence. He can hold steady to the logic of his views about social evils through long speeches wrought out of extraordinary language. Unlike Sganarelle in *Don Juan*, he does not go to pieces emotionally in the midst of an argument. Molière was writing a role that would allow him to play out of his deepest feelings and to express those feelings in the diction of a poet. Through Alceste, he sought to realize his personal despair at the pervasive lying that dominates the life of human beings in society, and to declare through word and action, scene and act, the madness of his passion for Armande. Alceste – which rings with an undertone that reminds one of the word "incest" – is a profoundly conflicted character. On one hand, Alceste is a name derived from the Greek, meaning – as described by Fernandez – a "man of strength, a powerful champion ... the sort of fighter who in the prize ring keeps boring in."[4] And on the other hand, he is the "Fool in Love" who can't tell the difference between being "honest" about a lady's hat and demanding that perfect love can only exist outside the ridiculous rules of society. He knows the wrongs of society, but knows little about his own nature. He finds he knows even less about the nature of Célimène.

Molière again begins the play with a debate between two "friends," but this time each is a person of clear intelligence, each representing a profoundly different argument about how to live in the world. This time they are social equals even though they are two contrasting theater types: the angry one and the reasonable one, the fool and the straight man. The actors debate the true meaning of friendship and the first scene of the play is a rhetorical masterpiece which pulls the audience's sympathy from one character's words to the other's. The debate format between master and servant – as in *Don Juan* (or *Don Quixote*) – is revisited here but now the two debaters are both *grands seigneurs* and both are equally persuasive. Undeterred by his emotional blindness and verbal extravagances we feel the moral passion of Alceste; we also respect the incisive intelligence of his friend, Philinte, played by that most seductive man-of-the-world, La Grange. Fresh from his role as Don Juan, he now tells us the truth about how it *really* is in society. Both men are clearly *au courant* with the works of Montaigne.

In his essay on "Friendship" Montaigne writes about his relationship with La Boétie: "If I were pressed to say why I love him, I feel that my only reply could be: Because it was he, because it was I."[5] These intense, idealistic words seem to directly echo in Alceste's (and Molière's) yearning for oneness. Montaigne in another instance writes about lesser, more quotidian social relationships: "As familiar company at table, I choose the amusing rather than the wise; in bed I prefer beauty to goodness; and for serious conversation I like ability even combined with dishonesty."[6] This is the part of the essay that Philinte seems to have read. Philinte will consistently argue that there are friendships that are intrinsically social and thus need not be held to such absolute idealism. It will be seen that the argument for absolute "oneness" is one that Alceste will make an absolute necessity for true love between a man and a woman.

The two men are at the richly furnished home of the young widow, Célimène, for a social gathering. Philinte seeks the pleasures of company; Alceste wants no company but Célimène's and hungers for Adam and Eve's private Eden. He has come with the intention of finding out whether Célimène is willing to give up everything and live for him alone as he would do for her. After witnessing in the next room her flirtations with those he deems as mindless idiots, he has stormed out followed by his concerned friend.

Jean Donneau de Visé, whose essay was printed in the first edition of the play, wrote that Molière "begins with the title character whose actions let everyone know that he is a misanthrope before he even opens his mouth."[7] It is most likely that Alceste came on first and that Molière as Alceste attacked the stage space with ferocity, plunking himself down hard on the edge of his chair and presenting, before Philinte speaks the first words, a comical parade of angry facial expressions and physical gestures – probably in wicked imitation of the social behavior he has just observed in the next room: "form without content, effect without cause: not a moral position, but a grimace and a posture." Within a few lines his strong-willed hero, Alceste, is heard stating the absolute: "I choose to be rude, Sir, and to be hard of hearing." ("Je veux me fâcher, et je ne veux point entendre.") Sounds like the solipsistic infantilism characteristic of farce types. The statement is made more absolute in the French by the use of the word *point* to supply a more absolute negative than the usual *pas*. Another onstage example of this *atrabilaire* attribute was displayed in the eighteenth century, when an actor named Molé smashed that downstage chair. A critic commented with disdain on that performance: "Alceste is, after all, not a stable hand; there is a description of his elegant and aristocratic silk costume of grey and gold with green ribbons." But the fierce, farcical type is a compelling role and surely was a vital part of the character as Molière played him. We will see later how the man with the "green ribbons" – Molière's favorite color and also the color of jealousy – can be played in a somber, heroic posture.

Alceste's anger in the opening lines is not just based on a matter of abstract principle but is part of the given circumstances of the scene. As Alceste has watched Célimène so obviously enjoying the flattery of those around her, he hears Philinte, his "best" friend, talking with fawning and facile phrases to one of his rival suitors for Célimène's hand . He feels betrayed and disgusted. Seeing Philinte succumb to the artifice of silly social conventions, he can foresee Célimène also betraying him. She, too, might not be strong enough to leave the pleasures of her life in society and love only him. This is happening on the very day he has chosen for confronting her. He is highly motivated and filled with energy as the play begins. This is to be the tipping point in his life.

Philinte starts the first scene of the play by gently inquiring into the reason for his friend's rage and in the next line of verse is told to get out and leave

LE MISANTROPE

Figure 24. The Philinte vs Alceste
debate in the seventeenth century.
Comédie-Française Archives.

Figure 25. The Alceste vs Philinte debate in the twentieth century.
Photo © Laurencine Lot.

him alone. Thus begins a very long exposition scene, which is like a prize fight between two evenly matched contenders. La Grange, who speaks for society as Philinte, played lovers for good reason: audiences were drawn to his warmth and attractiveness. Molière played the comic roles and audiences loved the laughter he brought them. The public must have been intrigued to hear such a philosophical discussion between the two well-known actors. Each character is given carefully written speeches to completely explain his point of view and to make us clearly understand what each friend feels about the right way for men to behave with honor in society. The debate, however, is not only between two characters in the same social environment, but also mirrors the ambivalence that tortured Molière's own soul as it ricocheted between the demands of his quotidian and artistic roles. It is a debate within himself, expressed through the words of a dramatist and the craft of an actor.

For the actor, what lies under the give and take of the ideas and carries them along, is the "action." Alceste's "intention" in the scene – the spur to his action – is to propose to Célimène that she come away with him. This is what he "wants," and that subtext, like the spinal cord, channels the flow of emotion: the passion of desire and the yearning for love; the despair of loneliness; the deep hatred for the hypocrisy of society. Célimène is the real spark for the rage of the opening and makes manifest the subtext for the whole play with all its digressions and arguments. She personifies the passions that surge all through the action in the play; she is the theatrical embodiment of Armande. And she *is* Armande! As the new star of the company, Armande has been cast in her first great leading role, as Célimène. She and Molière have been married a little over four years.

We hear one man declaring one should always speak the truth from the heart and if one doesn't, one should be hanged. Well surely, says the other, hanging is a little extreme as punishment for a social misstep and surely one has to play by society's rules. No! says Alceste, I don't want to be like everyone else; I don't want to be mediocre, I want to be a man of honor. Well, says Philinte, surely we can't change the world by being rude and your extreme point of view is making you ridiculous. Good, says Alceste, "Je veux qu'on me distingue, et, pour le trancher net, / L'ami du genre humain n'est point de tout mon fait" ("I choose, Sir, to be chosen; and in fine, / The friend of mankind is no friend of mine").[8] Well, he is answered, you are just excusing your own bad manners and forgetting man's nature; one must accept the world as it is and forgive the weaknesses that are part of human nature.

Then they get into deeper waters by arguing about human nature. Alceste, a true Hobbesian, thinks that human nature is evil and that those who tolerate evil are equally evil. His explosive character argues that one should reject the world, since liars control it. Ha, well, says Philinte, you might as well blame monkeys for their love of mischief or wolves for their rage to kill. There is a Right way and there is a Wrong way, and no in-between, ripostes Alceste. Compromise and irony are better, counters Philinte. The scene inevitably moves into the crucial issue of his love for Célimène. Then why on earth do you love such a sinner, asks Philinte, she is a person who exhibits all the qualities you most abhor in human beings. At this point, the tone of the scene is no longer angry; it becomes very intimate and very understanding, as if their true friendship has finally burned through the slough of Alceste's "black-biled" temperament to the vulnerability of a man in love. Philinte, with great sympathy for the feelings of the lover, asks if he really thinks that she loves him, to which Alceste replies:

> ALCESTE.   … Heavens yes!
>   I wouldn't love her did she not love me.
> PHILINTE. Well, if her taste for you is plain to see,
>   Why do these rivals cause you such despair?
> ALCESTE. True love, Sir, is possessive, and cannot bear
>   To share with all the world. I'm here today
>   To tell her she must send that mob away.
> PHILINTE. If I were you, and had your choice to make,
>   Éliante, her cousin, would be the one I'd take;
>   That honest heart, which cares for you alone.
>   Would harmonize far better with your own.
> ALCESTE. True, true: each day my reason tells me so;
>   But reason doesn't rule in love, you know.[9]

The last couplet is so well-known in French it has to be repeated in that language: "*Il est vrai: ma raison me le dit chaque jour; / Mais la raison n'est pas ce qui règle l'amour.*" With no disrespect to the acknowledged brilliance of Richard Wilbur, it's clear that to end the line with the length and richness of the word for love, "*amour*," with all its connotations, is stronger than the phrase "you know," though there is a possibility for ruefulness in those extended vowel sounds. In Neil Bartlett's modern view of the play as taking place in Hollywood, the phrase is also lighter than the French: "You're right. That's what I tell myself every day. / It's true. But as the song says, 'Love's funny that way.'"[10] Love is not so funny for Alceste, however, and in the great scenes in acts 4 and 5 his pain may overrule the comedy. In almost any interpretation, the audience then watches his defeat with more sorrow than laughter.

In the theater, we all live by T. S. Eliot's phrase, "The wheel turns and still is forever still." The wheel turning in the interpretation of Alceste began only a few years later, in 1672 – one year before his death – when Molière replaced himself with the young Michel Baron who played Alceste in a reprise of the play. Molière had seen Baron as a child actor at age 12 and had immediately brought him into the company. While Armande was not happy with him and even slapped him silly at one time, the boy actor remained very close to the aging head of the troupe, and even shared time with him out at Auteuil. Baron, with his experience as a child actor and later as a juvenile in the company, was an exceptionally handsome youth who was to become a great tragic actor long after Molière's death. He would never have played Alceste as a crusty, choleric, black-biled character. He began the tradition of playing Alceste as a romantic or glamorous figure. Baron may have played an elegant thirteen-year old in Molière's unfinished *Mélicerte* in 1666, so he was not yet twenty when he played Alceste. A nineteen-year old Alceste was a very different idea, especially against Armande who had reached the great age of twenty-four. How strange it must have been to see his two adopted children playing out his love story. There are many, since Baron, who have weighted the play with Alceste as a suffering hero, but few have been able to duplicate Molière, who knew just how to recreate a man's suffering, and then deflate it with laughter.

One of the important productions in the twentieth century was at the Comédie-Française in 1977 under the direction of Pierre Dux, who had begun his work on the play in 1933 playing Oronte, the foppish poet that so irritates Alceste. In later years he played Alceste. When he came to direct the play, he wrote in the program that "nowadays, Alceste no longer makes us laugh." After playing Molière's play before, during, and after World War II, it is not surprising that he and many others came to such a point of view and that he chose a powerful actor, Georges Descrières – with iron grey hair, a subdued puritanical costume, and a deep bass voice – to play the role in a new production. Mr. Herzel, in the publication of the Modern Language Association, found the interpretation to evoke a reaction similar to the one for the Ghost in Hamlet: no one laughed at his presence. Mr. Herzel describes the relationship between Alceste and Célimène as follows:

> This was not one of those coquettish Célimènes who keeps all her suitors impartially at arm's length; she may touch Clitandre on the forearm or allow Acaste to kiss her hand, but with Alceste we see her in one tight embrace after another as a willing, even aggressive participant. These physical displays cease, of course, when other characters enter and she becomes kittenish again, but the audience is entirely convinced of her love for Alceste even though Alceste himself is not. When he finally refuses her (in Act 5), she crosses to him, places her left hand on his left breast while he stares stonily ahead; she inclines her head briefly on his shoulder, her face averted from his (and from the audience). Then,

the picture of dejection, she makes her long, slow, painful progress upstage and off, leaving not a dry eye in the house.[11]

Molière might have had some problem with the choices made by these players, but he would have held these later thespians in the greatest respect as members of his extended troupe.

The great scene between Célimène and Alceste onstage – and the hidden presence of Armande and Molière felt in the subtext – takes place in act 4. A compelling production of the play was presented in 1988 in London, and was re-created in 1989 at the La Jolla Playhouse. The California production of the translation by Neil Bartlett was directed by Robert Falls, and Alceste and Célimène were played by David Darlow and Kim Cattrall facing off as a screenwriter and a movie star. The scene was played with a grown-up intensity, in a translation by Neil Bartlett that successfully married the rigors of the alexandrine line with American diction. The act 4 scene begins with Alceste storming on stage brandishing a letter he supposes to be a love letter from Célimène to the supercilious Oronte. He compares that "scrap of paper" to an earthquake.

ALCESTE.   Oh God. I'm going mad. I don't know what to do.
CÉLIMÈNE. You look terrible. What on earth is wrong with you?
           If looks could kill, just one look like that would fell me.
           Darling, is there something that you want to tell me?

One cannot help but think of Ms. Cattrall saying this in her role as the promiscuous sex goddess in *Sex and the City*.

ALCESTE.   Tell you that of all evils to which flesh is heir
           Your infidelity is quite without compare;
           Tell you Heaven has no rage like love to hatred turned,
           Nor Hell a fury like a lover who's been burned.
CÉLIMÈNE. You always did have such a clever turn of phrase.[12]

The almost Strindbergian man/woman struggle uncovers the reason for his burning jealousy: the letter. She moves so surely and with such ease to demolish both the letter and the man who has believed it. Simple! She wrote it to the woman, Arsinoé, who had given the letter to Alceste. She goes on with steely aplomb to tell him to stop "crashing around the place" and then, to finish him off, she reverses her tactics to tell him with a shrug, that, yes, she did write it to Oronte and to just "leave me alone, you give me a headache," unwittingly echoing his own opening statement on his first entrance. He crumbles and begs her to stop pretending she is guilty, but she goes on twisting the knife, telling him that she wishes she had had an affair so that he would have a real reason to make such a tiresome scene. He is now crumpled on the floor as she yells at him to "Get out."

Telling the truth – or pretending to tell the truth – leads to a transition from anger in each to a gentle and quiet attempt by each, standing close and holding hands, to make the other understand their differing ideas of love. Here is Bartlett's rendition of the scene (italics mine):

> ALCESTE. Oh, you're wicked! How strange that I should fall for you.
> When you are lying, I love it. What can I do?
> I give myself up to your scorn and derision;
> My love is in your hands; please, make your decision.
> I must know, and know now, what you're thinking inside;
> Must see what treachery your black heart can hide.
> CÉLIMÈNE. Oh! Why don't you behave like a lover's meant to! (*Shades of Pierrot!*)
> ALCESTE. No one ever felt the way I feel about you.
> I want to tell the world I love you so madly
> That I fantasize about hurting you, badly.
> I wish no one ever admired your loveliness.
> I wish I could watch you stripped of your happiness,
> I wish God had had you born in obscurity,
> With no home, with no wealth, no health, in poverty,
> So when I offered you the chance to be my wife,
> Offered, with that single gesture, to transform your life,
> I would be so happy, because then you would see
> That everything you had, you had it all from me.
> (*Shades of Arnolphe!*)
> CÉLIMÈNE. What a strange way you have of making me happy.
> I hope you never have the opportunity—[13]

She is interrupted by the phone ringing.

To see these two people on stage standing close, holding each other's hands, yet disagreeing so profoundly, is surely to witness one of the most unusual love scenes in all of dramatic literature. They can no more go on to domestic tranquility than could Romeo and Juliet but here one does not have the clarity or the chill of the tomb at the end. The Alceste in La Jolla wore a trench coat like Columbo and Célimène wore a designer dress; Monsieur Descrières in Paris wore a puritanical coat; and Baron and Armande were elegantly dressed and very young. So the wheel turns from irony to romantic tonalities, and back to its roots as comedy and is still the same play.

The ending of this mysterious and marvelous work has had many kinds
of staging. While the play may end in ambiguity, the production has to make
more specific choices. Some modern versions, including my own, have left
Célimène in the loneliness of her deserted "salon" after all the other characters
have gone – a slip of a twenty-year-old girl in a dark corner of the room,
deserted by everyone of importance in her life. Her long silence after the exit
of the happy Philinte and Éliante gives her pathos and brings her a little rueful
sympathy. Ms. Cattrall was no such girl. Here's the text Bartlett gave his actors
at the end of act 5 (italics mine):

> CÉLIMÈNE. Me? Live in a desert? Darling, what would I do?
>   Sit quietly down and grow old? Alone? With you?
> ALCESTE. But if your life was only fired by my passion,
>   All this would seem empty – prestige – people – fashion.
>   We would have each other and that will be plenty.
> CÉLIMÈNE. Solitude is too much to bear when you're twenty.
>   I'm neither old enough nor strong enough to cope
>   With the thought of us living off just Love and Hope.
>   If the promise of engagement would be enough
>   To start with, I could agree to that, perhaps Love
>   And marriage…
> ALCESTE.   Please, spare me all the rest. I'll just go;
>   Your answer tells me ev'rything I need to know.
>   Since you are not able to do what you're asked to,
>   To live for me alone as I have lived for you…
>   *(Ms. Cattrall, at this point, simply turned and left the stage, and Alceste yelled
>   after her.)*
>   All right, I'm leaving you. The blow you've just dealt me
>   Severs the chain of obligation; I … am … free.[14]

Astonishingly, he turns and proposes an affair with Éliante, which is, of course,
rejected.

The same scene in French with Mlle Mars, who played at the Comédie-
Française for decades before and after the French Revolution – and who not
only might have been a bed-mate for Napoleon, but had the beauty and the
voice to play young roles until she was past sixty – took another direction. Her
exit as Célimène is still described by editors of Molière's works:

> All the pride of a woman-of-the-world, who would never confess to the wound
> she suffered at the rage of Alceste was shown in the way she prepared for her
> exit. She began a deep bow as Alceste starts his last angry speech and she finished

Figure 26. Célimène in the early nineteenth century. Comédie-Française Archives.

Figure 27. Célimène responding to Alceste's passion in the early twentieth century. Comédie-Française Archives.

Figure 28. Célimène responding to Alceste's passion in the late twentieth century. Photo © Micha Langer.

the bow on his last word. As she moved to her exit she regained her appearance of defiance, and her fan looked as if it had much to say while the final gesture confirmed that she was ending her conversation with him.[15]

I dare say none of the older generation actresses would, like Kim Cattrall, simply turn and walk out on him. They waited patiently, as he tells them that he detests them and that he is through with them before they leave sadly accepting the impossible like the Célimène for Monsieur Dux, or defiantly gaining control at the end like Mlle Mars over one hundred years earlier, or, since the word "exit" is not actually written in the text, an actress could stay in place until all the stage was empty and once alone wonder if she had done the right thing.

Trying to understand the process that produced this enigmatic and mysterious play, biographers and scholars have wrestled with a document written by "Anonymous" in 1688, which contains a section purportedly about a conversation between Molière and Chapelle about the nature of love. This section some think was the work of La Fontaine and therefore tend to give it credit; others, who think Chapelle himself might have been the author, discount it because Chapelle was a drunk and could not be relied on. Still, Chapelle was a lifelong friend of Molière's and knew him from school days at the Collège until the day Molière died – and it was Chapelle who wrote him the verse quoted earlier about the moss and the willow tree, warning him to share the suggestive lines only with Armande. That letter was written in 1659 when Armande was only 15, three years before the couple married. So the two friends must have shared a rare intimacy about this love before it came to be known by others. Chapelle spent a good deal of time visiting with Molière at Auteuil – sharing other marvelous conversations about suicide and drinking – and the passage certainly rings true for a writer for whom sexual feelings are the core of his four great central plays, from *L'École des Femmes* to *Le Misanthrope*. I share with you the concluding part of the passage as translated by Virginia Scott in her chapter about Marriage (with my interpolations in italics).

"I see," answers Molière, "that you have never been in love and you have taken the appearance of love for love itself." He (*Molière*) agrees that he has studied human weakness, but personal experience convinces him that not all weaknesses can be overcome. "I was born with the utmost disposition for 'tendresse' (*a code word for sexual desire*) and as all my efforts have not been able to conquer the penchant I have for love, I have tried to be happy, that is to say, as much as one can be with a sensitive heart" (*also a code phrase for one who is vulnerable to sexual desire*) … Molière describes how he raised Armande to be the kind of wife he needed, innocent and untouched by self-interest, ambition, or vanity. "As she was still young when

I married her, I did not perceive her bad inclinations" ... But after marriage "I found so much indifference that I began to perceive that all my precautions had been useless and that what she felt for me was far from what I needed to be happy ... and I attributed to her nature what was an effect of her lack of sexual feeling for me" ... Now he is determined "to live with her as if she were not my wife. But if you knew what I suffer, you would pity me ... I tell myself perhaps she has the same difficulty suppressing the penchant that she has to be a coquette, and I find myself more disposed to be sorry for her than to blame her. You will no doubt say that one must be a poet to love that way? But, for me, I believe there is only one kind of love, and that people who do not have a weakness like this have never truly loved: everything in the world is related to her in my heart; my mind is so occupied with her that nothing can divert me in her absence; when I see her, an emotion and ecstasy that I can feel but never express takes away my power of reason; I have no eyes for her defects, I only see what is lovable in her. Isn't this the extreme of madness? And don't you admire the way my reason shows me my weakness, without being able to triumph over it."[16]

Sounds a little like Alceste.

In the center of his life's work Molière touched this deepest core of his being – the agony of unanswered, unreturned love – and whoever was that Anonymous who wrote those words must have understood the man he was writing about. What hovers over the burning words of *Le Misanthrope* is the inexpressible presence of Armande in his life and on stage, caught up in the mysteries of love in the human experience; and while the emotions of such experience are inexplicable, so too is the overwhelming need to write a play like this, if you could. Molière has fused this all together in a poetic burst of truth-telling from some unconscious place that has kept this play alive over the centuries and given great joy to actors and actresses and audiences who have shared the thrill of knowing and receiving these characters in their hearts and souls.

As we have seen, dramatists can work from the inside out, or from the outside in; or they can do both at the same time as Molière did when he wrote – and acted in – *Le Misanthrope*. The end result at many times brought about that ecstatic experience when the actor, the actress, and the audience all breathed in the same rhythm and the art of acting brought release and healing to Molière's heart if not to his lungs. In *Le Misanthrope*, as Alceste, Molière finally took the title role and played out his own love story, and the tidal wave of turbulent love seemed finally to subside. After playing Alceste to Armande's Célimène for twenty-one performances, Molière opened a new play. He never again wrote a play about love. When he comes on stage again, he is a different man, with a different story.

Act Three

THE COMIC RELIEF

XI

BLESSÈD LAUGHTER

Le Médecin Malgré Lui
as conceived by Molière
as echoed by the Empire Burlesque, Newark

Alceste did not leave the stage triumphant like Mascarille; he lost the capricious love of Célimène and the steadfast loyal devotion of Éliante as he marched off into the silence of the empty desert life that awaited him. It is generally accepted that it was about this time he and Armande chose to live apart. Almost as if he had visited the temple of Aesculapius – the god of healing located in sanctuaries near most Greek theaters – the actor, to ease the pain of his mounting personal and business problems, seemed to pay the cock to Aesculapius and go back to the basic lecheries that had nothing at stake for the man behind the mask of comedy. He found nourishment in the pure, simple joy of being on stage and getting the thunderous laugh at the same moment in time from everyone in the audience. The ironic smile is gone. The belly laugh is heard in the land.

It's not difficult to imagine that following the gasping needs of Arnolphe, the lecheries of Tartuffe, the power trips of Don Juan, the passions of Alceste, as well as all the poisonous reactions to these four masterpieces about deadly serious issues – plus all that time on milk – Molière might have felt pressured not only to recover his own health but also to develop a healthier box-office. Maybe laughter became more attractive to him than dramatic ambiguities. Molière climbed on stage again in the ancient clown make-up of good old Sganarelle, this time in the costume of a woodcutter. He went back to his roots and found the always-dependable foibles of the "Doctor" that work so well with the public – whether the doctor is flying, loving, or imaginary – and a new play hit the boards at the Palais-Royal to packed houses. This play came to be performed more often than any other play in his repertory, with the exception of *Tartuffe*. It is often paired at the "House of Molière" with one-acts from the nineteenth-century repertoire. Even today you might see, at the Comédie-Française, this romp by Molière featuring large-breasted milk nurses, combined with a one-act by Feydeau about a manufacturer of chamber pots for the French Army: *On Purge Bébé* (*Going to Pot*).

Many older critics, from Grimarest to Voltaire, believed that Molière was essentially a philosopher. Voltaire thought that Molière was a philosopher and wrote plays like *Le Misanthrope* for an elite audience, but unfortunately was also forced to write farces to lure the less sophisticated to fill his theater's seats. (One should remember that Voltaire wrote many plays and not one has a breath of life.) Boileau, a close friend of Molière, agreed with Voltaire. He always scolded Molière for his tendency to pander to the public. Louis Racine, in his book about his father, reports on a conversation with Molière that took place only a month before Molière's death:

> BOILEAU.   The profession of actor exhausts you, why don't you renounce it?
> MOLIÈRE.   Alas, I'm prevented by a point of honor.
> BOILEAU.   What point of honor? What! You dirty your face with the mustache of Sganarelle in order to come on stage to be beaten? There's a fine point of honor for a philosopher like you.[1]

As a man of letters, Boileau would have no concept of a theater manager's sense of honor. As the head of the king's company of actors, it was Molière's job to fulfill the unspoken mandate behind that gift given by the king: which was to make the king laugh and then do the same for the king's subjects in Paris. It also speaks to a love for his extended family of fellow actors and a feeling of responsibility for their well-being, offstage as well as on.

In a story in Virginia Scott's book taken from La Fontaine's *Les Amours de Psyché et Cupidon* (*The Loves of Psyche and Cupid*), four friends talk about comedy and other issues concerning the arts. The spokesman for comedy is Gélaste, and since Molière and La Fontaine were friends, these views may well have been inspired by the playwright and written down by the writer of fables. Ms. Scott translates some of what the defender of comedy has to say:

> Oh, immortal gods, I do not say that Sophocles and Euripides do not divert me more than many makers of comedy, but things being equal, would you leave the pleasures of seeing a funny fellow like Phormio trap two old men, in order to go weep for the family of old Priam.

Naturally, the spokesman for tragedy would, but Gélaste goes on, sounding exactly like Molière:

> The healthier people always prefer comedy to tragedy ... Ha, my friend, don't you see that one is never tired of laughter? One can tire of gambling, rich food, women, but of laughter, no. Have you ever heard anyone say, "We've been laughing for a week; I beg you, let us weep today."

The argument goes on, bringing in the gods and mortals, but Gélaste finally wins with this clincher:

> The gods never weep. Their portion is laughter ... Blessedness consists of laughter.[2]

That's one that's hard to beat: "blessedness." Maybe it's even better than sexual bliss?

When Molière left the stage as Alceste it seems as if he dropped his yearning for oneness with the beloved; the black bile of the *atrabilaire* was banished. He must have cherished the feeling of ecstatic experience when he was in charge of the stage and his audience. Since he did not find this experience in private life – where he was surely not in charge of Armande's feelings – at this point in time, August 1666, he turned to his old friend, the ancient role of Sganarelle, and feeling the "laughter in his soul,"[3] wrote one of his pure farces without a touch of bitterness or social comment and with no shade of melancholy about the loss of love. We are astonished to find no Armande shining through – just the delight coming from the small grinning mask of Comedy.

From all reports, Molière's body on stage had what Michael Chekhov said was the essential for the mimetic actor: "the extreme sensibility of the body to psychological creative impulses."[4] Those impulses may originate in the inner core and radiate out to form the gestures of the body, or the external gestures dictated by the outer mask of characterization may awaken that inner core. Acting is a body thing. One loves to act because it makes you feel alive, connecting soul to body. Acting in public, you break down the isolating walls and respond directly to someone else; you become larger as you connect with a larger community. You are carried along by a tempo-rhythm that is immensely pleasurable to the body and all its organs in a "fluid exchange of emotions." And you are in control – a vast difference from private life. The lightness at the center is joy, and joy is what actors feel when they are performing Molière. They feel connected to that center illuminated so brilliantly for them by the master.

The contrasts in this new play with *Le Misanthrope* are astonishing. His wife Armande, the newest star of the company, has no long, coolly intelligent speeches in perfect verse, but comes onstage as Géronte's aphasic daughter in the middle of act 2 for a consultation with Sganarelle, waving her arms in some sort of hysterical form of sign language. The first line her adoring public hears is, "Han, hi, hom, han, han, hi, hom." As the woodcutter forced to assume the role of an imaginary doctor, Molière glares at his young wife in the role of the tongue-tied Lucinde, and says, loudly, "What did you say?" She repeats the sounds and he imitates her savagely. He then tickles her neck and makes her laugh before launching into his clinical diagnosis, which begins with the color and copiousness of her urine, and goes on to quote Aristotle in Latin, creating a kind of Rube Goldberg contraption of human anatomy, as translated by Albert Bermel:

> … the vapors traveling from the left side where the liver is to the right where the heart is and it transpires that the lungs, which in Latin we call *armyan*, being connected to the brain, which we call *nasmus*, by way of the *vena cava*, which in Hebrew we call *cubile* … and that is precisely why your daughter's dumb. [5]

The confused father, Géronte, reacts:

> The position of the liver and heart. I thought you reversed them. The heart is on the left, no? And the liver on the right?

Sganarelle has the perfect retort of the consummate intellectual:

> They used to be. But we've changed all that.

Doctor William Harvey, of course, had recently done just that, by postulating in the early 1600s that the blood circulates all throughout the body!

Armande stayed on stage all through this scene about her urine and the description of her vapors until, with obvious relief, she was able to exit with a prescription for bread and wine. Later in the play the new star was given a scene in which she has miraculously recovered her voice after a walk with her young man. For her explosive climactic speech Molière writes a stage direction for her character: "*Parlant d'un ton de voix à étourdir.*" That is, she speaks in a tone of voice that stuns, deafens, astounds or staggers the others in the scene. Thus she vociferously refuses everything in life except her young lover, saying to all other possibilities "No! No way! Nothing doing! You're wasting your time. I won't listen. And that is that!"

This is a young girl who knows what she wants, and it's not what Daddy wants. And even if it isn't Célimène, it's a delicious role.

If the first scene in *Le Misanthrope* was structured as a debate between two highly intelligent men who speak in long reasoned pieces of magnificent rhetorical poetry about how to live in society, the first scene in *Le Médecin Malgré Lui* is a burlesque fight between a husband and wife that demonstrates how to hold the stage and get the laughs:

> SGANARELLE. No! I won't do it. And what I say goes. I'm the master here.
> MARTINE.   You will do it. You may be the master but you'll do as I say.

Figure 29. Molière as Sganarelle. Bibliothèque Nationale de France.

Figure 30. The Sganarelle vs Martine debate at the Comédie-Française. Photo © Laurencine Lot.

> SGANARELLE. What is a wife? A sharp instrument for cutting a man down.
> Socrates hit it when he said; Marry a woman, live with a demon.
> MARTINE. Listen to the clever man with his bonehead of a Socrates.

We can note that while the first two lines are probably done nose-to-nose, the second two are to the audience, with each actor trying to woo the public. In a battle on stage, the object is to win the audience to your side. Since Martine may well have been played by his former mistress and closest artistic collaborator, Madeleine Béjart, we know that the battle is even – or we may even suspect that the man may have gotten the worst of it. In my production at the University of California at Los Angeles, we chose to show his strength by having the actor heft his woodcutter's ax and bury it in a woodblock; to establish his manliness he pumped the stick of the butter churn up and down, thus demonstrating his physical prowess on the wedding night. Martine's speeches were supported by a waggling bosom and wiggling hips which she used to establish her superiority in such combat. The traditional business is full of sexual struggle with mops and much goosing. It all reaches its first climax with this domestic squabble:

> MARTINE. Gambles and boozes from morning to night.
> SGANARELLE. Better than being idle.
> MARTINE. And while all this goes on what do you expect me to do with the children?
> SGANARELLE. Anything you like.
> MARTINE. I have these four little ones on my hands.
> SGANARELLE. Let 'em drop.
> MARTINE. They're always crying for a crumb to eat.
> SGANARELLE. Give 'em a taste of the whip.

This kind of comedy comes out of Aristophanes but also has been seen in our time on stages like the Empire Burlesque in Newark. I sneaked in there as a sixteen year old – sitting among the old men with newspapers in their laps – and saw something approximating the following scene:

> A clown rocks a baby in a carriage; a stripper crosses the stage and bumps and grinds with the side curtain; the clown wants to go to her; the baby cries; the stripper leaves and the clown raises his arms to heaven; another stripper sashays across stage; baby cries again; the stripper leaves and the clown sobs out-loud; for the magic third time, the star stripper slowly bumps and grinds across the stage and uses the side curtain for sexual relief; the baby cries louder; in despair, the clown punches baby; the baby retaliates by unloosing a stream of pee in the

clown's face; the stripper leaves; both clown and audience go ape, each in their
own way. Moral for 2000 years: Sex is better than child care!! And he not only
doesn't get the sex ... he gets a face full of pee.[6]

Well within the tradition, Molière's scene ends with a spanking that feels more
like fun for the wife than pain for a beaten woman, and certainly would not be
played in front of their four children:

SGANARELLE. Shall I make you murmur in pain?
MARTINE.   Gut rot!
SGANARELLE. Then hammer you into silence?
MARTINE.   Big lip, double-crosser, chicken-hearted chiseler, sponger, gasbag,
                     wastrel, worm, thief.
SGANARELLE. (*Beating her with his stick*) So you enjoy punishment?
MARTINE.   Stop, stop, stop, stop!

Lots of skirt-lifting and tickling and assorted shrieks make the short scene
fun. Then Monsieur Robert comes in and tries to rescue the "poor woman
in distress." This brings about a major transition. As the happy "victim" lifts
her head and sees the "intruder" trying to rescue her, she starts chasing him
around the stage. Sganarelle also goes in pursuit but steps in a bucket and does
the classic clown-in-a-bucket routine and the rest of the scene resembles a
badminton game – smacking the outside do-gooder from side to side. The tag
for the scene: *Good guys always finish last*. We are, indeed, as far from Célimène's
salon as we can get.

   In playing farce, if it is to be closer to Mozart than to heavy vulgarity, the
"lightness of touch" is all. If an action is played with only naked aggression and
pain there is no laughter. The scene has to dance; the scene has to be played with
joy and spontaneity; the idea has to tap into our collective desire to strike at –
but not kill – whoever interferes with our wants, our pleasures, our intentions.
Monsieur Robert was at the wrong place at the wrong time and stuck his moral
nose into the Rabelaisian actions of a happy man and woman playing the eternal
game of "Hump the Hostess." Even the scene in Newark was played with a light
tongue-in-cheek awareness by both the clown and the strippers – that sex is on
everybody's mind, and that it really doesn't matter all that much anyway but it's
fun when you can get it. No emotional angst involved. If painless beatings are a
part of farce, pure, plain, lusty sex – unadulterated by the contorting, complex
rules of society's attempts to control lascivious love – remains the center.

   Rabelais would have loved the scene when Sganarelle meets the wet nurse
of the family who is married to the malapropish husband who can never say a
sentence without using the wrong word. What we get is a scene about bosoms

and the neglect of grammar. The role of Jacqueline, the "Lady" referred to in the following scene, was played at the Comédie-Française in the 1940s by the famous Béatrice Bretty who was, in size, a ringer for a Wagnerian soprano. She played often with Jean Meyer, another sociétaire, who was skinny as a bean-pole. Her breasts were like great shelves of pulchritude. Note that Jacqueline doesn't have any lines in this little scene, yet there is little doubt who had the focus.

SGANARELLE. And who's that sizable woman there?

GÉRONTE.   My little one's milk nurse.

SGANARELLE. What a splendid specimen of milkiness! Oh, milk nurse, you tantalizing milk nurse, my doctorate is the humble slave of your milky abundance. What I'd give to be the lucky brat who sucks the milk (*He touches her breasts*) of your human kindness. All my remediation, all my burning wisdom, my very professional touch – these are yours if–

LUCAS.   (*The husband*) Please, doctor, not so dispassionate.

            (*The two men do a little hide and peek around her.*)

LUCAS.   Doctor, lay off her.

SGANARELLE. I'll willingly lay off her!

Sounds like Groucho Marx on a tear. It taps into the fantasy dreamscape of farce where all the forbidden delights are seen devoid of risk and anxiety. As Robert Jouanny said in his preface to this play, Molière was, once again, "happy like a fish in water,"[7] swimming effortlessly through the glistening shoals of comedy and feeding off the coral swirls of laughter in one of his perfect little farces about doctors.

XII

CLASSIC ROUTINES

Amphitryon
as directed by *Jean-Louis Barrault*
as translated by *Richard Wilbur*

L'Avare
as adapted by *David Ball*
as directed by *Dominique Serrand*
as acted by *Stephen Epp*

In the last seven years of his life and in spite of continually failing health, Molière wrote fourteen plays, mostly to fulfill the desires of the king. Of these fourteen plays, seven were rewarded with an ongoing life into modern times. It is an amazing accomplishment: these seven plays were all fascinating explorations of a radically new style; five were unique and incomparable comic gems; one, the last written, has been termed an out and out masterpiece. Under much pressure from the king's unending demands for entertainment, Molière goes back further, before his days as Sganarelle in the provinces, to his roots in the dusty classrooms of Clermont and the unfettered boyhood renderings in Latin of works by Plautus for much-needed inspiration. Early in 1668 he used Plautus' *Amphitruo* as the basis for his own French *Amphitryon*. This is a play by Molière that reads as well as it plays and the irony is: its theme is the mystery found in the art of acting. How can someone be someone else and also at the very same time be one's own self? And which representation is the truer? And perhaps in a nod to his contemporary, Descartes, which part contains the soul? How can the public representative be so admired and adored while at the same time the private performer is so beset with carping critics, angry creditors and a cold, indifferent wife? All this is couched in free verse, a rare form of presentation for Molière who with the genteel lyricism of romantic comedy tells the story of the contented wife who can tell no difference between her husband and a god. One can sense his increasing fascination with his own developing power as an actor. In our time we have been fortunate enough to have had an exquisite production of *Amphitryon*, by the Madeleine Renaud–Jean-Louis Barrault Company, brought to New York in 1953, and also to have the recent superb translation of this delightful play by Richard Wilbur.

The point in *Amphitryon* is the lust of the King of the Gods, Jupiter, for a married woman. He decides he will take on the appearance of the famous General Amphitryon and act the role of the husband in the bed of the general's lovely wife, Alcmena. With the help of Mercury and a character called "Night," who will slow the passage of time, Jupiter not only cuckolds the human but also spends the longest night of lovemaking in the recorded myths of heavenly time. Thus the God turns himself not only into a human being but into an actor in the role of the Husband, and he is such a good actor the perfect "Wife" spends the long amorous night never suspecting a substitution. Poor Jupiter! He has a great night in her bed but the next morning he has to prove to himself that he is the greatest lover. He initiates a lengthy discussion with her about how she must have preferred the "lover" he was last night to the usual "husband" he is on all the other nights. The actor's ego, however, is somewhat bruised. She says words to the effect of "Honey, don't worry; to me you are always great." Such constancy is not in Jupiter's comprehension. Was she really paying attention? He must be better in the role of Lover. He tries to woo her to his side; he pleads his case eloquently. He speaks as the hero of many clandestine loves – i.e., a god, a matinee idol, a Star, not some wimpy, lowly, utility actor of a Husband. Onstage was our Don Juan, La Grange himself, trying to convince Catherine de Brie as Alcmena whose virtue is absolute even when compromised by the head of the gods, just as Catherine's role as a wife in life was not compromised by her affairs over time with the head of the troupe. Romantic comedy is not working out too well for Jupiter.

The acting metaphor is also explored in another even more fascinating way with the god Mercury acting the role of the man-servant, Sosia. Molière plays the human servant who is robbed of his identity right there in front of him. Sosia arrives to tell Alcmena that her husband is on the way home. But upstairs Alcmena is still making divine love with the god acting her husband, Amphitryon, and out in front of their house is none other than … another Sosia. The conflict between the real servant and the "acting" servant played by Mercury is all too familiar; on one hand, the god beats the human and the human gives in and concedes that he is not himself – the same mechanism used when the two men beat Sganarelle until he admits that he is "really" a doctor, which he isn't, and not a woodcutter, which he is. Sosia, however, can't play the game like the sharp woodcutter and he can't believe that the other person on stage is "really" him. He keeps worrying over the idea that "I can't be someone else than me" and in spite of the cowardly metamorphosis caused by

Figure 31. A midnight dream of godly love in *Amphitryon*. Barrault Archives: Rights reserved.

Figure 32. A nightmare vision of earthly greed in *The Miser*. Photo © Michal Daniel.

the beating, Sosia still can't quite accept what's happening and he goes on to argue:

> No matter. I can't annul myself for you,
> Or listen to more fantasy and sham.
> How can you be the person that I am?
>   Can I cease to be myself? Not true!"[1]

The game played in this scene suggests the tension in acting between the "self" of the actor and the "soul" of the character. In the great actor they become the same. Morris Carnovsky of the Group Theatre told the story of how, when playing Shylock one night after an exhausting day, he decided to go onstage with all his gestures, costumes, and make-up for Shylock and just be Morris. The rest of the cast all descended on him after the performance, telling him how "real" he was that night, so believable. Everyone always spoke of how "real" Molière was as an actor. "Self" and role fused into one. Sometimes that "self" was a despairing lover and sometimes a theatrical "type" but both are in the core of the actor/man. As a writer he also, as we have seen over and over, fuses his "self" with his "plays."

The all-powerful King Louis, being both a general and a god, must have enjoyed it greatly, since he was in the throes of an affair with a married woman, Marquise de Montespan, whose father-in-law, upon hearing of the affair with the king exclaimed, "At last Fortune has entered our House!" – a line that could be in a play by Molière.

The third play Molière wrote in 1668 – a very busy year indeed – was *L'Avare* (*The Miser*) based on Plautus' *Aulularia* (*Pot of Gold*). It is the one Molière play that almost everyone has seen. But oddly it was not popular in Molière's day, while *Amphitryon* was hugely popular in the seventeenth century and is seldom seen today. *L'Avare* carries identity crisis a step further in that one actor plays three different people, changing his hat, his costume and even his personality right on stage to fit the occasion's desperate needs. This is the role of the servant Monsieur Jacques-of-all-trades, who upon occasion disguises himself as the chef and the chauffeur. This obvious role-playing is motivated by his employer's extreme miserliness: three for the price of one.

The miser is Harpagon and Molière played this role in which the acting metaphor is carried to deeper and even tragic dimensions. Some think, with good reason, that Harpagon is a characterization based on the kind of deep feelings stirred up by Alceste's final exit into the desert saying:

> Meanwhile, betrayed and wronged in everything,
> I'll flee this bitter world where vice is king …

Many have commented on the bitterness of Molière during these months – the never ending dispute over *Le Tartuffe* which he knew would support his actors, the illness, the milk diets, the pain of his love for Armande: any or all of which could have motivated his work on a big play about a miser of vicious selfishness who treats everyone in the world, including his own children, with withering indifference. We have heard it asked what happens to Nora when she walks out and slams the door on her *Doll's House*. *L'Avare* could be Molière's answer to what happens to Alceste. If he transformed his sexual desires into a language for Tartuffe, he could certainly channel his life's resentments into a monster like Harpagon.

Harpagon's miserliness could not be further from Molière's own nature. He was known by his friends as an extremely generous man, one who was particularly vulnerable to other theater people in need, but he creates here a true monster of egoism, a character who is not just obsessive but a madman. And the catalyst is not love, lust, power or truth, but money. His hard "pot of gold" has replaced the soft body of Armande, and avarice has taken over his brain. However, *L'Avare*, unlike the passions of *Le Misanthrope*, is heartless, and when the play opened in 1668, it ran for only eight performances. Audiences then may have found the bitterness and hatred in the soul of Harpagon to be too uncomfortable for laughter. Maybe their favorite actor was playing a role too far away from his nature. This time the obsession tipped into madness. Being estranged from Armande, the work of the theater and the pot of gold needed for the survival of his troupe took over all his thoughts. For a sick man, his schedule of work in these last years is mind-boggling. Yes. Money was a big concern in his role as company manager, but it does not seem to have been a personal obsession. The "pot of gold" is not from his inner nature, but from the classics.

In any event, today the play is done a great deal. Maybe it is because our society is possessed by cravings for cash. The 2005 production presented on tour by the Théâtre de la Jeune Lune at the La Jolla Playhouse was brilliantly directed by Dominique Serrand, and it fused the darkest terrors of cruelty in the obsessed Harpagon with the company's formidable skills at physical comedy. It is the best performance of this play I have ever seen. Stephen Epp as Harpagon was a virtuoso. His face, like Molière's, was an instrument of extraordinary *plastique*: it could freeze with his tongue hanging far out; it could move through thrashing waves of emotion; it could – and often did – suddenly drop all such characteristics and stand nakedly on stage and face the audience with total simplicity. He drove the character beyond obsession into dementia, yet kept the audience awed and delighted for three hours.

Molière created the glory of this starring role for himself and for the many actors that followed, including Mr. Epp. In 1668, the challenge of Harpagon's addresses directly to the public might have been too strong to take. Today, laughter can be found in the mind-boggling absurdity of those soliloquies, such as the long one in act 4 when Harpagon weeps over the loss of his money as if it were the loss of all consolation. He doesn't know who he is or where he is. He thinks he is dying; then goes on to say, "No. I'm dead. I'm buried." But the actor in him pulls the character out of the morbidity of a snake pit by suddenly seeing the audience:

> Look at all those eyes. Thieves' eyes. Staring. What're they staring at? For more to steal? Who are you? You've a stench like thieves. All right, which one of you has my gold? Everyone innocent raise your hand. Hah! I knew it. Never so many lying thieves in one place outside jail. Vultures! Buzzards. Staring. You're looking at yourselves, don't you know that? Someday this will be you. Yes, you. And you and you and you. You will wake up with everything gone. You won't even be able to breathe. You too will be dying. Remember I warned you.
>
> I saw you over there sneak in. YOU BETTER CONFESS. We do not mollycoddle robbers here, we hang them. From one foot, with your pockets turned inside out!
>
> Oh, please, please, dear God, please if anyone knows anything, please make them just tell me? I'll be good. I am begging on my knees.
>
> You there. Why are you looking at each other? Is she my robber? Is he? Why are you hiding my robber? Please, look under the thief next to you. Is he sitting on my money? Look in his pocket. There, that one, look under her skirt.
>
> Hah! …
>
> (*Confronting audience*)
>
> Laughing at me? You thieves can laugh together, but one at a time you will hang.[2]

Molière knew how to work an audience. We can remember his first little play before the king, with Molière, in a stiff black half mask, his tongue hanging out below it, on his knees begging for a smile from the perfectly made-up king who, with his extreme white make-up, looked almost masked himself. Surely here, on his knees in his own theater with his own public, he must have been astonishingly charismatic. We remember Arnolphe on his knees to Agnès, or Alceste abjectly begging Célimène to give up all and follow him. In those roles, Molière failed to get the love he sought, but now the actor, pleading with the audience to help him get back his cash box, receives the golden reward of laughter, the unmistakable measure of their love for him. We can imagine Molière wondering, with a bemused smile, why it was that he was so beloved onstage and so beset with anxieties offstage.

Mr. Serrand staged the opening scenes between Harpagon and his servant, La Flèche (the arrow), as pure farce, using the age-old techniques of comedy. La Flèche, played by Nathan Keeper, who moved with the effortlessness of a loose-limbed puppet and at times with the startling speed of an arrow, and Harpagon, who combined the gestural language of age with the unpredictable energies of infancy, were both costumed by Sonya Berlovitz in layered rags-over-rags of bygone glory. The two actors whizzed through a litany of comedic *lazzi*:

a. Chase scenes full of invectives and insults (sprinkled with scatological words describing bodily functions)
b. Daemonic energies (speed and manic rhythms from start to finish; the devil is energy and it's the only thing that makes Harpagon human)
c. Tunnel vision (versus reason and common sense)
d. Rigidities and fluidities of all sorts (anal and infantile behavior)
e. Primal emotion (fear of Master; fear of losing money)
f. Repressed sexuality (money as a substitute sexual object)
g. Costume jokes (La Flèche has the money in his pants where his sex is; the shoes don't match; patched patches etc.)
h. Sight gags (extreme exaggerations of all sorts; mechanical malfunctions in the scenery)

At the end of the play, in an absolutely bleak and "tragic" atmosphere, Harpagon, after the frantic chase for his gold, dove into a long box with his money, the box became a coffin, and in a funereal light his coffin was born down stage by all his abused servants, to the death music borrowed from Mnouchkine's film on Molière.

The space in which this play lived was a huge and totally empty room in a crumbling eighteenth-century mansion, designed by Riccardo Hernandez with great artistic precision in both scale and detail. For instance, the only chair was nailed high up on the back wall, onto which La Fleche would fly up and perch from time to time. The ceiling had plastic sheeting which had been put there to stop the rain leaks and was holding pools of yellowing water. Doors didn't open; they came off. Floor boards sprang up as they stepped on them, a *lazzo* which culminated in the last act with the entire upstage area seesawing dangerously under the actor's movement. The scenic metaphor was based on this Harpagon's refusal to spend anything on anything, and so he lived in a space with a disintegrating structure, devoid of all furnishings so no one could steal them.

Sadly, this brilliant American company is no longer with us. No benefactor like Louis was available and all that talent is now dispersed around the country. A company manager's nightmare.[3]

XIII

MUSICAL COMEDY

George Dandin; ou, le Mari Confondu
Le Bourgeois Gentilhomme
as conceived by Molière
as ordered by Louis XIV, King of France

Here we deal with what might be called the first stirrings of musical comedy. While Molière's personal choice as an actor, playwright, and company manager, was for farce and the classics, he was increasingly subject to the choices made for him by Louis XIV. The King was Absolute. The king was not a modest man. His philosophy of life was set down in his *Memoirs* (italics mine):

> In my heart I prefer fame above all else, even life itself ... Love of glory has the same subtleties as the most tender passions ... (*code for sexual pleasure*)[1]

Louis dictated much of what, when, where and even how Molière was to write during the next five years. Between 1667 and his death in 1673, eight of his remaining fourteen plays were court entertainments given in the gardens of various palaces, and his collaborator on six of them was Jean-Baptiste Lully. Lully had been for some time the supervisor of music for the king, and when, back in 1661 at Vaux-le-Vicomte, he and Molière hurriedly devised a new form that alternated interludes of music and dance with the novel addition of comic acts, the two artists became an ongoing team working at the pleasure of the king. Their collaboration may have begun in *Les Fâcheux* (*The Bores*) with a simple scheme in which the play stopped now and then and the dancers came out and did a short number. The king may have put the owner of Vaux-le-Vicomte in prison for embezzlement, but he liked the entertainment. Beginning with *Le Tartuffe* in 1664, the spectacles became more and more complicated and awe-inspiring.

The main purpose of these events was to glorify the Sun King, and, at times, even to allow his Majesty to join in, transforming himself into a daring knight winning a joust, or into a dancer showing the well-turned royal leg. The king was the focal point around which the audience and the performance revolved. There in his magnificent regalia he listened to the music, watched the dancers move, and was dazzled by the scene shifts. He also got quite a few laughs from his favorite comedian, Molière.

This chapter talks of two of those plays with leads both seeking a move up the social ladder: M. Dandin, a darkly bitter, disappointed man; M. Jourdain, radiantly happy and confident of his success. George Dandin comes alive in *George Dandin; ou, le Mari Confondu (George Dandin; or, The Confounded Husband)*: it is a world full of recriminations and humiliations. M. Jourdain lives in *Le Bourgeois Gentilhomme*: this delightful fool is happy in a world dedicated to the celebration of … himself. Molière played both parts. We will first go to Versailles – where Louis had commanded that an event was to take place on April 18, 1668 – to look at *George Dandin*, written in the same year as his two Roman plays.

The Festival surrounding *George Dandin* was modestly titled Le Grand Divertissement Royal de Versailles (The Royal Grand Festival of Versailles). The evening was to celebrate both Louis' victory in Flanders and the opening of the newly landscaped gardens. After a sumptuous dinner the three thousand guests – should one describe them as demigods? – poured into a theater space fashioned out of tons of greenery and flanked by massive fountains. Twelve hundred papal emissaries, ambassadors, great lords of France, members of the court and the numerous members of the royal family surrounded the king, enthroned at the center of the front row on a raised dais. Behind them were arrayed a host of minor luminaries. Molière and Lully had noted what was happening in the new creations of Italian opera, and were expanding some of those ideas to craft these extravagant entertainments for the king. The opening prologue began with the appearance of thirty-nine dancing Bacchantes, a chorus of twenty nine singing lovers costumed as shepherds and shepherdesses, all giddily extolling the romance of love by acting out the quintessential Hollywood story: Boy meets girl, boy loses girl, and most importantly, boy gets that girl. Royalty tended to lose their heads over shepherds; we can look forward to Marie Antoinette and her Trianon.

The dramatic form chosen for this production was the alternation between a brutal domestic three-act farce in prose called "The Comedy," interrupted and framed by the lyrical romance of the lengthy interludes of music and dance featuring, in verse, the eternal loves of shepherds and shepherdesses. The contrast between the savage farce and the pastoral skits is extreme. To give the reader a sense of the style I'll quote a few lines from our production at the University of Washington. The opening prologue is in light and silly pastoral verses and was adapted for us in a manuscript translation by Angela Paton from Molière's text in a version that limits the Versailles' cast of hundreds to a more manageable four, graced with music by Matthew Goldsby that he termed contemporary/period with a little bit of harpsichord thrown in:

(*Enter two giggling shepherdesses followed by two stalwart shepherds*)

CLIMÈNE.	No, Philène! Never return
CLORIS.	Both of you. Leave us Alone
TIRCIS AND PHILÈNE.	(*Two boys sweetly singing in harmony*)
	Are their beautiful breasts so firm
	Because their hearts are made of stone?
	Ladies, hear us out! Change your tone
CLIMÈNE AND CLORIS.	Why on earth should we watch you squirm?
TIRCIS AND PHILÈNE.	(*Again singing even more passionately*)
	Our hearts burn
	Like an eternal flame, we yearn
	For you. Forever and a day
	We'll cherish and honor and obey.
CLORIS.	Heavens! What a pretty choir!
CLIMÈNE.	I have to say they sang with zest.
PHILÈNE.	The sparkle in your eyes lights my heart with fire!
CLIMÈNE.	I'll close my eyes. Give your heart a rest!
PHILÈNE.	Sweet lady, do not hide those starry eyes!
CLORIS.	I think I like their tuneful sighs.
CLIMÈNE.	Shepherd, I find your love too callow.
	Enough! You fellows mustn't follow!
TIRCIS.	Cloris! I'll follow you anywhere!
CLIMÈNE.	(*Sternly to Cloris*) Come. We'll show we do not care!

The two buddies, after a momentary loss of stalwartness, decide on a fool-proof way to soften those female hard hearts. Happy with their plan, they march stoutheartedly off singing:

To the lake! To the lake!
Why should we be left here crying!
To the lake! To the lake!
We'll show those two by dying!

This prologue/interlude is followed by what Molière titled "The Comedy" in the program he wrote for the event, with George Dandin appearing alone down center saying directly to the king and the very well-born audience:

Ah!! What a wretched thing it is to have a well-born wife! Let my marriage be
a lesson to everyone who wants to rise above their station and join themselves,
as I did, to a House that claims Nobility. Nobility, by itself, is all right; everyone
says it's a big deal. But it comes with so many nasty surprises. ... Ah, George
Dandin, George Dandin, you big booby! What a mess! Going in the front door
of my house is like stepping into a wasp's nest![2]

Armande played Angélique, the wife. Need I say more.

Like the starkness of *Le Tartuffe* and its threat of loss in the midst of
outrageous luxury, here again the three short twenty minute acts each end in
a mortifying defeat for the husband. The tone of the farce is as harsh as the
interludes are soft, pretty, silly and comic; the atmosphere of the play is dark,
wintry and savage. Molière, of course, did it in a magnificent theater setting
with rich court costumes, but even in rich garments and in front of astonishing
vistas, the play is the kind of farce that takes the skin off.

If one remembers the passionate love story of Alceste and Célimène only
two years prior as one watches the same married couple playing in this farce,
one can sense the profound change in their personal man/wife relationship
as it is reflected on stage. There is not one shred of sexual yearning left.
By the end of the play, standing alone and in despair, he, like the two
shepherds, decides to end it all by drowning. What saves him is not the
situation, not the king, not the *deus*, but the world of theater. The two worlds
that have alternated for three acts end with a giant spectacle with all the
lovers in the make-believe world of poetic license joining all the players in
George's real world of pain, coming on stage to sing to him about getting
drunk and forgetting Love. Wine replaces Love, and the bitterness of the
marriage is replaced by the conviviality of the cast party. So be it. Nobody
saved Arnolphe or Alceste, Don Juan or Tartuffe.

Having staged this play twice, once with the interludes and its music and
dancing, and once without, I found that without the interludes the play is
doubtful as comedy and doesn't elicit much laughter from an audience
watching a man forced to kneel and apologize for his actions.[3] Without the
interludes, nothing saves the play; with them, it is undeniably listed properly
by the author as "The Comedy." Many versions exist without the interludes
including the famous production by Roger Planchon who did it in an über-
realistic seventeenth-century farmyard. Again, not so funny. George Dandin
seems to need theatricality to save it.

Another change lightened the Washington production. In my Berkeley
production, which was translated by George House who maintained the
original names for the lapsed noble family of Sotenville (drunk-in-town) and
his wife's family name of Prudoterie (with its obvious connection to prudery).

Both these names would have tickled the French funny bone but for the American funny bone, Angela Paton, as translator, changed the noble couple to M. and Mme de Totalasse and Mme's family name to de la Frigidaire in my second production.

Later I worked with Matthew Goldsby as he turned his contemporary/ period music into honky-tonk, the low-down music of lost love in the world of unfortunate low-borns, and wrote a libretto based on *George Dandin*, calling it *Makin' Hay* and setting it in Texas. The shepherds and shepherdesses became cowboys and housemaids and were integrated into the action of the play. George Dandin, a farmer made rich by the oil discovered on his property, was never made to kneel by the substitute characters to represent nobility, a self-important country judge and his Southern belle wife who was no-longer a Southern belle. Texans don't bend their knee to anyone.[1]

But all three versions keep intact the showdown scene between Angélique and George which makes you feel you are eavesdropping on Armande and Jean-Baptiste as they argue over breakfast. That is the scene in which Angélique pleads with George – who has locked her out of the house because she has been off with another man in the middle of the night – to let her come back in. She swears absolute fidelity if he does. "Lo! How the crocodile smiles before she eats you!" says George, deaf to her pleas and promises. In off stage life, sometime in the two years after *George Dandin* opened, it so happened that Armande came to Molière and they became reconciled. He opened the door to her. Again the precise dates and venues of their personal life are vague. Were there promises made? No matter. By 1670 the mood has changed. That is the year he creates his only joyful, happy, sensationally funny character in *Le Bourgeois Gentilhomme* which was presented for the king's pleasure out-of-town at Chambord.

Molière and Lully successfully fused comedy, music and dance into a sublimely successful musical comedy. This time the music and dancing were included within the situation as well as between the acts, and the king told the actor that this was his best work! The uniqueness of this work lies in the title character, Monsieur Jourdain. This is the first obsessive leading role for which the obsession creates Happiness – with a capital *H*. Monsieur Jourdain is the quintessential expression of the *nouveau riche*.

A seminal production of *Le Bourgeois Gentilhomme* starring Louis Seigner was done at the Comédie-Française in 1951, and was subsequently made into a lovely film. In acts 1 and 2, floating about the stage in an Indian house-dress over a violent red and green undergarment, Seigner is attended to by fencing masters, tailors, music and dance instructors, and above all by a Master of Philosophy. The music and dance masters teach the would-be gentleman about music and dance by presenting him with dancers and singers – and inviting him to join in as the king was wont to do during the festivals. Here is some of the dialog, as done by Nick Dear for a production at the National Theatre in England (italics mine):

MUSIC MASTER.	The first piece is an exercise in the portrayal of the passions, musically … you must envisage them dressed as shepherds.
MONSIEUR JOURDAIN.	Not shepherds again. It's always bleeding shepherds. Can't I have water-nymphs?
MUSIC MASTER.	No. It is called the pastoral convention. They are expressing their innermost passions in song. Would it seem natural to have water-nymphs expressing their innermost passions in song? It would not. It must be shepherds.
	(*A duet follows about two exquisite flowers in love which is followed by a little ballet on the same subject. All are costumed as shepherds.*)
MONSIEUR JOURDAIN.	That wasn't quite as pathetic as I expected. Some of those shepherds can wiggle very nicely.[5]

His obsession to rise in society was treated with a sense of buoyant joy. Even those who made fun of him were caught up in his fascination with himself and the society around him that he so wished to join. He had the innocence of a child entering a splendid magical funhouse. He was a portly, aging Peter Pan. Monsieur Jourdain is introduced in a series of scenes to the Pedants. We watched Seigner dance like Dumbo the elephant with the rehearsing shepherds, and sing off-key with the singers in his delighted and atonal "LaLaLaLaLaLaLaLaLaLa." He learned the hard way that in fencing it is better to give than to receive; he was dressed by four tailors, played by a corps of dancers in a choreographed "dressing scene." And he met the "Master of Philosophy."

This famous cameo role is always taken by one of the major *sociétaires* of the Comédie-Française. I was fortunate to see it with the fabulous Robert Hirsch in the part. Hirsch portrayed him as a ferocious, almost hysterically frustrated teacher who began by angrily quoting Seneca on the benefits of avoiding anger and paraphrasing the Stoic Epictetus about enduring calmly all things over which you have no control. He then fell into a towering rage at the other teachers. He quickly became involved in a stage-wide brawl with all of them, only to end up thoroughly beaten but still clinging to some shreds of dignity. Sweating and panting, he struggled to remember his Epictetus. After girding his loins against adversity, he proceeded with the lessons of the day. Clad in black – in contrast to everyone else in the play – Hirsch drenched the

Figure 33. Dandin's unhappy marriage in the seventeenth century. Comédie-Française Archives.

Figure 34. Dandin's unhappy marriage in the twentieth century. Photo © Laurencine Lot.

Figure 35. M. Jourdain's giddy rise in society. Comédie-Française Archives. Photo by François Darras. Rights reserved.

Figure 36. M. Jourdain fights for respectability. Comédie-Française Archives. Agence Roget-Viollet: Rights reserved.

first rows of the audience in perspiration as he strove, like Ionesco's murderous teacher in *The Lesson*, to drive some simple point into this would-be gentleman's bone-head. Finally, after we are all in the aisle, we witness the climactic discovery in the Academy of Higher Learning, as the two of them set out to write a love letter to a countess and debate whether the letter should be in prose or verse.

MASTER OF PHILOSOPHY.	You want the letter to be written in verse.
MONSIEUR JOURDAIN.	No, no. No verse!
MASTER OF PHILOSOPHY.	You want it in prose?
MONSIEUR JOURDAIN.	No, I want neither prose nor verse.
MASTER OF PHILOSOPHY.	It has to be one or the other.
MONSIEUR JOURDAIN.	Why?
MASTER OF PHILOSOPHY.	Because, Monsieur, in order to express oneself, one has to use either prose or verse.
MONSIEUR JOURDAIN.	Isn't there something besides prose or verse?
MASTER OF PHILOSOPHY.	No, Monsieur: everything that is not prose is verse, and everything that is not verse is prose.
MONSIEUR JOURDAIN.	And when I'm talking now, what's that?
MASTER OF PHILOSOPHY.	Prose.
MONSIEUR JOURDAIN.	No! You mean when I say to Nicole, "Fetch my slippers and get my nightcap," that's prose?
MASTER OF PHILOSOPHY.	Yes, Monsieur.
MONSIEUR JOURDAIN.	My God! You mean I've been speaking prose for forty years and didn't know it!⁶

By the time the scene ends the poor teacher is beside himself, but he doesn't kill the student; he agrees to come back tomorrow for another lesson. Greed is always with us. It is too bad Jackie Gleason or Buddy Hackett were never called on to play Monsieur Jourdain. Either one would have proved an American treasure.

The supporting characters in the play consist of three pairs of lovers but it is never questioned that they dwell in an atmosphere of true lovingness. It is all too apparent that Molière is not playing the lover even though Armande is playing the beloved. But it is usually assumed by scholars that Molière and Armande were again living together in a grand apartment near the theater, which might explain the aura of happiness and joy that pervades this work and the loving ode to Armande's special beauty that Molière wrote to be said by Armande's young stage lover.

In all the world I love only her; I think only of her; I want to talk only of her; my dreams are only of her; my heart is totally hers; she is my life.

This scene goes on for two pages of equally ecstatic descriptions of love, and it is the kind of love Pierrot talked about when he said in act 2 of Don Juan that "that's how one loves when one loves how one ought to love."

David Richards wrote a Sunday *New York Times* piece about the Seigner production which is so appropriate for our discussion, I want to share it with the reader:

> Any age that produced Molière would be a golden age of the theater. There are no better comedies than his ... He was the first playwright to speak to me loud and clear across the gulf of time. I was eighteen and acquiring the rudiments of French in Paris and the *matinées classiques* at the Comédie-Française were a mandatory part of the process. One afternoon, I happened to be seated next to a French schoolboy, no older than twelve, and a white-haired woman I assumed to be his grandmother. The play was *The Would-Be Gentleman* – Louis Seigner played the title role – and I remember laughing very hard at this dolt who wanted to acquire highborn airs. The schoolboy and his grandmother were laughing equally hard. We couldn't have been a more disparate trio, and yet a 300-year-old voice had brought us together for a while and made us one. Time had been erased, social differences negated, and any language barriers, which were real in my case, shattered. That is what the best theater does, I now know. The sense of communion I felt that day was a revelation, however.[7]

Stanislavski, in his "System," used the term "communion" very prominently as a way to define what was created by the work of an actor before the public: an expression of the "life of our soul, on stage." What David Richards has described is "the fluid exchange of emotion" which usually is ascribed to what happens between two actors on stage, but in this case I apply it to the process between the actor and the audience, or what Alfred Lunt and Lynn Fontaine called "playing together." That's what audiences feel today in the art form that Molière and Lully's experiments opened up: musical comedy. The wonder of *Oklahoma*, the pulsing heartbeat of *Spring Awakening*, the artistry of *Sunday in the Park with George*, the theatricality of *Kiss Me Kate*, the magic of *Wicked*, all bring us together in their worlds as one. We leave the theater feeling like kings. And that is the pure gold found in live theater that every theater artisan – from writer to propman – works to bring you each night: community; communion; ecstatic experience.

XIV

THE BONES OF FARCE

Les Fourberies de Scapin
as directed by Jacques Copeau
as acted by Louis Jouvet
as directed by Louis Jouvet
as acted by Jean-Louis Barrault
as translated by Lady Gregory

In 1671, Molière and Armande, although again living together as man and wife, went their separate ways on stage. The last play in the cycle of musical collaborations was *Psyché*, an ambitious and expensive baroque court spectacle written by Molière in collaboration with Pierre Corneille and Quinault and for the last time working with Lully as the composer. It opened for the king's pleasure in Paris at the Salles des Machines at the Tuileries in January. The vast production cost Louis hundreds of thousands of francs. It was a mind-boggling extravaganza that lasted five hours and gave Armande the opportunity to do the thing she loved to do: wear many sumptuous costumes and be admired for her comedic talents. Virginia Scott quotes the ambassador from the Court of Savoy, who reports on the last scene:

> It is the most astonishing thing, for, in an instant, more than 300 persons appear suspended in the clouds and making the most beautiful music in the world with violins, theorbos,[1] lutes, harpsichords, oboes, flutes, trumpets, and cymbals.[2]

Armande was the star, reigning above it all, almost as radiant as the Sun King himself.

A few months after *Psyché* opened, Molière chose to come down to earth and tread the boards of his newly remodeled Palais-Royal in a three-act, prose, bare-boned farce, letting Armande stay on dancing through the heavens in her very own hit as the appealingly lovelorn Psyché. He became Scapin in *Les Fourberies de Scapin*, doing it without a commission from the king. He took on the role of the arch manipulator, arch con man, arch rogue, with his roots in the earthiness of good old Italian *Commedia*. He is a man completely in control; he is home again.

What holds up the body of comedy are the all important bones of farce, the rewarding mechanics that get the laugh. From Aristophanes to sitcom; from the pair of buddies climbing into the land of *The Birds* to Abbot and Costello watching baseball; from the first farce of Molière to the last scene he wrote – the same devices can be found: the age-old tricks, the sure-fire gimmicks, the sweet little *lazzi* that help make an entrance alive with brilliance and make an exit leave the public wanting more. Farce celebrates the physical body, and nobody who wrote plays was more at home in his body than Jean-Baptiste Poquelin *dit* Molière. As an actor, he brought the dry bones of technique to vibrant life and left them as a pattern for bringing laughter to the hearts of future audiences. We will look at some of those bones in his last pure farce, *Les Fourberies de Scapin*, written and played by Molière late in his career, in May 1671.

The English language text we will refer to in this chapter belongs to an Irish woman who translated a version for W. B. Yeats in 1907, at the Abbey Theatre in Dublin, Ireland. From *Les Fourberies de Scapin*, Lady Gregory turned her lilting Irish version into *The Rogueries of Scapin*. The French title comes from the word *fourbe*, which the French dictionary *Le Littré* defines as "one who has the resources to deceive by even odious methods."[3] Farce loves the odious, and a *rogue* has the scent of a *fourbe*, and when I re-imagined the play in 1958 in Berkeley, I chose the Lady's version because it has the music and the mischief of the original, and its slight Irish flavor gave the performance a roguish speed and bounce.

In the following pages, this play's life passes through Molière's production at his own theater in Paris, to Lady Gregory's translation, to Jacques Copeau, the most influential French director in the twentieth century who was responsible for throwing out heavy nineteenth-century scenery and putting the focus back on the text. Copeau directed and performed in his production of Molière's play in New York in the middle of World War I and in Paris in 1920 at his own theater, Théâtre du Vieux-Colombier. It was there that Copeau worked with the great Louis Jouvet, as a young actor playing the old man, Géronte. Later, in 1951, Jouvet directed Jean-Louis Barrault's celebrated performance as Scapin for the first season of the Renaud-Barrault Company at the Marigny Theatre in Paris. Louis Jouvet then published Jacques Copeau's prompt script in the 1950s which I used in my own production as a director at the University of California at Berkeley when, as a beginning director in 1958, I unashamedly stole material from both the prompt script and the Barrault production I had seen in Paris: transportations; transmigrations; transformations! All these live performances circled back through time and connected to the original creator. Great artists like Jouvet and Barrault and the spirited Berkeley students – all were joined with both Copeau and Molière.

To examine how some of those bones that make up the skeleton of farce speak to us let us turn to the first scene between a young man hopelessly in love and his not-too-sympathetic servant as translated by Lady Gregory:

OCTAVE.   Oh! What news for a lover! What a fix I am in. You say, Silvester, you have just heard at the port that my father has landed from his voyage?

SILVESTER. Just so.

OCTAVE.   And that he is on the point of coming to the house?

SILVESTER. Just so.

OCTAVE.   And that he has made up a match for me?

SILVESTER. That's it.

OCTAVE.   A daughter of Géronte's?

SILVESTER. Of Mr. Géronte.

OCTAVE.   That they are bringing her from Tarentum?

SILVESTER. That's what I said.[1]

Here we can look at how the words are chosen (the diction) and what the sentences say to us (the syntax). Many elements comprise the dialog. In this scene we begin with tempo and contrast. Rhetorically, the speed is clued by the run-on sentences, alternating with staccato replies, heightened by the danger of the situation as indicated by the words. Contrast is in the length of sentences and the differing emotional stances of the two characters. There is also the basic contrast of the upward inflection of a question and the flat authority of the down inflected answer. The syntax gives us clarity and helps get the story line set in a minimum number of words. This scene, in both French and English, swiftly develops the master-servant relationship, defines the missing Father as a bully, and tells us that neither of these characters has the wit to get out of what is a very undesirable marriage for the young master, who we soon learn has already married a gypsy girl while his father was away. All this is facilitated through the unbelieving questioning of Octave and the reassurance of Silvester that he has been heard correctly.

To re-create a text from the past in the present as we have been doing has been vital to our understanding of how Molière stays alive on stage. To go even deeper, let us turn to the master: Jacques Copeau. Another means of communication is the unspoken language of gesture which is demonstrated in Jacques Copeau's written *mise-en-scène* describing how he staged the scene:

The juvenile, Octave, enters with huge strides and moves rapidly and passionately up and down across the stage. His servant, Silvester, enters slowly, stays in place, and slowly cracks and spits sunflower seeds to punctuate his terse replies. Just

before the entrance of Scapin they both freeze and turn upstage almost as if they
know that Scapin is waiting to enter. And he does![5]

In farce, the above, taken from Copeau's prompt script, describes what is
called a pacing scene. It physically illuminates the text; it contrasts two bodies
moving in space; it uses repetition as a comic device; and if done precisely, it
makes absolutely clear the given circumstances of the scene.

If the opening scenes are to communicate a text vividly for the audience
through movement, one of the essential decisions for the director is the
ground plan or the geography of the playing space. Copeau's theater at
the Vieux-Colombier was a series of permanent architectural planes with
side stairs and a bridge over a center archway. Christian Bérard, who did the
set for the later Jouvet/Barrault production, simplified it but used a similar
alignment of spaces. Both ground plans are perfect for this little introductory
scene. The two subordinate characters of Octave and Silvester are blocked on
the floor level downstage. The rapidly pacing lover turns upstage, in a final,
arms uplifted prayer to the gods, and cries out, "What am I to do? What can
I do? How can I help myself?" At that moment Scapin is revealed in the most
powerful stage position – full front upstage center on the highest level – we all
immediately know that help has, indeed, arrived. Out of Roman and Italian
comedy, we have a fresh French version of the traditional street-wise servant:
the all-powerful *homme de théâtre*, whether Molière or Jean-Louis Barrault. For a
small pause, a breath, we take in his vibrant presence, then he jumps into the
scene and takes absolute control of the stage and the situation. He will solve
the problems of not one, but two young men, and get them the money they
need to save their threatened love affairs. Scapin, the archetypical con man,
knows how to talk birds out of trees and get blood from turnips with ease.

Molière decides that for his version of the *fourbe*, Scapin, he will immediately
show how the character reacts to the story of love. The juvenile, Octave, played
by the young Baron in Molière's production, recounts at length his and his friend
Léandre's many adventures; how they both met with young gypsy girls; how his
gypsy girl's tears aroused great feelings of pity in him; how he fell in love and
married her without telling his father; how his father is now coming home; etc.
etc. We don't know how Molière as Scapin played the scene, but his character's
attitude toward romantic love is clear from the text: he couldn't care less. Scapin
is a pragmatist and a cynic. Copeau, playing the role, sat on the edge of a
platform in *front* of the young lover. As the boy ardently described his plight,
Copeau as Scapin started watching an imaginary fly buzz around him. Such
fly-catching is typical scene-stealing business – Charlie Chaplin was a master –
and it successfully and succinctly indicates that, for the comic über-servant, love
is a big bore. This no doubt added to the young lover's frustration. Jouvet with

Barrault chose to play the same scene directly *behind* Octave who played front to the public carried away with the fervor of his story. As the unaware juvenile goes on totally absorbed by his story of true love, Barrault transformed himself into the young girl, simpering and quivering and using Silvester as a very willing sex object. He performs a similar mime in his film *Les Enfants du Paradis* (*Children of Paradise*). This convention of playing an attitude in counterpoint to another – at the same time and in the same space – is used throughout the play. This is a play of contrasting duos: two overbearing fathers; two servants; two naïve sons; two ingénues of mysterious origins; and two cons.

Michael Chekhov believed that the deepest foundation of the art of acting was in the concept of "transformation." Jean-Louis Barrault told actors to study the way kittens instinctively transformed themselves into jungle killers by arching their backs and hissing. This occurs before the kitten ever sees any such killers; the instinct to terrify the opponent is in their bones. The mimetic human actor can similarly feel the gesture coming out of an even deeper instinct than a mere literal "imitation."

Stanislavski called one principal key to unlocking the action of transformation the "magic if." Molière twice invents a scene employing the device of the "magic if." At one point he turns Scapin into a stage director rehearsing a not-too-bright Silvester as a would-be actor, showing him how to play the role of a bully in order to terrify his master, Octave's father. He corrects the way Silvester walks: "Walk like a King you would see in the theater," he tells him, with a wink to the public – and mayhap to King Louis. Copeau had Silvester go wild stomping about. They go off to rehearse some more with Scapin saying "I know all the ways of disguising the face and the voice" as an underplayed remark by the superior man of the theater who knows just how to get the last big laugh by confiding his very apparent power *sub rosa* to his public. As kids say, "Let's pretend!"

Scapin also uses the "magic if" to help the son win a debate against the ogre of a father. He tells the boy he will pretend to be the father so that Octave can rehearse his defense and they begin to rehearse the scene *as if* it were a play, and Scapin will act *as if* he were the Father. "Pretend I'm your father and answer me firmly."

Scapin goes upstage, turns around, and appears transformed into the choleric Argante. Lady Gregory renders that transformation thus:

What's that? You fool, you dog-boy! You ill-conditioned idiot! Would you dare come before me after your behavior, after the dirty trick you played and my back turned? Is that the harvest I get for caring for you, you hound? Answer me, you villain. Answer me, I say? Let me hear now your grand excuses – Oh, the deuce take it – have you nothing to say?

All this is played by the actor *as if* he were the old obstructionist figure in a rage, stomping up and down and waving his arms while the son, totally believing, melts down into a quivering mass of submission. When scolded, the son querulously defends himself saying, "It's because I keep thinking it is my father who is speaking." Then Octave runs away. That is the power of transformation in its simplest form.

The mark is set up and, presto, right on cue, who does Scapin see coming toward them but the "real" father, the terrible Argante, played for Molière by, of all actors, the charming La Grange, who probably relished playing a comic role for the first time in his career.[6] Scapin and Silvester find a place upstage to spy on the unsuspecting villain who enters thinking himself alone, and we can see how much he is like the character Scapin pretended to be. Molière has Argante simply say, "Did anyone ever hear of such a thing?" Copeau staged the entrance like this:

> Argante enters in a passionate cross identical to that of his son at the opening of the play. He strikes the floor with his cane. He is out of breath and sweating. He pulls off his straw hat, wipes his brow with a madras handkerchief as he sits on the bench down stage and with a great sigh he continues, "Did anyone ever hear of such a thing?"

And for a good page of dialog the two servants move upstage of him where they listen to his fulminations and comment to each other and to the public. He doesn't see them of course, because he is blinded by his own ego. It is like the scene in *Twelfth Night* when Sir Toby, Florian and Feste comment on Malvolio from behind the hedge. This is a classic mechanism for farce: to have the witnesses in a superior place in relation to a comic character blinded by his obsession.

We can identify here another tool popular with writers of comedy. One might call it a "strand." A strand in acting is like a little surprise that you don't quite see but which heightens enjoyment; it's like the red dots in a Seurat painting, the gold thread woven through a tapestry, or the truffle in a sauce. It offers complexity to the character and vividness to the scene. It is an opportunity for subtle contrast and for highlighting clarity. It may be as short as the blink of an eye, but it is always revelatory. Molière has the note on Argante's entrance that he "believes himself alone." Copeau filled this in with the following suggestion:

> Argante enters slowly grumbling to himself. He turns in circles and with his back to the public, he makes strange gestures with his arms. Scapin, watching him, says to the public, "Meditatin' he is."

Scapin's tone of voice might be called a "strand" of "sarcasm." The idea of taking the skin off someone through sarcasm – and revealing the bones – comes from the cruelty found in ancient farce. The strand is swift here, not Swiftian, a glancing comment, but it surely gets a laugh for it has ingredients of superiority, contrast and surprise. It successfully strips off the pomposity of the old man.

The scene shifts to a long scene between the real adversaries, Scapin and the oppressive Father. To flatter his opponent, Scapin brings up sex, never far from any farce. It is always good for getting a rise out of any old bones that might be lying around. Molière uses it here to try and convince Argante to forgive his son by reminding him that although his son was chasing a girl, look how he, the father, used to chase the girls. "Weren't you yourself young one time, and didn't you play your little pranks the same as the others?" Argante smiles. "I heard it said you used to be a terror among the ladies." Argante modestly laughs. "Well able to coax them you were." Argante roars with delight and is thus revealed as an emotionally vulnerable character. He becomes the object of attack in the following famous scene-within-a-scene in which Scapin uses Socratic questioning to lead Argante into a towering rage. This scene is famous partly because it is superb comic writing, and partly because it is borrowed and inserted almost verbatim in Molière's last play, *Le Malade Imaginaire* (*The Imaginary Invalid*), which he wrote as he was dying when he quickly needed a scene between the invalid, Argan, and his servant, Toinette. We'll look at this dramatic rhetoric when we study his luminous last work.

Scapin tries out other favorite roles to achieve his objective of getting money out of the old miser. We now meet Scapin the philosopher, as he presents himself as a stoic "*raisonneur*" to the emotionally explosive Argante. While in life Molière was interested in thinkers like Lucretius and Descartes, on stage he gives "Philosophy" short shrift so not too much stage time is given to playing a version of Epictetus. The playwright goes on to furnish Scapin with an idea which will bring "fear and trembling" to the father. The weapon of choice will be the terror of the law felt by all the French middle class. The law, like medicine and the church, posits that it has the absolute answer for human life. Each of these respectable occupations dwells on rigid formulations of rules and regulations expressed in opaque, turgid Latin and therefore not understandable by the ordinary human being. In Molière's view, such rules and regulations are instilled in an effort to dam up the flow of human life; they are as ridiculous as sticking a worm-eaten plank in the mud to stop a river. Scapin uses the idea of the law sharply and swiftly, to terrify the father into giving the needed money to him.

Scapin falsely claims that he will give the money to the bride's brother, who has promised to stop the marriage to his sister, the gypsy girl – if he gets the

money soon. He sets up the brother in a dramatic description straight from the
Braggart Soldier in the Italian theater with all his "strokes and slashes." Then
carried away, as usual, by his own lies, he seeks to get more money by inventing
a bogus story about how the brother needs even more money to buy armor …
and then a horse … and then a mount for his servant … and then a mule for
his luggage. When Argante blows up over the mule – "Not even a little mule!"
he roars – Scapin moves into a Daumier-like description of the legal system
and the two-legged asses in the courtroom. The speech is a classic tirade, with
the intent to crush Argante. Here is a description of how Copeau, who calls
this "*le grand jeu*" (the grand style), decided his Scapin should play this speech,
which begins after Argante, like a stubborn bull, digs in his heels and says he
will go to court and will not pay a cent to the brother.

> Scapin stops sharply, his arms extended outward in terror. He strikes his brow. His
> voice changes. He plays in the grand style. He makes Argante dizzy, going round
> and round him, pressing him, seizing him by the arm, by the jacket. He goes away,
> comes back, counts on his fingers, throws out little cries. Then when he seems to
> have stopped, he starts again with even more passion and volubility. Argante's
> head begins to roll on his shoulders; his legs begin to give out beneath him; he
> begins to rock and tremble, his brow wrinkles; his voice warbles and he puts up his
> hands to ward off calamity. Scapin shows him no pity. He undoes him.

While Argante appears to be totally smashed by Scapin's rhetoric about the
law, he instantly regains full energy when the amount of the money is spoken:
"Two hundred pounds?" This time he refuses all entreaties by Scapin, each
entreaty using a repetition of the word money; all Argante can hear is "money
this, money that, gimme, gimme, gimme money." Argante, however, resists,
and in a last effort tries to dam the flood by announcing with absolute certainty,
"I will not give two hundred pounds."

When language fails to persuade, bring on the bully. The tone and style of
the play shift from rhetoric to gesture as a masked Silvester stomps on as the
Brother completely immersed in the role of the Braggart Soldier. In Molière's
production this character was played by La Thorillière who got kudos for his
furious sword-wielding pyrotechnics. Aggressive movement replaces aggressive
diction. Silvester thrashes and clomps about the stage until, at its climax, both
Argante and Scapin fall flat on the floor as Silvester goes stomping about in
circles swinging his sword. He was directed by Copeau to do a full-scale battle
dance, raising his mask from time to time to wink knowingly at Scapin. Think
of *Seinfeld*'s Kramer or Art Carney in oversize boots. Silvester joyfully finishes
by flattening his employer, Argante, when he attempts to rise and the newly
inspired actor roars off stage wiping his sword on his sleeve and bellowing,

"I'll show what it is to dare play with me!!" A huge crashing sound offstage is followed by a fear-laden silence, and then this exchange between Scapin and Argante, who are both kneeling facing each other downstage center:

> SCAPIN. You see how many people will be killed for the sake of two hundred pounds. ... I wish you luck
> ARGANTE. (*Trembling*) Scapin.
> SCAPIN. What is it?
> ARGANTE. I have decided to give him the two hundred pounds.

Scapin, exhausted by the struggle, graciously accepts the money as well as the huge laugh that welcomes his victory. Argante staggers off stage.

The triumphant servant exults, drunk with triumph: "One bird caught. I have but to look for the other!" Then, by coincidence, he sees his next mark approaching and in Lady Gregory's lilting phraseology confides to the audience, "Well, if he isn't coming this way! It's like as if (*Lady Gregory's phrase!*) heaven itself was sending them one by one into my net." As the unsuspecting Géronte comes in, Scapin turns to take on his own master, played for Molière by Du Croisy, who was also playing Tartuffe now successfully in the repertory. Soon all hell will break loose.

Géronte's entrance in act 2, scene 7 of *Les Fourberies de Scapin* marks the beginning of one of the most famous scenes in all of French farce. In writing about performance, we are always caught in the tension between the time it takes to do such a scene in performance, and how much patience the reader has with all the details going into the creation of that "doing." I have chosen, as a guide to this scene's primary elements, to follow bit by bit, block by block – or, if you will, vertebra by vertebra – the spine of the interaction between two characters: Géronte and Scapin and a host of imaginary assailants. I have broken it down to ten "beats," to use the actor's terminology for the process of analyzing bits or units which one strings together as the through-line – or the spine – of the scene. In looking at these details, artists also begin to see the "whole" of the play and to sense the answer to the question "What's it all about?" or as Ted Hoffman – the former chairman of the New York University Theater Program – used to say, "What's it *really* all about?"

What this scene between Géronte and Scapin is really all about is the invention of strategies by Scapin to achieve his goal, i.e., to get the money from Géronte, (and Molière to entertain his public.) Despite its outrageousness, the scene adheres to an age-old dictum of farce: the plot of farce is always improbable but it must never be impossible. What follows is based on Jacques Copeau's prompt script and represents for us the orchestration of those strategies which come like variations on a theme, like a theme constantly reappearing and changing in a Beethoven symphony. Each "beat" marks a shift in intention or emotion on the part of the characters who are both involved in actions and strategies to attain their singular and individual over-all intention: Scapin's being to get the money; and Géronte's being to keep his money.[7]

Beat 1

As Géronte makes his entrance, Copeau sees him as comic counterpoint to the bull-like emotional Argante. Louis Jouvet, who plays Géronte, is calm and bony, takes little bitty steps, carries a parasol, and speaks in a pinched voice – a stick figure that contrasts with Argante's corpulence, and who offers the perfect foil to Scapin's fluidity. The scene will make vivid the comic journey, from the tightness in clothing, body and mind evident on the entrance of the character, to the wildness and chaos that will possess him at the end of the scene with the loss of his money and identity.

Henri Bergson, in his essay, "Le Rire" ("Laughter"), writes of the life-force of the human soul in comedy as always being seen as flowing against the "mechanical inelasticity" of body, social rigidities, and human obsessions, as if the warm-blooded human being is trying to escape from behind a fixed societal mask.[8] Géronte is in every sense a stick "stuck" in his miserly role. His entrance shows us no trace of emotion; Jouvet's mask-like face is secure in an expression of all-consuming greed. Such characters are always the best ones to have slipping on a banana peel.

Molière opens the scene with a game that has delighted countless children from time immemorial. One person enters while the other races about the stage pretending not to see him. Jean-Louis Barrault, in a later production directed by Jouvet, used a ladder he propped up against the side stairs to climb up and pretend to look for Géronte while Géronte, with his tiny steps, clicks and parasol, is right behind him trying desperately to get his attention. The public sees the game and feels immediately that it's a reversal of the game played earlier, when the obsessed Argante keeps on talking to himself and ignoring what is in front of him. Both of the old men have a problem with reality. Here Scapin "plays" the game of manipulating the mind, not the emotions; he controls the scene like a director. We realize we are going to see a tug-of-war between the resilient strategies of a highly imaginative intelligence and the life-denying mental rigor mortis of a rich and rickety old man. This "prologue" entrance ends with the delightful surprise of their "accidental" meeting, no doubt with an aside gesture by Scapin commenting to the public about the giant intellect of his prey.

Beat 2

Scapin has a story all ready in his mind and he begins a narrative about the make-believe misadventures of Géronte's son, Léander, who has the gall to be in love with the wrong young girl. Story-telling as a strategy comes out of a long tradition in literature beginning with the Greeks. The audience is waiting to see how Scapin goes about getting money out of his second antagonist, Géronte, knowing all along that he will. The struggle with the powerful Argante used sexual flattery, stoical reasoning, satire about the law, and finally physical violence. What begins the first beat in this later scene is a simple blind-man's-bluff game. The second beat moves into imaginative fiction, sometimes known as the "big lie." The story seems innocuous as Scapin describes the visit by the son to a rich Turkish galley, and Géronte listens, in full control of his superior responses. The last line, however, reverses everything when Scapin hooks him with the message that he must send 500 crowns or the Turks will carry his son off to slavery in Algiers. "Money" is the climax. Géronte, for an unmistakable moment, loses his mask to sheer panic. Horrified gasps and wheezing breath identify the quivering human being behind the rigid respectable mask of the miser.

Beat 3

We are into an exquisite torture scene continually interrupted by Géronte's repetition of the sentence, "Que diable allait-il faire dans cette galère?" ("What the devil did he want going into that galley?") We see Géronte panic and his bones begin to jiggle like Jell-O. This old man has none of Argante's shrewdness; he believes totally in the story and his response is the wailing question, "Que diable allait-il faire dans cette galère?" This phrase is repeated seven times during the scene lifting the farce toward the condition of music.

Beat 4

Scapin plays the next part of the scene dryly and swiftly, since he knows he has no real resistance. The fish has taken the hook of the story and now the man with the fishing pole just lets him thrash around. Géronte eventually pulls himself together and has his first "bright idea." Long a staple of farce, the "bright idea" is an evasion of reality symptomatic of what we might call "denial" in today's jargon. It could be argued that Aristophanes always developed his plays with one big "bright idea." In *Lysistrata* the "bright idea" was "Let's stop screwing men so they will give up war." In *The Birds* it was "Let's go live among the birds, this world sucks." Géronte's energy is revived by the power of his first "bright idea" which is "Go tell this Turk I will bring him to justice." After Scapin, with exaggerated ease, demonstrates the hopelessness of carrying off such a "bright idea" out on the open sea, Géronte seizes upon his second brilliant "bright idea": "Tell the Turk to send back my son and take you in his place." "Are you kidding? I'm not worth anything," confides his tormentor. Géronte cannot deny that: two "bright ideas" are defeated; Molière moves on.

Beat 5

The next subject for the actors to mine is the all-important money. We have another repetition of the slowly-dying phrase about the devil, followed by shocked questioning of the amount; as if it were totally gargantuan; as if the Turk has no conscience and doesn't know the meaning of money; as if the Turk thinks that such a sum is to be picked up off the ground. Copeau specified that this part of the scene should be played with "careless ease" by the totally relaxed Scapin, as Géronte begins to wriggle more and more spastically under the fear of losing his precious money.

Beat 6

This section flows out of the last as Géronte, seeking a new strategy, invents his own story, which would have Scapin taking his key to find another key behind the door which will open another door where he will find old clothes in a hamper which he can take to sell for the money needed. Having so easily solved his problem, Géronte does a "turn-and-go" exit in triumph. Scapin catches him and reminds him of the lack of value in the used clothes market and that time is pressing. A third "bright idea" downed. Géronte piteously stops and whines out for the sixth time the curse on that oft-mentioned devil that brought all this upon him.

Beat 7

By this time Scapin is getting bored and wants this finished. So, of course, he, as an actor, drops his straight-man tone of providing information and transforms himself into the grieving servant for his lost master on the way to being a slave in Algiers: wails, tears, and lamentations change the emotional tone of the scene into a more intense fight to the death.

Beat 8

Géronte begins the final struggle, with evasions and misunderstandings erupting out of his increasing desperation. He flails at the amount of money; he bewails the stupidity of his son; and finally, he appears to give up and pulls out his purse. We go into the final sector which could be titled, "the mime of the purse."

Beat 9

The old man, holding the "magic prop" – a purse of jingling coins – between himself and Scapin, begins the following dialog, which is classic Molière:

GÉRONTE. (*Holds out purse*) Take it and ransom my son.
SCAPIN.   I will, sir.
GÉRONTE. (*Still keeping purse*) But tell this Turk he is a villain.
SCAPIN.   (*Holding out hand*) So I will.
GÉRONTE. A wretch.
SCAPIN.   I will.
GÉRONTE. A traitor. A thief.
SCAPIN.   Let me alone.
GÉRONTE. That he is dragging this money out of me against all right.
SCAPIN.   I'll tell him that.
GÉRONTE. That I don't give it of my own free will.
SCAPIN.   All right.
GÉRONTE. That if ever I take him, I'll make him pay for it.
SCAPIN.   That's it.
GÉRONTE. (*Putting purse in his pocket and going out*) Go at once and bring back my son.

Beat 10

The final *lazzo* is still focused on the purse, which has made it back into Géronte's pocket; with infinite reluctance, the crushed old man comes out with the innocent question: "Didn't I give you the purse? No? Oh!" Then he searches in the wrong pockets. Finally he surrenders it to Scapin, who takes it and turns to go – but discovers it is still chained to Géronte. Crippled in agony, Géronte finally releases it as he cries out the seventh reprise of the devil curse, and makes his exit – destroyed. Scapin has won. He completed his intention. He got the money away from the second old man and the "beats" of act 2, scene 7 are completed. Like a circus performer, Scapin juggles the two purses he has won from the two old farts. As one audience member shouted during a performance of *Les Précieuses Ridicules*: "That's real comedy, Molière!"

After giving the two young men their money, Scapin decides to play another "game," one with a thrilling taste of danger about it. He uses the famous "sack" scene of act 3, scene 2, simply to have the pure fun of turning himself into multiple personalities. The actor, above all, is the core of Molière, as W. G. Moore said in his famous book, *Molière: A New Criticism*.[9] For hundreds of years many scholars agreed with Boileau, who wrote, "Dans ce sac ridicule où Scapin s'enveloppe, je ne reconnais plus l'Auteur du Misanthrope" ("In that ridiculous sack in which Scapin wraps himself, I cannot recognize the author of *The Misanthrope*").[10] Boileau was Molière's friend, but he didn't like the "silliness" of Scapin; he preferred the literary quality of the verse play. Obviously he wasn't paying attention to the stage: Scapin was not in the sack.

Farce deals with the ABCs of life, those dirty little secrets common to all: sex, money and fear of death, releasing their pain into laughter. That's why it is so popular. Some older critics clearly did not appreciate the real emotional desperation of the basic situations that whip the plots of farce. But for Copeau, and many others like Professor Moore who have looked into the art of acting as vital to understanding this writer of comedy, here is a scene that has no other reason for being than to offer a time for the two virtuoso actors to entertain their public. Jouvet complained that, in his time as a leading actor of Molière, he found nothing in 250 years of French criticism that was of any use in performing the plays. Jouvet preferred to use the ideas of Copeau and Jean-Louis Barrault to make the farce of physical comedy work as a brilliant piece of dramatic art. The idea is not very profound: an old fool thinks he has found safety in a burlap sack and he gets beat up. But in the playing, it is realized as a complex work of art, one that has remained vital for centuries.

Géronte is the ultimate fool. He re-enters in act 3 wanting to know what happened to his money. Scapin instantly invents another story about a brother to the slave girl Géronte's son wants to marry, who is now recruiting a band of warriors to find and kill Géronte. The old man, his button pushed, instantly trembles and asks the fatal question, "Ha, Scapin, what can I do?" Géronte "runs" about with stiff knee joints while Scapin moves with "ease and entirety," or simply stays in place, relaxed and waiting. Géronte is frantic to find some way to escape even if it means Scapin will be killed in his place. To that end, he offers his coat to Scapin, then decides to wait until he's "had a little more wear out of it." Miserliness never dies. He is so frightened he even gets into the sack that Scapin just happens to have on hand so that Scapin can carry him safely back to his house. Too late!! Scapin sees the imaginary bully coming from offstage and pushes Géronte's head into the sack. There is an exchange of pushing the head into the sack and it popping back out. Head goes in; we wait; head pops out; we laugh. Henri Bergson calls it the "Jack-in-the-box" technique for making laughter, and uses the toy to illustrate the way energy acts out of rigidity: you push the puppet on a coiled spring down into a rigid box, put the top on, turn the handle to music, and then the child shrieks with

Figure 37. Scapin by Copeau. © 1950
Éditions du Seuil: Rights reserved.

Figure 38. Copeau's Scapin with
Jouvet's Géronte. © 1950 Éditions
du Seuil: Rights reserved.

Figure 39. Scapin by Barrault. Barrault
Archives: Rights reserved.

Figure 40. Barrault's Scapin with
Bertin's Géronte. Barrault Archives:
Rights reserved.

laughter when the puppet pops out. All the panic and fear of the rigid old man is stuffed into the sack and pops back out – first laugh. Then Copeau had him open his parasol to protect himself in the sack – second laugh. Scapin takes it away and stuffs head back in again; Scapin waits for it to reappear; it doesn't and after some editorializing gestures out it pops – third laugh.

Molière regales us with three actions to make up this "punishment scene." First, the scene is played using a rough version of ventriloquism: with little movement, Scapin assumes two voices embroiled in an argument. He speaks in a heavy voice as if he were the imaginary bully, then answers lightly in his own voice as the loyal servant to Géronte that he is. After playing this scene between Scapin, one imaginary character, and one shaking sack, Molière switches to physical comedy and starts to beat up the stingy old man in the sack with the ancient "baton."[11] There is lots of violence in comedy, but the suffering can't be real. Barrault played with the gestural style and skill of a mimetic artist. He swung the baton and then six inches away from the sack, he stopped and pulled it back in a smooth fluid move; the sack reacted with little jumps and cries against the idea of being struck. This is orchestrated and repeated in different variations, adding the idea that Scapin is also being hit and is crying out in as much pain as Géronte. Finally, the sack and Scapin both collapse on the floor. A pause. Géronte's head slowly reappears in response to the silence, and the two argue about who was hit the hardest.

The scene shifts quickly when Scapin suddenly yells that the bully is coming back. This time the imaginary character takes over the scene and yells loudly about running his sword through the quivering sack; growing in his role, Scapin leans on the sack, then sits on it, then circles it – all the while making vicious and horrifying threats. Again the head starts to poke out and this time is immediately shoved back into the sack. The third and final action gives Scapin the chance to play as if he were half a dozen soldiers, all with funny accents, until Scapin's joy in acting takes off into just doing the moves for the fun of it and not noticing that Géronte has finally come out of the sack and is watching what he is doing. The key to the scene is not just the Bergson mechanics, but the full spontaneous joy of the actor and the high performance skills of a star. And Molière slyly has let us know that even the superior mind of Scapin is done in by his ego and his lack of self-awareness. Shades of Alceste. Shades of Jackie Gleason.

The joy of the actor onstage before an audience convulsed with laughter, is reinforced when Zerbinette – played for Molière by his new company member, Mlle Beauval, hired to replace the ailing Madeleine Béjart – comes in to tell the aching Géronte the hilarious story of how Scapin duped some old idiot with the story of the galley. The scene is used to allow the soubrette to play what is known in comedy as a "laughing scene." Mlle Beauval was famous for her infectious laughter, and to this day actors at the Comédie-Française are trained to begin scenes like this in giggles, working up to guffaws, and finally achieving the moment when the audience "breaks" and joins in with the hilarity. No real motivation for this scene in terms of the plot is offered, but that's not the point. The point is the pure joy of the theater.

Molière closes his ode to pure farce with another example of a literary fiction, in which Scapin makes claim to being hit by a hammer falling off a building in order to escape – successfully, of course – the wrath of the two fathers. Cyrano de Bergerac met his death from a falling hammer, and with this little tag to the play Molière thanks Cyrano for the use of his play, *Le Pédant Joué* (*The Scholar Fooled*), from which he lifted the "galley scene" that so undoes Géronte and so amuses Zerbinette.

It is all the wonderful stew of laughter made delicious with the bones of farce: diction and all the modulations and semi-quavers of the voice; pace with all its variations; action and all the contortions of the body; reactions and all their emotional revelations of the vulnerable soul; and the magic transformations of all those frogs turning into princes. These are the bones that give strength to an actor's craft.

Act Four

AND LEAVE 'EM LAUGHIN'

XV

THE DANCING SKELETON

Les Femmes Savantes
as translated by Richard Wilbur

Early in Mnouchkine's film on Molière, in a harrowing scene, a group of doctors bleed the young boy's mother to death. They throw the blood out into the courtyard before returning to the house to gluttonously gnaw on dripping red meat for their lunch. The kindly grandfather gets Jean-Baptiste out of this house of death, taking him down the street to see a makeshift stage set up in a cobblestone square. On the stage is an old man, reminiscent of Pantalone in *Commedia*, doddering about with a long white beard, making important harrumphing sounds as he talks to himself and goes about his business. Also on stage is an actor dressed as a skeleton with a grinning skull mask. The old man does basic human things like squatting on a chamber pot, while the skeleton shrieks with laughter and jumps about the stage with joy. He points at the old man, and then at the public. The moral is clear: you may think you are a Very Important Person but Death will get you in the end! The scene gave ecstatic experience to the actor playing the skeleton and it amused the public. Pantalone was upset but he's an old man and so who cares. He's the straight man. And he is the obstacle to fun. So the "*fourbe*" will win – even if, in this case, the *fourbe* is not Scapin, but a hard-masked type called "Death."

What is Death? How are we to portray – or write about – death? In art, as in life, death is never very far away however rarely we admit it. It is the ultimate reality; the ultimate challenge for the art form that is closest to life itself: the theater. One way, as we saw above, is to mask him. We have a great symbol throughout the vast times of dramatic art – prehistoric, savage and civilized – the outer mask over the naked inner face. In the primitive farce that Mnouchkine's ten-year-old fictional Molière saw, the mask was the skull-like rigidity of Death on top of the extreme elasticity of the live flowing actor. The actor is the life; the mask is the idea of Death. Molière, having given up the outer mask as a tool in his playing, does not resort to the skull-like mask of death to hide the living face. For him, that very elastic, lively, ever-reacting, quick-to-laugh flesh is the mask that covers and protects us from the bony, unsmiling skull beneath.

While writing his next-to-last play – a major play in verse, *Les Femmes Savantes* (*The Learned Ladies*) – Madeleine Béjart, his long time lover, friend, and mother of his wife, took to her deathbed after a long illness. In early January 1672, she made her will, put all her affairs in order, and renounced acting to the "Mother Church" to assure her burial rights in sanctified ground. She died on 17 February 1672. Molière was summoned back to Paris from performances in Versailles to follow her funeral cortège to the cemetery. What went through his mind as he walked behind her body, struggling as he was in the last stages of tuberculosis? We can only guess at how he felt seeing this beloved person and long-time working partner put into the ground. Little did he know that exactly one year later on 17 February 1673, he would be struck dead by consumption and Armande would have to follow his body in the black night to unconsecrated ground.

Armande and Molière's third child, a son, was born in September of that fateful year of 1672 but only lived one month… so two hard deaths in one year. Between these losses, he put *Les Femmes Savantes* into the performance repertory of his theater. It was a play that recalled Madeleine's great triumph with him in their first huge Paris hit, *Les Précieuses Ridicules*.

Long ago, in the good old days, *Les Précieuses Ridicules* used three unworldly, boisterous new-comers to the ways of Paris to lampoon literary pretensions; in *Les Femmes Savantes* Molière returns to that theme of literary pretentiousness, but after his own stay of twelve years in Paris, the players have become urbane, sophisticated, and even sillier. In *Précieuses*, two ridiculous young country girls yearn to be learnèd and Parisian; in *Femmes Savantes* he writes of Parisian ladies who consider themselves already learnèd. In *Précieuses* it is the young innocents, still wet behind the ears, who fall wholeheartedly into the trap of faddish pretensions; in *Femmes Savantes* it is the older generation, who should know better. The clickety dry bones of the skeleton are poking through. Molière's comic vision returns to themes of literary satire and fraudulent poets, as well as to middle-class folk pretending to the life of the mind, and to the hypocrisy of those who trumpet ideas about virtue and rail against the desires of healthy bodies.

Les Femmes Savantes would surely have included Madeleine as the matron, Philaminte, but since she was terminally ill even as he worked on the play, she was replaced in rehearsal and performance by a male actor, Monsieur Hubert. Molière added to the ladies' salon the dry-as-bones character of Trissotin, the morbidly intense poet, hell-bent on killing all joy in life and art. Irony of ironies, Molière cast himself, not in the starring comic role of the ridiculous Trissotin, the poet who grew out of the ebullient Mascarille, but as the rather ineffectual father, and he put Armande in the role of his daughter – a warm, sensible, loving girl who wants only to love a husband and to have children. Neither have the starring roles. We are indeed very far from Alceste and Célimène.

The play is a special piece. Its origins may be in the wild farce of the earlier one-act but the language in this play is supple and lucid French verse. It belongs to the world of those masterpieces we looked at earlier – his three central verse plays: *L'École des Femmes, Le Tartuffe, Le Misanthrope*. He must have worked on *Les Femmes Savantes* for several years while writing various other prose or entertainment pieces specifically for the king. The underlying feeling of hatred for all forms of hypocrisy has returned to his work, and although this play has less darkness than *Tartuffe* and *Don Juan*, the scorn for pretentiousness runs deep. I love the idea that Molière cast himself as the husband and a man as his wife. He is obviously no longer centered in his obsession with love and desire.

There is another intriguing aspect to the casting. One would assume, of course, that the character named Armande would have been played by Armande, but it was Catherine de Brie who played the sharp, anti-sex sister named Armande, and Armande played the good-humored Henriette. Maybe when Armande read the play, she decided she didn't want to play another spiteful character whose costumes would be too puritanical and not at all attractive. Or maybe Molière, always the consummate professional, knew that de Brie was the better character actress. Or it may just have amused him to start the buzz about why Catherine played Armande and not Armande.

With age comes the desire for simplicity. Laurent Mahelot, who recorded what was needed to produce plays in Molière's time, noted that *Les Femmes Savantes* needed only "a room, four chairs, two books, and some paper."[1] Not a spectacle play by any means but one deeply cherished by the *sociétaires* of the Comédie-Française, who often keep these roles for a lifetime. When my friend, Mlle Nadine Marziano, was assigned to replay Philaminte, she said she hadn't done the part in a year or more and asked if I would hold book for her. She handed me the text and then went through the whole play absolutely letter-perfect. She had what Jean-Louis Barrault called the "docility of the great professional," as well as the discipline of all those actors fortunate enough to be performers in the "House of Molière."

Richard Wilbur, who has done so much to keep Molière alive for English-speaking audiences, did a version of this play which, to my mind, is among the best of his translations; one that keeps the comedic tone and also gives a good actor the tools to play the emotional and realistic relationships Molière built into this play – which, like *Tartuffe*, is about a good middle-class family threatened by the hypocrites in society. Wilbur beautifully translates the husband's great long speech about his middle-class view of life; he creates an imaginative language for Trissotin, the ridiculous poet with verses longer than those of Mascarille, and whose veins are filled with the sinister, black blood of Tartuffe; and he gives the women in the company brilliantly comedic verse shining with irony and wit.[2]

The Learned Ladies begins with a conversation – i.e., another debate – between two sisters: Henriette, played by Armande, a sensual young woman who is ready to get married, and Armande, played by Catherine, a high-spirited and strong-minded woman who holds on tenaciously to the Augustinian duality of human nature. She believes that the mind and body are two separate parts. One might argue that "division" is the curse of the Western World; indeed many with more learning than Armande, the character, have so argued: Mind is good; body is bad. Starve the body and its animal appetites and nourish the mind with faith and reason.[3] I quote some lines from Wilbur that are spoken by Armande (the character) to her sister, Henriette, who wishes to follow the dictates of her heart and marry her handsome suitor:

> Oh dear, you crave such squalid satisfactions!
> Oh, can you choose to play a petty role,
> Dull and domestic, and content your soul
> With joys no loftier than keeping house
> And raising brats, and pampering a spouse?

Armande goes on for half a page about the yet-to-be-seen dominating mother, Philaminte, "to whom all pay honor," and why her sister should model herself on that gorgon of a mother. She counsels Henriette on the advantages of "loving learning" over desiring those gross, physical body things:

> Why marry, and be the slave of him you wed?
> Be married to philosophy instead,
> Which lifts us up above mankind, and gives
> All power to reason's pure imperatives,
> Thus rendering our bestial natures tame
> And mastering those lusts which lead to shame.

One can sense, even in these few lines, an energy and a will supporting the words. If we remember how Cathos, in Les Précieuses Ridicules, poses the question about marriage with the plaint "How can one imagine sleeping next to a man who is completely naked?" and then how she giggles and trembles with the very real desires of a country wench for naked sex, we can see in this play how Molière has changed his tone and point of view toward his subject. Here affectation runs deep in the blood, and is not put on just to impress a visitor. "Society Triumphant," as Fernandez titles his last chapter, has become a truth.[4]

Molière takes the role of the henpecked husband, Chrysale, who is unable to stand up to the dominating, alpha woman he has married. She fires the servant for using improper grammar and he has to agree. She intends to marry the sensible daughter, Henriette, to the fop, Trissotin, and we greatly fear this husband will be forced to give his daughter away to this literary Tartuffe. Before the action comes to its climax in act 5, Molière gives himself a two page speech protesting what this "intellectualizing" has done to his quality of life. The speech is a star turn and Wilbur does it so well. He starts the speech addressing his wife, but sensing danger he changes course and … :

> CHRYSALE. (*To his sister, Bélise*) Sister, I am addressing *you* …
>   The least mistake in speech you can't forgive,
>   But how mistakenly you choose to live!
>   I'm sick of those eternal books you've got;
>   In my opinion, you should burn the lot,
>   Save for that Plutarch where I press my collars,
>   And leave the studious life to clerks and scholars.

The man who wrote these lines was a reader. Molière's inventory of books was large and included many works in other languages, ranging from plays to philosophy and poetry. The great rumor was that he worked on a translation of the Roman philosopher, Lucretius, all his life. Who knows if that is so, but they would make a great pair of minds facing an atom-based physical reality. In Lucretius, death is only a dispersal of heavier and lighter atoms, an immortality without the visions of Christian angels or Islamic houris. Death is simply a return to the physical universe.

Molière's unlettered fictional husband, however, goes on to bewail that his roast beef is always burned because even the servants in his house have their noses buried in the dictionary. He declares the women in his house are "mad as hatters!"

I'm tired of visits from these pedants versed
In Latin, and that ass Trissotin's the worst.
He's flattered you in many a wretched sonnet;
There's a great swarm of queer bees in his bonnet;
Each time he speaks, one wonders what he's said;
I think, myself, that he's crazy in the head.

Speaking, as we were, of Lucretius who was famous for his atomic theory, Chrysale's sister, Bélise, puts her brother down with Lucretian disdain:

> Could particles more grossly be combined,
> Or atoms form an aggregate more crass?
> And can we be of the same blood? Alas,
> I hate myself because we two are kin,
> And leave this scene in horror and chagrin.

One cannot ignore Trissotin, who dominates the entire third act reading wretched verses and communing with his muses – the three learnèd ladies. He finishes the act in a full-scale physical fight with the Greek-speaking philosopher, Vadius. Mascarille in *Les Précieuses Ridicules* has a five-line impromptu that sends him careening around the stage. In this later play, all is magnificently expanded. Quoting a little part of it is like playing a melody out of Beethoven's ninth, but Wilbur does a splendid job and a flavor may be helpful, especially a sample of the immortal writings of Trissotin, a poet in the tradition of Oronte in *Le Misanthrope*:

> SONNET TO THE PRINCESS URANIE
> REGARDING HER FEVER
>
> Your prudence, Madam, must have drowsed
> When you took in so hot a foe
> And let him be so nobly housed,
> And feasted and regaled him so.

Two pages of swooping *explication du texte* by the three ladies follow before the pretentious poet is able to continue with his feverish sonnet.

> Say what they may, the wretch must go!
> From your rich lodging drive away
> This ingrate who, as well you know,
> Would make your precious life his prey.

I would love to have seen Molière's expression, sitting quill in hand and coughing his life out, as he mouthed the words he was writing for this inane description of a "fever." Onstage, the discussion is fervid and the trumpet voice of Philaminte blares out repeatedly the cacophonous phrase "*Quoi qu'on dit, quoi qu'on dit*" which Wilbur renders as "Say what they may, say what they may." The French words allow the actor to hit those beginning consonants like a duck's "quack, quack" and may well be the inspiration of Beckett's Lucky when he tries to think and comes up with "qua, qua, qua." In Wilbur, a good actor could elongate the ending vowels like a howling wolf singing Wagner. And a Wagnerian wolf (or a braying ass) can be just as funny as a self-important duck.

The poem concludes after four more pages of almost demented appreciations by the three ladies, who utter phrases as titillating as those found in the scandal sheets. Trissotin finishes his epic, killing off the insulting fever with bubbling fervor:

> Shall he afflict you night and day,
> And shall you tolerate such things?
> No! To the baths you must repair,
> And with your own hands drown him there.

The ladies all faint, delighted and ravished.

The play ends with Trissotin unmasked and, like Tartuffe, defeated. In *Le Tartuffe* the king provides the *deus ex machina*. Not so here in a play written not for the king but for the Parisian audience. The family of *bons bourgeois* all join together to force the hypocrite's removal from the scene. The family wins without any intervention from a king or god.

What is not bourgeois is the transformation of Chrysale from the docile husband to the magnanimous older man who seizes control of his own house, quiets the critical sister, and says these astonishing verses directly to the two young lovers, Clitandre and Henriette – who is actually his wife, Armande – as they stand facing him on stage:

> Come, take her hand, now. After you, my boy;
> Conduct her to her room. (*To Ariste*) Ah, Brother, this is
> A tonic to me; think of those hugs, those kisses!
> It warms my old heart, and reminds me of
> My youthful days of gallantry and love.

I happened to see two productions of this play since originally writing this chapter. One by the Comédie-Française at the Vieux-Colombier; the other at a workshop for the Antaeus Theater in Los Angeles. Both productions taught me something I had not realized; i.e., that the relationship between the two sisters was highly charged emotionally and that both were possessed by physical desire for the same passionate young man – Clitandre. Henriette admitted it; Armande fought it. But it left both girls literally trembling with desire: one with the words and one against the words. Otherwise the two approaches

Figure 41. A choleric Chrysale.
Photo © Brigette Enguérand.

Figure 42. A cool Philaminte.
Photo © Brigette Enguérand.

Figure 43. A choleric Philaminte.
Photo © Alyson Aliano.

Figure 44. A querelous Chrysale.
Photo © Alyson Aliano.

were vastly different. In Los Angeles the interpretation of the husband and wife were more closely aligned to Molière's representation of the wife as a dominating, shall we say, castrating female determined to order her world to her wishes, and the husband resigned and meekly doing what he could to avoid a battle. In France the Chrysale was rendered as a younger Molière would have approached it – highly choleric in sweating frustration at his very beautiful, sleek, sophisticated, opinionated, contrary, surprisingly young and very soft-spoken Philaminte. The two Trissotins also offered a sharp contrast in the two productions. On the French stage, he was truly a menace, a real swindler conning his prey and in the United States he was almost as stupid as the misguided ladies. The French version did not receive a single laugh; the North Hollywood one was hilarious. Strangely, the recent French productions have all seemed to be played against the comedy: this one, *The Miser*, *Don Juan*, Mnouchkine's *Tartuffe*, *The Imaginary Invalid*. Maybe, as Pierre Dux noted, the world is in too serious a state for the French to laugh any more.

This last verse play entered the company's repertory with a good box-office, and Molière worked to finish what would be his final play. He chose to write a role in which, because of his illness, he could sit down for most of the play, and whereby he could make mock of the fact that he was dying. Now lust, love, greed, power, and social climbing are replaced by another obsession; it is fear of dying that anchors his last play – fear of death whether imminent or imaginary.

XVI

THE IMAGINARY INVALID

Le Malade Imaginaire
as conceived by Molière
as translated by Mildred Marmur
as directed by Robert W. Goldsby
as translated by Morris Bishop

Le Malade Imaginaire (*The Imaginary Invalid*) is a masterpiece. André Gide thought it "the" masterpiece. It is an astonishing compilation of comedic knowledge, a beautifully structured plot, and astonishingly alive characters; it is Molière's last word in confronting private agonies with public laughter. The private moments now are not about Armande; his attention is not on new forms of theater; he is not writing pure farce for the "joy" of it, or fashioning perfect verse lines for the old themes of hypocrisy and societal foolishness. He is now facing Death at the core of his being. And he turns it into the perfect subject for laughter. That's his job.

Way back in time when he was on tour in southern France, Molière began by playing little farces about flying doctors. They were sketches for comic *lazzi* inspired by the Italians. They were mostly action, few words and very close to improvisation. His last would-be doctor begins with a page-long scripted analysis of various kinds of medical enemas and their exact ingredients.

Before the imaginary invalid speaks, however, there is a long section of music and dance by a large cast. Molière continued the court entertainment convention of Versailles and called it a comedy with a *mêlée* – a free-for-all, a mix-up, a confused brawl – of music and dance. He hired twelve musicians and seven singers and, for the first time, he premiered a musical comedy work at his own theater instead of at the court. Out in Versailles, Lully had won the fight for the king's favor, so Molière used Charpentier as a composer in Paris, permanently sealing a split with his old partner. A greatly expanded *Églogue* opens the performance with singers and dancers and mythic characters like Pan; a nightmare chase scene with violins in the middle of the play; a Moorish entertainment about seizing the moment because time is passing as an interlude before act 3; and finally, after the play-acting deaths in act 3, the work finishes with a joyful grand spectacle in which the patient becomes a pig-Latin-quoting doctor. Two of these "interludes" feature the "true-love" shepherds and shepherdesses so favored by Louis. Within act 2, a make-believe opera also has a shepherd and shepherdess as its characters, but they are sung by the principal actors pretending to be imaginary shepherds. He meant it to be a *Comédie Mêlée de Musique et de Danse*, and it may seem like a *mêlée*, but it is a structure of great sophistication in the theater.

Molière was back starring in the title role as Argan, the Imaginary Invalid, the soul-brother of Orgon from *Le Tartuffe*. His opening monologue touches on the memories of the child watching the street theater with the old man and the skeleton. Then the old man squatted on a chamber pot making farting noises and the skeleton howled with laughter. Now the great professional actor/ writer/theater manager has composed an aria to bowel movement, complete with rhapsodic descriptions of the many recipes of emetic ingredients. In *Don Juan*, Sganarelle did a short riff on the new "emetic wine" which efficiently killed off patients. Now Argan is taking many flowery potions up his rear end and loving his trips to the commode.

Not so incidentally, there are three essentials for a ground plan for this play: a solid chair (the only solid thing left of Molière's life is the chair he used in this performance, which is now displayed in a glass box at the current Comédie-Française); a comfy bed that Argan likes to be tucked into; and a commode that can be seen or curtained off. The great French film actor, Raimu, was once invited to play this role at the Comédie-Française, and he had a toilet in front of which was a half-curtain – so his face could be seen puffing away while he did his duty as if it were an ecstatic experience.

At the conclusion of this opening "tragic tirade" featuring herbs and enema tubes, Argan, wanting instant service, starts ringing his bell and shouting as if he were himself a bell, "Drelin, drelin, drelin!" He transforms in front of us from a powerful, healthy, happy businessman to an over-sized infant bawling for his "Mommy." Toinette, one of Molière's great soubrette creations, comes on pretending to have hit her head and the two howl together for a long beat in which sound replaces sense and language disintegrates into animal noises. The scene finishes with a rush to the "john."

Following these two extreme scenes in which the two main characters are revealed to us in both rhetorical and tantrum mode, the daughter enters to begin the plot-line. This Angélique, again played by Armande, is a glassy-eyed twit in love with another "Cléante." As she helps Toinette make up Papa's bed, a charming exposition scene takes place wherein the comedy-of-infatuated-love replaces the farce-of-the-loo. The plot is strongly anchored, and when Argan returns we have a classic cross-purpose dialog between the father and the daughter about marrying her off. She thinks he's talking about Cléante, whom she loves; we know he is talking about the doctor's idiot son. When she hears that her husband-to-be speaks Latin and Greek, she realizes he's no handsome juvenile but the idiot son of the clownish doctor. She promptly melts to the floor, where she remains prostrate and struck dumb for a long time, as Toinette berates the Father.

The first argument in this confrontation between the master and the servant is lifted from *Les Fourberies de Scapin*. In Mnouchkine's film, the dying Madeleine and an exhausted Molière sit on the stairs of their mutual apartment building. He says he's stuck on a scene. She tells him, "Just take the scene from Scapin. It worked." He says, "People will know." She says, "No one will know and if they do they'll laugh anyway." Here are two small scenes to compare from each play:

From *Scapin*		From *Malade*	
Translator: Lady Gregory		Translator: Mildred Marmur[1]	
ARGANTE.	That's a good joke. I'll not disinherit my son?	ARGAN.	Just listen to her. I won't put my daughter in a convent?
SCAPIN.	I say you will not.	TOINETTE.	No, I tell you.
ARGANTE.	Who will stop me?	ARGAN.	Who will stop me?
SCAPIN.	Yourself.	TOINETTE.	You, yourself.
ARGANTE.	Myself?	ARGAN.	Me?
SCAPIN.	That's it. You will not have the heart to do it.	TOINETTE.	Yes. You won't have the heart.
ARGANTE.	I will have the heart.	ARGAN.	Oh, yes I will.
SCAPIN.	You're making fun.	TOINETTE.	You're fooling yourself.
ARGANTE.	I'm not making fun.	ARGAN.	No, I'm not.
SCAPIN.	Fatherly tenderness will gain the day.	TOINETTE.	Your fatherly affection won't let you.
ARGANTE.	It will do no such thing.	ARGAN.	Affection won't sway me.
SCAPIN.	It will. It will.	TOINETTE.	A little tear or two, her arms around your neck, a "papa darling" said with the right note of sadness.
		ARGAN.	It won't do a thing.
		TOINETTE.	Oh, yes it will.
ARGANTE.	I tell you it shall be done.	ARGAN.	I tell you, I won't give in.

SCAPIN.	Good morrow to you.	TOINETTE.	Nonsense.
ARGANTE.	You must not say "Good morrow to you."	ARGAN.	There's no use saying "nonsense."
SCAPIN.	I know you well. You are kind by nature.	TOINETTE.	I know you very well. You're naturally kind-hearted.
ARGANTE.	(*Furious*) I am not kind. I am wicked when I have a mind.	ARGAN.	(*Angry*) I'm not kind-hearted; I can be mean when I want to be.

While these two scenes by two different translators have some slight variations, the thrust of the scenes is identical. Obviously, the lines about a "little tear or two" would not be appropriate to the son in *Scapin* but are perfect for Angélique. Like Shakespeare in his last play, *The Tempest*, it's as if Molière drew from all his former plays and all his experience as an actor. Sometimes he used full scenes like the above, and sometimes an old farce *lazzo*, for example Argan's second wife, Béline, while helping Toinette gently tuck the old man into bed suddenly loses her self control and starts a violent pillow fight. He put in a notary scene sounding eerily like the one in *Le Tartuffe*, also transforming the theft of a family's assets by the second wife into a legally approved boondoggle. Thus we have pure comedy rooted in ancient farce; we have the evolution of hybrids and mutations; we have a theater born of transformations!

In act 2, the games move more into "let's pretend," riffing on acting metaphors as the young juvenile arrives disguised as a music teacher come to give the daughter a lesson. In this role he later makes up an opera in which the make-believe teacher and the willing student assume the roles of two lovers singing of their undying love for each other. But before that theatrical deception, we have the medical deception of the two doctors: Diafoirus and his idiot son, Thomas.

This scene, between three demented male clowns, begins with a simultaneously run-on dialog between the two fathers as they greet each other, and then moves into inane declarations of love for Angélique by the mindless son, who decorates his memorized oration with all sorts of classical Latinized jargon to mask the perennial male lust that exists even in a fool. Henri Bergson classifies this kind of pedantic mask as "something mechanical encrusted on the living."[2] The dunce of a son starts off on the wrong foot by confusing the mother-in-law-to-be for the bride-to-be, but he does zero in on the young one when it comes to presenting his case for love's physical needs. He is so obnoxious and so slobbering about the prospect of sexual fulfillment that Cléante, Angélique's secret suitor, almost leaps forward to kill him but thinks better of it and decides to present his case to his beloved by improvising the operatic romance through which he and Angélique can declare their love. So we are treated to an opera of made-up shepherd lyrics done off-key by two characters who are not singers, to a tune that neither of them knows for sure. This is pure "feel good" playwriting from head to little toe, and has convulsed audiences from 1673 to the present day. Molière might have staged it accompanied by twelve musicians; my students did it *a cappella*; but the effect remains the same.

Towards the end of act 2, a number of scenes begin to have reverberations which can only be described as melancholy. The scenes all remain comedic but they may make those of us who love Molière weep as well as laugh. The play moves into a more dramatic tone and atmosphere when Angélique confronts her wicked stepmother and, instead of being the weak vessel of act 1, she stands up to her. The daughter's honesty and integrity shine through the absurdities of the comedy. This Angélique is not the Angélique of *George Dandin*. She now speaks of marriage quite differently: "I want a husband I can love dearly and I hope to make him the one love of my life." This is more like Henriette in *Les Femmes Savantes*. Of course this is "in character," but we can't help but be touched when we remember that Armande would be burying her husband within a few days of performing this, and that she was the one he sent for when he was coughing up too much blood.

The play may evoke Armande in another way altogether from the wife who has shared three children and many days and many performances with her husband. In act 2, scene 8, the stepmother has bribed their little daughter to go tell Argan she has seen her older sister, Angélique, with the music teacher. Here is another acting metaphor. The scene has the powerful male star, who is the head of the company and the greatest actor in France, sitting in his solid chair. In comes a little eight-year-old girl, probably the daughter of the new actress in the company, Mlle Beauval, who started with the company as Zerbinette in the laughing scene with Scapin and is now playing Toinette. The little girl is a child in the company, as was Armande. Her name is Louison, and she plays the role of Louison. She sits at Molière's feet and they play a scene about pretending. He wants her to confess to him; she wants him to tell her a fable by La Fontaine. Getting nowhere with the little girl, he picks up a birch rod to spank her and she cries out:

LOUISON. Forgive me, Papa!
ARGAN. No.
Louison. Please, Papa, don't hit me.
ARGAN. You deserve it.
LOUISON. Please!
ARGAN. (*Pulling her closer*) Come here.
LOUISON. Papa, you've hurt me. I'm dying. (*She plays dead.*)

ARGAN.   Oh my God! Louison, Louison, what have I done. Oh Lord! Louison,
my daughter. What sort of a monster am I? This accursed rod, if only
I had never seen it! My poor baby, my poor little Louison!

LOUISON.   (*Sitting up*) Don't cry; I'm not dead all over.

He forgives her, needless to say, but we have seen how quickly and completely
he believes in what is clearly imaginary – and how quickly he can forgive
and get out of that belief. This is a good thing to remember at the end of the
play. As the scene goes on, his little finger is transformed into an omniscient
voice. Louison plays along with the game of "let's believe the little finger"
until finally she gets exasperated as any eight-year-old would and says to him,
"Your little finger is lying, Papa!" That quite finishes off their game of "let's
pretend." We can't help but remember that Armande was once an eight-
year-old in the company not all that long ago and also learned about the
magic of imagination in the theater from the very man sitting on the stage in
1673, playing this delicate scene with yet another child of the theater. As we
remember the little nymph played by Mlle Menou, the stage name of the ten-
year-old Armande, we find some sadness here, too, even if the death in the
scene is a game. We know it is ... and it isn't.

Following that totally original scene comes a formulaic interlude: Argan's
brother brings in a troupe of Moorish girls to entertain him. Polichinelle sings
about what joy it is to kiss a girl who's twenty, and the ensemble of girls reply
to him:

We must submit.
We must give in.We must take the good with the bad;
For the good when it's good, is so very good
That the bad when it's bad, can't be bad.
(*The girls dance and play with the monkeys they have brought with them.*)

To mix up kissing young girls and dancing with monkeys is not far from the
Theatre of the Absurd – and a lot funnier. Memory is evoked of other young
girls appearing in his life and on his stage: Armande, a bride at nineteen;
Célimène, a triumphant creation of twenty. There is no pathos in that memory –
just lost time.

Act 3 begins with another long debate like the opening scene of *Le
Misanthrope*, this time played between two brothers. For the first time the
straight man (or the reasonable man) is being played not by La Grange but by
La Thorillière, the company clown, fresh from his triumph playing Trissotin
in *Les Femmes Savantes*. After Molière's death, this is the actor who took over
Molière's role when *Le Malade* went back into performance.

After the two comic actors debate old arguments from previous plays –
"hypocrites are everywhere" – Molière gives the brother a passionate speech
about the terrible hypocrisy of those in medicine:

> BÉRALDE. When the doctor talks to you about helping or easing Mother Nature,
> about removing harmful influences from her, about giving her what
> she needs, about restoring her to full control of her functions; when he
> talks to you about restoring the blood, adjusting the intestines and the
> brain, soothing the chest, repairing the liver, strengthening the heart,
> re-establishing and maintaining normal body temperature and knowing
> the secrets of longer life; when he talks to you about all this he is merely
> telling you the story of medicine. And when you find the truth out by
> experience, you'll see that none of it is true; you'll be as disillusioned as if
> you had awakened from a beautiful dream only to find it wasn't real.

Argan refuses to give up on doctors, and Molière polishes off this scene with
an amazing variation on "dreaming" when, sitting on stage as a character
who imagines he is sick, he brings up himself as a famous author and actor of
comedies about doctors, who is also, as everyone knows, in real life actually a
sick man. It is a situation that gave Pirandello an entire life's work:

> BÉRALDE. I was going to amuse you and take you to see a comedy by Molière on
> the subject.
> ARGAN. That Molière of yours is a scoundrel with those comedies he writes. I find
> his habit of poking fun at honest men like doctors very impertinent.
> BÉRALDE. He's not poking fun at doctors; he's poking fun at the practice of
> medicine.
> ARGAN. It's all right for him to stick his nose into medical matters; the insolent
> rogue laughing at examinations and prescriptions, attacking the medical
> profession and putting these respectable gentlemen into his plays!
> BÉRALDE. Whom should he put into his plays if not people from all walks of life?
> Kings and Princes are portrayed every day and they're certainly equal
> to doctors.
> ARGAN. What a rascally whelp. If I were one of his doctors, I'd revenge myself
> for his impudence and let him die without treatment if he became ill.
> Whatever he said, whatever he did, I wouldn't prescribe the slightest
> blood-letting, or the smallest enema, and I'd say to him, "Die, die!
> That will teach you to make fun of the Faculty."

Neither the actor nor the audience at that time knew that after the fourth
performance of this play, Molière would die – without the help of doctors

or anyone else – but we know it today and it makes a difference. The scene ends with Béralde saying about the man Molière, whom he is facing on stage, "He himself has just enough strength to bear his sickness." Molière as Argan replies "in character" that Molière the dramatist "heats up my bile and only makes me sick."

As if this scene, still securely in the comic light, were not surreal enough, the light darkens toward another kind of dream when the doctor himself arrives in a rage. Monsieur Purgon – patterned after a real-life doctor who killed his wife and daughter with a dose of antimony – comes in, followed by his assistant, Fleurant, carrying a giant enema tube, and the play descends toward nightmare. After scourging his patient for disobedience, the primal Biblical sin, Purgon drives the scene by threatening to abandon poor Argan to the "bitterness of your bile and the turbidity of your humors." The almost Satanic ritual takes place with the Doctor towering over the kneeling patient, quivering with terror:

MONSIEUR PURGON.	In less than four days you will be incurable!
ARGAN.	Have mercy on me!
MONSIEUR PURGON.	That you will develop bradypepsia.
ARGAN.	Monsieur Purgon!
MONSIEUR PURGON.	Bradypepsia will lead to dyspepsia.
ARGAN.	Monsieur Purgon!
MONSIEUR PURGON.	Dyspepsia will lead to apepsy.
ARGAN.	Monsieur Purgon!
MONSIEUR Purgon.	Apepsy will lead to lientery.
ARGAN.	Monsieur Purgon!
MONSIEUR PURGON.	Lientery will lead to dysentery.
ARGAN.	Monsieur Purgon!
MONSIEUR PURGON.	Dysentery will lead to dropsy.
ARGAN.	Monsieur Purgon!
MONSIEUR PURGON.	And dropsy will lead to the loss of life, and that is how far you will have brought yourself by your folly.
	(*Exit the Doctors.*)
ARGAN.	Oh, I'm as good as dead. Brother, you have murdered me.

He is prostrate on the floor like little Louison had been, though not, perhaps, with so much volition. What cures him is comedy, not medicine, even with its shower of threatened diseases loaded with painful consonants.

The nightmare of abandonment is dispelled by the scene in which Toinette does a "turn and go" scene, racing out one door as Toinette and back in another door disguised as a Traveling Doctor who has come to cure him.

Figure 45. Argan, the happy hypochondriac, reviewing his purgatives. Photo © Carol Rosegg.

Figure 46. An old Molière. Photo © akg-images.

She fools him completely, in spite of her transparent disguise. He is, after all, the same obsessive as the miser, Harpagon, who catches his own arm as if it were the thief. She goes along gaily reinventing the mechanisms of the body as if she were in the *Doctor In Spite of Himself*. They play a little scene about the "lungs." This scene can be played just as a mechanical repetitive device to get laughs but it surely has far more melancholic overtones – and if the scene is played intimately, with Toinette really embracing him and taking care of him with great love, the scene is both comedic and very moving:

TOINETTE. (*Loosely disguised as a Doctor*) It's your lungs.
ARGAN. My lungs?
TOINETTE. Yes. What are your symptoms?
ARGAN. I have head pains occasionally.
TOINETTE. Exactly. Lungs.
ARGAN. And sometimes I feel that there's a fog in front of my eyes.
TOINETTE. Lungs.
ARGAN. Sometimes I get heart pain.
TOINETTE. Lungs.
ARGAN. Sometimes I feel weak all over.
TOINETTE. Lungs.
ARGAN. And sometimes I have terrible pains in the stomach.
TOINETTE. Lungs. Do you have a powerful appetite?
ARGAN. Yes, sir.
TOINETTE. Lungs. Do you like to drink a drop of wine?
ARGAN. Yes, sir.
TOINETTE. Lungs. You take a little nap after meals and fall asleep easily?
ARGAN. Yes, sir.
TOINETTE. Lungs, lungs, lungs.

The actress playing Toinette knew that the situation was absurd and funny. She also knew that the man under her hands was deathly sick with a disease of the lungs and she knew the character was listing the author's own symptoms. So did the rest of the company and so, I imagine, did many in the audience. She cures him in the scene by hugging him and prescribing lots of meat and wine, Dutch cheese and oatmeal; and then decides what he really needs is to have his left arm amputated to cure the pain in his right elbow and to have his right eye gouged out to help the ailing left eye. Argan, finally showing a bit of sense, says, "There's no hurry for that," and she rushes off to see a man who died yesterday.

The final scenes in the play continue the idea of theatrical imagination as the cure for illusions and obsessions. Argan is persuaded to play dead twice: once for his wife and a second time for his daughter. The mean-spirited wife falls for it and expresses relief he is dead. She is glad to be rid of his "disgusting" habits, and besides, what good was he, "always with a medicine or an enema in his stomach, wiping his nose, coughing, spitting, dull-witted, ill-tempered, boring, tiring everyone out." She can now take his money and go. He sits up like Louison and says "not so fast" and she does go – with incredible speed. He plays the same death scene for his daughter who, of course, being honest in her love for both father and lover, weeps softly over the loss. On his unexpected recovery from death all are instantly reconciled and ready for the final "bright idea." Why not make Argan himself a doctor? Then he will not need to marry his daughter off to one. It just so happens that Béralde knows the whole College of Medicine and they just happen to be right offstage dressed in cap and gown, ready to conduct the initiation.

The Grand Finale is a joyful interlude with a stage full of well-attired doctors all chanting in what we used to call "pig-Latin." Morris Bishop many years ago wrote a witty English version of this scene in which the doctors ecstatically question the candidate about illnesses and their cure. The cure is always the same refrain to a question about the best method of confronting particular symptoms. The answer is the proclamation repeated by Argan as the candidate, and the chorus of Doctors, over and over.

ARGAN.	Give 'eman eneman,
	N'enemam bleedeman,
	N'enemam purgeman,
	N'enemam bleedeman purgeman-againe-man.
CHORUS OF DOCTORS.	(*Singing and dancing in "mêlée"*)
	Bene, bene, bene, bene respondere,
	Dignus, dignus, est entrare,
	In nostro docto corpore.[3]

And they proceed to the swearing-in of the new doctor. They do some mumbo jumbo about "ancieni opinione." Then, at that precise moment, Molière the actor uttered the fatal word:

Juro!

And that was Moliére's last word on stage. He started coughing blood. He "covered" it; he made every effort to disguise his difficulty; he went on acting. The scene played out with him hiding his face and coughing blood while the Doctors sang and danced, and the audience laughed because they thought it was all part of the comedy.

Jean-Baptiste was carried to his home on Rue Richelieu, a short way from the theater. La Grange asked him if he wanted a bit of soup, and he said, "No. Armande makes it too peppery. Bring me a little dry Parmesan cheese." Just moments prior Toinette had been offering him a cure of "good Dutch cheese." He then started hemorrhaging blood; he told La Grange to get his wife. When La Grange went to get Armande, Molière died alone. He bled to death alone, in a bleeding that started in full view on stage that was thought by the laughing audience to be "imaginary." Jean-Baptiste goes home after his fourth performance of the play in which he plays a hypochondriac plagued by imaginary illnesses, and he dies of very real tuberculosis. After Armande's efforts to get church approval for a Christian burial failed – even the king demurred by saying it was up to the bishop – a small group of people gathered at night to take the wooden box with the actor inside to a small grave at St. Joseph's in Montmartre – where he was buried without church rites next to, of all places, a street called on the old maps la rue du Temps Perdu (The Street of Lost Time).[1] This is the story of his final hours as it was told me by the actress at the Comédie-Française who took me to the celebratory performance of *Le Misanthrope* in 1947 and later that night wept as she spoke of Molière's death. Joy and grief. Both are there in this wild play described by Molière as a *Comédie Mêlée de Musique et de Danse*.

The Palais-Royal remained dark for one week after his death. It reopened with *Le Misanthrope* starring Armande.

XVII

FULL CIRCLE

On an ancient stone circle in Wales, there is a *graffito* that says, "Find your place and stand in it. When you do, the circle is begun, and once the circle is begun, the circle is completed." What century this advice came from is unknown, but it seems to speak with authority.

Following a grant from Louis XIV, Armande, La Grange and Catherine de Brie created Molière's living memorial with the founding of the House of Molière, also known as the Comédie-Française, a theater begun in 1680 and which still operates today, having survived enlightenments, revolutions, dictatorships, world wars, depressions and technological invasions. Even more of a memorial, perhaps, was the gathering together of Molière's complete works for publication.

But the eternal question still remains: Is there life after death? His body was exhumed, stored, moved around, pieced out in reliquaries, until there seemed to be nothing left, not even bones. But on stage, in his own theater, as well as in thousands of theaters all over the world, his spirit is continually being brought to life by the magic of what happens on stage. That is the greatest memorial a playwright can achieve.

It is the spirit of Molière, born from the agonies and joys of daily living that we all share in some way, that held 3,000 nobles rapt in the vast sculpted garden spaces of King Louis XIV's court in Versailles and, over 300 years later on the other side of the world near the border of the Pacific Ocean, could enrapture picnickers sitting on hard wooden benches in California's Marin County. That shared life in the theater is available to everyone; and that theater which is alive with the spirit of greatness is for all time and exists over time. It is like the seeds of wild flowers buried in the ground waiting patiently for the rain to bring them over and over again to another short, sweet life. While the authors are bits of bone and ash, their words and plays live in the sweating bodies and ardent souls of their actors – each loving the person who created the living, breathing words that bring audiences to share life with them.[1]

In 1973, three hundred years to the day after Molière's death, my wife and I stood by the memorial grave in Père Lachaise cemetery in Paris. A small plot of ground and a modest set of headstones marks the place for Molière and his friend, La Fontaine. At that time I assumed that his body was there but it seems likely, from Virginia Scott's expert sleuthing, that there is little or nothing of his body in that fenced-in piece of ground. I noticed a dirty piece of yellowing lined paper inside the space, and I reached in to pick it up. It said,

"'Allo, Molière! We miss you."

NOTES

I " 'Allo, Molière"

1 "*Dit*" means "called," "stage name" or "known as."
2 The Comédie-Française is the national theater of France created by King Louis XIV in 1680 when he put together Molière's company and the actors from the Hôtel de Bourgogne. It is also known as "The House of Molière" or "Le Théâtre Français" and is still performing at "La Salle Richelieu" adjacent to the original theater in the Palais-Royal.
3 Aimé Clariond was the 398th sociétaire of the Comédie-Française from 1937 until his death in 1959. The first sociétaire was Catherine de Brie from Molière's original company. Clariond's picture in the role can be seen in the chapter on *Le Misanthrope*.

II The First Stages

1 Virginia Scott, *Molière: A Theatrical Life* (Cambridge: Cambridge University Press, 2001).
2 W. G. Moore, *Molière: A New Criticism* (Oxford: Clarendon Press, 1949).
3 Ramon Fernandez, *Molière: The Man Seen Through the Plays*, trans. Wilson Follett (New York: Hill & Wang, 1958); originally published in French as *La Vie de Molière* (Gallimard, 1929).
4 *Molière*: a film written and directed by Ariane Mnouchkine with Le Théâtre du Soleil in 1978. (DVD video *Bel Air Classiques*, 2005).
5 The principal theater of Paris in the seventeenth century. It was founded in the sixteenth century when Les Confréries de la Passion produced mystery plays. In Molière's time it was the theater that produced Racine and Corneille. Among its actors of that time was Montfleury, a recipient of Cyrano de Bergerac's wrath and Molière's scorn.
6 The improvisational farcical style of the Italian touring troupes who established themselves in Paris in 1653. It was a form of theater that employed masks, acrobatics, sharp one-liners, either witty or scatological (or both), and stock characters such as Harlequin and Pantalone. It was a great influence on Molière.
7 Stephen Greenblatt, *Will in the World: How Shakespeare Became Shakespeare* (New York: W. W. Norton & Co., 2004), 26.
8 François Rey, *L'Album Molière* (Paris: Éditions Gallimard, 2010), 40.
9 The Théâtre Illustre was located on the unfashionable left bank on the rue Vielle-de-Temple in a building that no longer exists.
10 Fernandez, op. cit., 25.
11 The Petit-Bourbon was located on the rue des Poulies opposite the convent of Saint Germain des l'Auxerrois. Molière and his troupe played there from 1658 to 1660 on the off days of the week.

III Finding His Light

1 Montfleury was an overweight tragedian in the troupe that was resident at the Hôtel de Bourgogne. As that troupe had been long reigning in Paris there was a great deal of disdain and resentment felt by them towards the new guys on the block. And vice versa.

2 Scott, op. cit., 58.

3 Fernandez, op. cit., 113. Molière, a wondrous clown onstage, was quiet, attentive, and very serious and dignified offstage.

4 The reader might wonder how something superficial can be described as "deep" but as a guru once said in answer to a deep question, "What if there is no deep?"

5 Charles Varlet *dit* La Grange, *Le Registre* (2 vols. facsimile edition, edited by Bert E. Young and Grace P. Young. Paris: E. Droz, 1947).

6 Fernandez, op. cit., 60.

7 MS translation of *Les Précieuses Ridicules* by Robert W. Goldsby, done for performance by the University of Washington's Professional Actor Training Program in 1999. All passages in this chapter are from this translation. The author also directed this play as part of "The Molière Project" at the University of California at Los Angeles in 1993 at the Freud Playhouse.

8 A phrase used by Constantin Stanislavski in his long and intricate 1934 chart delineating the "Stanislavski System" and the elements necessary to attain excellence in the art of acting. Stella Adler, after her meetings in Russia with Stanislavski, brought this chart to America where it was taken up by Strasberg and Kazan and used as the basis for their work at the renowned Actors Studio and became known as "Method Acting." Robert Lewis, (as the French would say) *dit* Bobby Lewis, gave a series of lectures to explicate and analyze the chart as used by the Studio, all of which were held at midnight in order to accommodate the attendance of working actors. These lectures were later published as *Method – or Madness?* (New York: Samuel French, 1958). Sharon Carnicke in 1998 dealt with the chart in her book *Stanislavsky in Focus*, by referring to the literal translation of the Russian terms which many times shed new light on old problems or ambiguities.

IV The Actor Unmasked

1 Claude-Emmanuel Lhuillier, *dit* Chapelle, *Œuvres de Chapelle et de Bachaumont* (Paris: P. Jannet, 1854) as quoted by Virginia Scott, op. cit., 283. MS translation by Angela Paton.

2 Fernandez, op. cit., 111.

3 In 1660 the troupe was suddenly evicted in preparation for the building's demolition by M. Ratabon in order to make way for enlarging of the Louvre. However Molière had attained such a solid success in the preceding two years that he was able to remedy the sudden upheaval by obtaining from Louis XIV a new home in the Palais Royal, the former Palais Cardinal, home of Richelieu. It was opened as a refurbished Palais-Royal on 20 January 1661 and became the home to his succession of masterpieces.

4 Donald M. Frame, trans., *Tartuffe and Other Plays* (New York: The New American Library, 1981). All translations from *L'École des Maris* are by Mr. Frame.

V Into the Mouth of the Wolf

1 The French, great lovers of farce and the body, are quite basic, wishing fellow actors simply *merde*, a five-letter word meaning a four-letter shit in English, perhaps an effort to offer relief from stress. The English "break a leg" is not as cruel as it seems. It refers to

the knee bending in a curtsey or bow, therefore wishing you a great curtain call ovation when you will bow ever deeper. Another form of relief.

2 Fernandez, 84–85.

3 Richard Wilbur, *Molière: Four Comedies* (New York and London: Harcourt Brace Jovanovich, 1978), includes four comedies by Molière translated into English verse by Mr. Wilbur. All quotations in this chapter are from Mr. Wilbur's translation of *The School for Wives* found in this collection.

4 It is interesting to note that Molière fashioned a coat-of-arms for himself which depicted three tall trees separated by two small trees, all in green leaf and all growing out of a mound of green moss. François Rey, op. cit., 142.

5 Woody Allen, interview by Richard Schickel (London: BBC, 2001).

6 For the French *bouchonner* has a double meaning hidden in it: *bouchon* is a cork, a plug, a stopper. When I worked with Jean Renoir on his translation of his *Carola* into English, and later as his assistant when he directed that play at U. C. Berkeley, he started his rehearsal with the "Italian method," which was to read through the script word by word very slowly, letting each word ring in the actor's heads with all its etymological and emotional reverberations. Some American actors cannot stand this process; those who give themselves to it are richly rewarded. Because of his celebrity and the lack of time constraints, Renoir was able to go through his entire play. I have used it only on a selected scene or two and suggested the actor pursue the course at home. It is a process that is echoed in Michael Chekhov's directive to actors to "love your words," which does not mean embellish them with the frills and furbelows of artful vocal tricks but take them to your heart. Actors should all learn their lines by heart.

VI "Go Saddle Yon Braying Ass!"

1 This might be considered as the first after-play discussion but without audience participation.

2 There is a well-known account of Mlle de Brie, at 60-some years, being led hastily from her lodgings to perform in her everyday clothes in the production of *L'École des Femmes* as Agnès one evening at the Comédie-Française, because the audience refused to let the show go on without her in it.

3 Morris Bishop, trans., *Eight Plays by Molière* (New York: Modern Library College Edition, 1957). All quotes for the *Critique* are from Mr. Bishop's version of *The Critique of the School for Wives* found in this collection.

4 Brécourt was a highly respected actor in Paris theater at that time, but highly unstable off stage. He was with the company for only two years, when highly dependable La Grange took over the role of Dorante. Herzel, op. cit., 11.

5 Jean Racine, "Correspondance" in *Œuvres complètes*, edited by Raymond Picard (Paris: Gallimard, 1950–2) vol. 2, 459. Translated by Virginia Scott, op. cit., 133.

6 The Prince de Conti was an early supporter of Molière and his troupe in the provinces, but after the Prince took the holy orders of the Catholic Church he became vitriolic in his criticism, going so far as to publish a treatise on comedy accusing Molière of the unforgivable sin of atheism.

7 "Molière, with Love" was a project in three parts for one evening's performance which ran for several weeks at the University of Washington's School of Theater in 2001. The prologue, "The Actors Prepare," is a brief fragment freely adapted in a MS translation by Angela Paton from the much longer one-act by Molière: *L'Impromptu de Versailles*.

It was conceived as an introduction to the uncut versions of *Les Précieuses Ridicules*, MS translation by Robert W. Goldsby, and *George Dandin*, MS translation by Angela Paton, which constituted the remainder of the evening. In 1980 the author staged the full version of *L'Impromptu de Versailles* at the University of California at Berkeley in a translation by Albert Bermel accompanied by *George Dandin* in a MS translation by George House.

8   Albert Bermel, trans., *One-Act Comedies of Molière* (New York: Frederick Ungar Publishing, 1981).

VII Entrances...

1   Fernandez, op. cit., 122.

2   All quotes from *Le Tartuffe* in this chapter are translated by Richard Wilbur, op. cit., 313–470.

3   Olivier Schmitt, *Le Monde*, Paris, Nov. 7, 1995. My translation.

4   Mr. MacDougall was composer-in-residence at the Berkeley Stage Company and director of that theater's acclaimed Festival of New Music.

5   Monsieur Loyal has been the household name of the uniformed ringleader of every circus in France from the time of Astley's Hippodrome in Paris.

6   Georges Mongrédien and Jean Robert, "Recueil des textes et de documents du XVIIe siècle relatifs à Molière" *XVIIe Siècle* (1973): 98–9. A priest, Father Roullé, in reaction to *Tartuffe*, wrote that Molière was "a devil, cloaked in flesh and dressed as a man, and is the most outrageous, free-thinking heretic of all the centuries past who has had the impiety and abomination to put his diabolical spirit into a play and put it on in a public place ... And he and his play should be burned at the stake." A review any actor would cherish.

7   One wonders how Father Roullé would have reacted to Mr. René Auberjonois' choice as an actor in William Ball's production of *Tartuffe* at the American Conservatory Theater in San Francisco in 1966: After Orgon had given Tartuffe all his worldly goods, including the deed to the house, René took a holy water sprinkler and sprinkled Orgon and then, as the rest of the family gathered, he sprinkled all of them, at first slowly and reverently and then, finding himself in ecstasy over his inheritance began to go wild and leaping about as if he were an exuberant two-year-old, he took over the stage, wildly flinging water everywhere as the lights went out. Obviously the audience could not wait to come back for the second half of the play.

8   Dussane, Mlle de la Comédie-Française, *Un comédien nommé Molière*; translated from the French by Louis Galantière, *An Actor Named Molière* (New York: Scribners, 1937).

9   A Soviet poet, playwright, graphic artist and political activist whose work greatly influenced Russian Futurism. In 1930 he died of his own hand at the age of 34, apparently no longer believing in the future.

VIII ...And Exits

1   *MOLIÈRE: Œuvres Complètes*, Bibliothèque de la Pléiade, vol. 2, text and annotation by Maurice Rat. (Paris: Éditions Gallimard, 1956), 2.

2   Sharon Carnicke, in her book *Stanislavsky in Focus*, tells us the true interpretation of the Russian word is not "the objective" but "the problem."

3   *La Muse Historique* was a weekly gazette that included satirical verses and gossip about goings-on in the arts and the court between 1650 and 1665. Jean Loret was the creator of the paper and its contents.

4 Eugène Despois and Paul Mesnard, eds, *Œuvres de Molière*, vol. 5, *Les grands écrivains de la France* (Paris: Librairie Hachette, 1880), 256–9.

5 This production, which I saw at the Old Globe Theatre in San Diego in 2004, originated at the Seattle Rep in Seattle, Washington and was also presented at the McCarter Theatre in Princeton, New Jersey.

6 A production of *Don Juan* by the Marin Shakespeare Company in San Rafael, California. Directed by and based on a MS translation by the author and Angela Paton. Costumed by Julie Weiss. All translations in this chapter are from this 2003 version of the play. The author staged his own translation of this play at the University of California at Berkeley in 1962 with Stacy Keach, then a young student, playing Sganarelle. This production was later taken on a tour of the then existing nine campuses of the University of California. In 1965, the author reworked his translation for a staging at the Actor's Workshop in San Francisco by John Hancock.

7 Olivier Schmitt, Review of the Paris production, *Le Monde*, Paris, October 25, 1993.

8 Michel Cournot, Review of the production at Avignon, *Le Monde*, Paris, July 12, 1993.

9 *Les Échos*, (Paris, May 28, 2002).

10 Schmitt, op. cit.

11 Jean-Léonor Le Gallois de Grimarest, *La vie de M. de Molière: Édition critique par George Mongrédien* (Paris: M. Brient, 1955), 79–80.

12 Mikhail Bulgakov, *The Life of Monsieur de Molière*, translated by Mirra Ginsburg (New York: Funk & Wagnalls, 1970), 175.

13 Julie Weiss is a designer nominated for a Tony award for her work in *Elephant Man* on Broadway, and in film nominated for 2 Oscars for *Frida* and *Twelve Monkeys*.

IX She Loves Me... She Loves Me...

1 This character we named D'Assoucy. D'Assoucy was an entertainer in the salons of Paris, composing verses and poems which he accompanied on his lute. The happy-go-lucky eccentric, nicknamed Phoebus Wardrobin, achieved a certain fame in that city as much for his lifestyle as for his performances, but he decided to leave Paris at the age of fifty for a carefree life on the road, part vagabond, part minstrel. He fell into many misfortunes, lost his money through carelessness or outright robbery and finally, destitute, was adopted by the Molière troupe for one winter. He always paid tribute to Molière's generosity of spirit.

X ...Not!

1   Nel mezzo del cammin di nostra vita
        mi ritrovai per una selva oscura,
        ché la diritta via era smarrita.

  From *The Divine Comedy of Dante Alighieri, Volume I: Inferno*, Italian text with English translation and commentary by John Sinclair (New York: Oxford University Press, 1959).

2 In the Concise Oxford French Dictionary, it is listed as "Artrabile [L. atra bilis] (and. Med.) Black bile. Hypochondria." The mention of hypochondria intrigues me; I immediately thought of *The Imaginary Invalid*.

3 Robert Brustein, *Letters to a Young Actor: A Universal Guide to Performance* (New York: Basic Books, 2005), 18–19. My italics. Brustein was the Founding Director of the Yale

Repertory Theatre and the American Repertory Theater and served for twenty-three years as the director of the Loeb Drama Center at Harvard.

4 Fernandez, 153.

5 Michel de Montaigne, *Essays*, translated by J. M. Cohen (Baltimore: Penguin, 1958), 97.

6 Ibid., 102.

7 Roger W. Herzel, "'Much Depends on the Acting': The Original Cast of *Le Misanthrope*," *PMLA* 95 (May 1980), 349. Jean Donneau de Visé was an eminent French critic in Molière's time. He wrote these words about *The Misanthrope* in 1667.

8 Wilbur, op. cit., 156.

9 Wilbur, op. cit., 176–7.

10 Neil Bartlett, *The Misanthrope*, translation for La Jolla Playhouse in 1989, directed by Robert Falls. Neil Barlett is a leading British theater director and translator, with translations and stagings of Molière (*The Misanthrope*, *The School for Wives*, *Don Juan*), Marivaux, Racine, Genet, Kleist Dumas and Labiche to his credit, by companies including the Royal Shakespeare Company, the National Theatre in London, The Arena in Washington, La Jolla Playhouse and the Goodman in Chicago. His American version of *The Misanthrope* was published in *American Theatre* (July/August 1990); the original British version is published by Oberon Books, London. I directed a production of the American version at Pepperdine University in 1997.

11 Herzel, op. cit., 352–3.

12 Bartlett, op. cit., 13.

13 Ibid., 18.

14 Ibid., 20.

15 Molière, *Œuvres complètes*, vol. 1, ed. Robert Jouanny (Paris: Éditions Garnier Frères), 942.

16 Scott, op. cit., 217–18.

XI Blessèd Laughter

1 Louis Racine, *Mémoires sur la vie et les ouvrages de Jean Racine*, œuvres complètes, vol. I, 43; as quoted in Scott, op. cit., 304.

2 Scott, op. cit., 187.

3 Donneau de Visé, op. cit., 53.

4 Michael Chekhov, *To the Actor: On the Technique of Acting* (New York, Hagerstown, San Francisco, London: Harper & Row, 1953), 2.

5 Albert Bermel, *The Actor's Molière*, vol. 2 (New York: Applause Theatre Book Publishers, 1988), 3–40. *Le Médecin Malgré Lui*, translated by Mr. Bermel, was directed by the author at University of California at Los Angeles in 1988 as part of the previously mentioned "Molière Project." All translations in this chapter are from Mr. Bermel.

6 The origins for this skit are in the grave and the Empire Burlesque Theatre in Newark, New Jersey is long gone.

7 Jouanny, op. cit., 3.

XII Classic Routines

1 Richard Wilbur, trans., *Amphitryon by Molière* (New York: Dramatists Play Service, 1995).

2 Adaptation and MS translation by David Ball for production at the Théâtre de la Jeune Lune and later produced at the American Repertory Theater.

3 I have since learned that Dominique Serrand and Stephen Epp have reformed their theater in Minneapolis calling it the MovingCompany because they claim no permanent home.

XIII Musical Comedy

1 Louix XIV, *Mémoires pour l'instruction du Dauphin*, ed. Pierre Goubert (Paris: Imprimerie National, 1992).
2 Dandin, according to the *Littré*, is translated as "booby or ninny." See Émile Littré, *Dictionnaire de la langue Française*, abridged by A. Beajean, 13th ed. (Éditions Universaires, 1963).
3 Though in Molière's time, putting down peasants (who are not to be confused with shepherds) were considered fair game for provoking laughter from an audience.
4 *Makin' Hay*, a musical adaptation of Molière's *George Dandin* written and composed by Matthew Goldsby, was produced by Heather Chesley in 2009 at the Actors Co-op in Los Angeles, California which was directed by Linda Kerns. Prior to that production it received two workshop productions at Antaeus in North Hollywood in 2007 and 2008.
5 Molière, *Le Bourgeois Gentilhomme*, trans. Nick Dear (Bath: Absolute Classics, 1992). It was produced by the National Theatre in London that same year.
6 The next two passages from *Le Bourgeois Gentilhomme* are MS translations by the author.
7 *New York Times*, Sunday Art Selection, 10 April 1994. David Richards was the theater critic for the *New York Times*, the *Washington Post*, and the *Washington Star*. As a *New York Times* critic he won the Pulitzer Prize in 1989.

XIV The Bones of Farce

1 A long-necked, plucked instrument akin to a lute.
2 Scott, op. cit., 244–5.
3 Littré, op. cit.
4 Lady Gregory, *The Kiltartan Molière* (New York: Benjamin Blom, 1971). All translations in this chapter are from *The Rogueries of Scapin* as rendered by Lady Gregory. The author's staging of this translation was at the University of California at Berkeley in 1957 with a cast that included Sid Fields, who was to become a leading teacher of screenwriting in Los Angeles, and Jerry Evans, who was to become a leading director of daytime television in New York.
5 *Les Fourberies de Scapin*, collections "mise-en-scène" sous la direction de Pierre-Aimé Touchard et Paul-Louis Mignon (Paris: Éditions du Seuil, 1920). (Prompt script for Copeau's productions.) First performed in New York at the Garrick Theatre in 1917 and again in Paris in the Vieux-Colombier in 1920. All quoted passages are from this prompt script as translated by the author, while the text of the play is translated by Lady Gregory.
6 In San Francisco's American Conservatory Theater, the handsome leading man, Paul Shenar, was cast by Bill Ball as the ugly Tusenbach in *Three Sisters*. To the amazement of his fellow actors, Paul, with a bald pate masking his thick black wavy hair, was absolutely wonderful, doing some of his best work. When asked about it, he simply said, "It is the inner me."

7 It is said that Jessica Tandy, in her role as Blanche in *Streetcar Named Desire*, used for her intention in her opening scene the need to go to the bathroom (probably suggested to her by her director Elia Kazan, trying to help her satisfy Tennessee William's intention of creating a woman in desperate need of relief from the ills of her life). It lent her a strange and indefinable nervousness that piqued curiosity and added mystery.

8 Henri Bergson, "Laughter," in *Comedy*, edited by Wylie Sypher (New York: Doubleday Anchor Books, 1956). 90–91.

9 W. G. Moore, *Molière: A New Criticism* (New York: Doubleday Anchor Books, 1962), 33.

10 Nicolas Boileau, *Œuvres complètes*, ed. Françoise Escal (Paris: Gallimard, 1966), 178.

11 A theatrical prop sometimes also called a slap-stick, in the shape of a stick, and rigged to make a loud noise when it strikes against a person, but without offering any pain to the recipient.

XV The Dancing Skeleton

1 Lanson, Gustave. *Le mémoire de Mahelot, Laurent: et d'autres décorateurs de l'Hôtel de Bourgogne et de la Comédie-Française au XVIIe siècle*. Compte rendu, 1923.

2 Wilbur, op. cit., *Four Comedies*, translation of *Les Femme Savantes*. All passages in this chapter are from Mr. Wilbur's translation.

3 More echoes of the Jansenism that so plagued Molière.

4 Fernandez, op. cit., 163.

XVI The Imaginary Invalid

1 Albert Bermel, ed., *The Genius of the French Theater* (New York: Mentor, 1961). Passages from *The Imaginary Invalid* are from the translation by Ms. Mildred Marmur unless otherwise noted. The author directed productions of this translation for the Columbia Players at Columbia University in New York in 1991 and at the University of Southern California at Los Angeles in 1995. He also oversaw a workshop production of this play for the Antaeus Company in 1996 then located at the Mark Taper Forum in Los Angeles with Andrew Robinson as Argan and Lawrence Pressman as Diafoirus.

2 Bergson, op. cit., 67.

3 Bishop, op. cit.

4 Sylvie Chevalley, *Molière en son temps 1622–1673* (Paris: Éditions Minkoff, 1973). According to an old map of the district, the Cimetière St. Joseph where Molière was buried on that night in an out-of-the-way unhallowed strip of ground, was located at rue Montmartre and rue de Temps Perdus [*sic*] (374). According to a plaque in the nave of St. Eustache, the man who was the presiding curate at the time of Molière's death was one Abbé Pierre Marlin. Abbé Marlin thus may have officiated at both the christening and the burial of Molière's son a few short months before Molière's passing and then either willingly or unwillingly, may have had to follow the orders from above to refuse Molière a final resting place in his home church in 1673. A sad role to play.

XVII Full Circle

1 Hannah Arendt in *The Life of the Mind* (New York: Harcourt Brace Jovanovich, 1971) and in *The Human Condition* (New York: Doubleday & Co., 1958) talks in detail

of the battle of the human individual caught, as also spoken of in Lucretius, between the graven edicts of the past and the elusive promises of the future in a constantly moving present – *nunc stans* (this moment now). In the ever-changing moment it is possible to stop time and obtain a transcendence that reverberates with eternity when you slip away from the cares, demands, and needs of that moment into a deeper world of contemplation and thought that can be brought about by the epiphanies made real in art. Plato described that experience as *arrhēton* (unspeakable); Aristotle called it *aneu logou* (without word); Buddhists think of it as nirvana. Philosophers all through time have tried to explain the sensation that is beyond the limits of reason. The deep core that the artists go to in their work is really composed of that mystery. It is the moment of coming to life, not an individual life, but life itself. It is the achievement of those moments of eternity that reward the artist with immortality.

WORKS CITED AND CONSULTED

Adam, Antoine. *L'Histoire de la littérature française au XVIIe siècle.* Vol. 4. Paris: Éditions Mondiales, 1962.

Alberge, Claude. *Et Molière devint dieu.* Pézenas: Éditions Domens, 2009.

Alighieri, Dante. *The Divine Comedy of Dante Alighieri, Volume I: Inferno.* Italian text with English translation and commentary by John Sinclair. New York: Oxford University Press, 1959.

Arendt, Hannah. *The Human Condition.* Anchor Books Edition. New York: Doubleday & Co., 1958.

_____. *The Life of the Mind.* New York: Harcourt Brace Jovanovich, 1971.

Auerbach, Erich. *Mimesis.* Princeton: Princeton University Press, 1974.

Barrault, Jean-Louis. *Réflexions sur le théâtre.* Paris: Jacques Vautrin, 1949.

_____. *Souvenirs pour demain.* Paris: Éditions du Seuil, 1972.

_____. *Paris, notre siècle.* Paris: Éditions de Messine/Pierre Berge, 1982.

Benichou, Paul. *Morales du grand siècle.* Paris: Gallimard, NRF, 1948.

Bergson, Henri. *The Creative Mind.* Translated by Mibelle L. Andison. New York: Citadel Press, 1919.

_____. "Laughter." In *Comedy.* Edited by Wylie Sypher. New York: Doubleday Anchor Books, 1956.

Bermel, Albert. *Molière's Theatrical Bounty.* Carbondale: Southern Illinois University Press, 1990.

Biet, Christian, ed. *Le théâtre français du XVIIe siècle.* Paris: Éditions l'Avant-Scène Théâtre, 2009.

Blanchart, Paul. *Histoire de la mise en scène. Que sais je?* Paris: Presses universitaires de France, 1947.

Bloom, Harold, ed. *Molière: Modern Critical Views.* Philadelphia: Chelsea House, 2001.

Boileau, Nicolas. *Œuvres complètes.* Edited by Françoise Escal. Paris: Gallimard, 1966.

Bradby, David and Andrew Calder, eds. *The Cambridge Companion to Molière.* Cambridge: Cambridge University Press, 2006.

Bray, René. *La formation de la doctrine classique.* Paris: Librairie Nizet, 1963.

_____. *Molière, homme de théâtre.* Paris: Mercure de France, 1954.

Brisson, Pierre. *Molière: Sa vie dans ses œuvres.* Paris: Gallimard, 1942.

Brustein, Robert. *Letters to a Young Actor: A Universal Guide to Performance.* New York: Basic Books, 2005.

Bulgakov, Mikhail. *The Life of Monsieur de Molière.* Translated from the Russian by Mirra Ginsburg. New York: Funk & Wagnalls, 1970.

Cahiers de la Compagnie Madeleine Renaud–Jean-Louis Barrault. No. 15. Paris: 1953. Reissued in Paris: Éditions Juillard, 1988.

Carmody, Jim. *Rereading Molière: Mise en scène from Antoine to Vitez.* Ann Arbor: University of Michigan Press, 1993.

Carnicke, Sharon M. *Stanislavsky in Focus*. Amsterdam: Harwood Academic Publishers, 1998.

Caudwell, H. *Introduction to French Classicism*. London: Macmillan & Co., 1951.

Cervantes, Miguel de. *Don Quixote*. Ozell's revision of the translation by Peter Motteux. New York: Modern Library, 1930.

Chapelle, Claude-Emmanuelle Lhuillier. *Œuvres de Chapelle et de Bachaumont*. Paris: P. Jannet, 1845.

Chapman, Percy Addison. *The Spirit of Molière*. Princeton: Princeton University Press, 1940.

Chekov, Michael. *To the Actor: On the Technique of Acting*. New York, Hagerstown, San Francisco, London: Harper & Row, 1953.

Chevalley, Sylvie, ed. *Album théâtre classique: la vie théâtrale sous Louis XIII et Louis XIV.* Iconographie réunie et comentée par Sylvie Chevalley. Paris: Gallimard, 1970.

————. *Molière en son temps 1622–1673*. Paris/Geneva: Éditions Minkoff, 1973.

Chicago Shakespeare Festival. Program for the Comédie-Française production of *Le Malade Imaginaire*. Chicago: Chicago Shakespeare Festival, 2004.

La Comédie-Française: 30 ans de création théâtrale. Photography by Laurencine Lot and text by Joël Huthwohl. Tournai: La Renaissance du Livre, 2003.

Copeau, Jacques. *Les Fourberies de Scapin*. Mise-en-scène de Jacques Copeau. Présentation de Louis Jouvet. Paris: Éditions du Seuil, 1950. Seuil catalogue number 087123959. Collections "mise en scène" sous la direction de Pierre-Aimé Touchard et Paul-Louis Mignon. (Prompt script for Copeau's productions in New York, 1917 and Paris, 1920.)

Corrigan, Robert W., ed. *Comedy: Meaning and Form*. New York: Chandler Publishing, 1965.

Davenport, Millia. *The Book of Costume*. New York: Crown Publishers, 1956.

Deierkauf-Holsboer, S. Wilma. *Histoire de la mise en scène dans le théâtre français à Paris de 1600 à 1673*. Paris: Librairie Nizet, 1960.

De Jomaron, Jacquelin, ed. *Le théâtre en France du Moyen Âge à 1789*. Preface by Ariane Mnouchkine. Paris: Armand Colin, 1998.

Despois, Eugene and Paul Mesnard, eds. *Œuvres de Molière*. Vol. 5, *Les grands écrivains de la France*. Paris: Librairie Hachette, 1880.

Dock, S. V. *Costume and Fashion in the Plays of Jean-Baptiste Molière*. Geneva: Éditions Slatkine, 1992.

Dullin, Charles. *L'Avare*. Mise-en-scène et commentaires par Charles Dullin. Paris: Éditions du Seuil, 1946.

Dussane, Béatrix. *An Actor Named Molière*. Translated from the French by Lewis Galantière. New York: Scribners, 1937. (Originally published in French as *Un comédien nommé Molière*. Paris: Éditions du PLON, 1936.)

Fabré, Émile. *Notre Molière*. Paris: Éditions Albin Michel, 1951.

Féral, Josette. *Trajectoires du Soleil: autour d'Ariane Mnouchkine*. Berlin: Alexander Verlag/Paris: Éditions Théâtrales, 1998.

Fernandez, Ramon. *Molière: The Man Seen through the Plays*. Translated by Wilson Follett. New York: Hill and Wang, 1958. (Originally published in French as *La vie de Molière*. Paris: Gallimard, 1929.)

Frye, Northrop. *The Anatomy of Criticism*. Princeton: Princeton University Press, 1957.

Garapon, Robert. *La fantaisie verbale et le comique dans le théâtre français du Moyen Âge à la fin du XVIIe siècle*. Paris: Librairie Armand Colin, 1957.

Greenblatt, Stephen. *Will in the World: How Shakespeare Became Shakespeare*. New York: W. W. Norton & Co., 2004.

Grimarest, Jean-Léonor Le Gallois de. *La vie de M. de Molière: édition critique par George Mongrédien*. Publications de la Société d'Histoire du Théâtre. Paris: M. Brient, 1955.

Gross, Nathan. *From Gesture to Idea: Esthetics and Ethics in Molière's Comedy*. New York: Columbia University Press, 1982.

Grossman, Lionel. *Men and Masks: A Study of Molière*. Baltimore: Johns Hopkins University Press, 1963.

Guicharnaud, Jacques, ed. *Molière: A Collection of Critical Essays*. Englewood Cliffs: Prentice Hall, 1964.

———. *Molière: une aventure théâtrale*. Paris: Gallimard, 1963.

Herzel, Roger W. "'Much Depends on the Acting': The Original Cast of *Le Misanthrope*." *PMLA* 95, (May) 1980.

———. *The Original Casting of Molière's Plays*. Ann Arbor: UMI Research Press, 1981.

Howarth, W. D., ed. *French Theatre in the Neo-classical Era, 1550–1789*. Cambridge: Cambridge University Press, 1997.

———. *Molière: A Playwright and his Audience*. Cambridge: Cambridge University Press, 1982.

Howarth, W. D. and Merlin Thomas, eds. *Molière: Stage and Study: Essays in Honour of W. G. Moore*. Oxford: Clarendon Press, 1973.

Hubert, J. D. *Molière and the Comedy of Intellect*. Berkeley: University of California Press, 1962.

Janko, Richard. *Aristotle on Comedy*. Berkeley: University of California Press, 1984.

Jasinski, René. *Molière and the Misanthrope*. Paris: Librairie Nizet, 1963.

———. *Molière: connaissance des lettres*. Paris: Hatier, 1969.

Jouvet, Louis. *Molière et la comédie classique*. Paris: Gallimard, 1965.

Jurgens, Madeleine and Elizabeth Maxfield-Miller, eds. *Cent ans de recherches sur Molière, sur sa famille et sur les comédiens de sa troupe*. Paris: Imprimerie Nationale, 1963.

Kurtz, Maurice. *Jacques Copeau: Biography of a Theater*. Carbondale: Southern Illinois University Press, 1999.

La Grange, Charles Varlet de. *Registre*. 2 vols. Facsimile edition edited by Bert E. Young and Grace P. Young. Paris: E. Droz, 1947.

La Fontaine. *Œuvres complètes*. 2 vols. Paris: Bibliothèque de la Pléiade, 1954.

Lacour, Léopold. *Les maîtresses de Molière*. Paris: Société Française d'Éditions Littéraires et Techniques, 1932.

Lafayette, Madame de. *La Princesse de Clèves*. Préface par Antoine Adam. Paris: Garnier-Flamarion, 1966.

Lancaster, Henry Carrington. *A History of French Dramatic Literature in the Seventeenth Century*. Vol. 3 of 9: "The Period of Molière, 1652–1672." Baltimore: John Hopkins University Press, 1929–42.

Lanson, Gustave. "Molière et la Farce." *La Revue de Paris*, 1 May 1901. (Reprinted in *Comedy: Meaning and Form*, edited by Robert W. Corrigan. New York: Chandler Publishing, 1965.)

———. *Le Mémoire de Mahelot, Laurent et d'autres décorateurs de l'Hôtel de Bourgogne et de la Comédie-Française au XVIIe siècle, par Lancaster*. Compte rendu, R.H.L. 1923, Avril–Juin.

Lauter, Paul, ed. *Theories of Comedy*. New York: Anchor Books, 1964.

Laver, James. *Costume in the Theatre*. New York: Hill & Wang, 1964.

Lewis, Robert. *Method – or Madness?* Introduction by Harold Clurman. Hollywood, Toronto, London: Samuel French, 1958.

Lewis, W. H. *The Splendid Century: Life in the France of Louis XIV*. New York: Doubleday Anchor Books, 1957.

Littré, Émile. *Dictionnaire de la langue Française*. Abridged by A. Beajean. 13th ed. Éditions Universitaires, 1963.

Louis XIV. *Mémoires pour l'instruction du Dauphin*. Edited by Pierre Goubert. Translated by Virginia Scott. Paris: Imprimerie National, 1992.

Lough, John. *Paris Theatre Audiences in the Seventeenth and Eighteenth Centuries*. London: Oxford University Press, 1957.

————. *Seventeenth-century French Drama: The Background*. Oxford: Oxford University Press, 1979.

Lucretius. *On the Nature of Things (De rerum natura)*. Edited and translated by Anthony Esolen. Baltimore and London: Johns Hopkins University Press, 1995.

Lucretius. *On the Nature of the Universe*. Translated by R. E. Latham and revised by John Godwin. London: Penguin, 1994.

Matthews, Brander. *Molière: His Life and his Works*. New York: Charles Scribner & Sons, 1926.

McCarthy, Gerry. *The Theatres of Molière*. New York: Routledge, 2002.

Meredith, George. *An Essay on Comedy and the Uses of the Comic Spirit*. New York: Scribner's, 1897. (Reprinted in *Comedy*, ed. Wylie Sypher. New York: Doubleday Anchor Books, 1956.)

Michaut, G. *La jeunesse de Molière*. Paris: Librairie Hachette, 1922.

————. *Les débuts de Molière à Paris*. Paris: Librairie Hachette, 1923.

————. *Les luttes de Molière*. Paris: Librairie Hachette, 1925.

Mnouchkine, Ariane. *L'Art du présent: entretiens avec Fabienne Pascaud*. Paris: Plon, 2005.

————, dir. *Molière*. DVD. Written and directed by Ariane Mnouchkine with Le Théâtre du Soleil, 1978. Bel Air Classiques, 2005.

Mongrédien, Georges. *Daily Life in the French Theatre at the Time of Moliere*. Translated by Claire Eliane Engel. London: George Allen & Unwin, 1969.

Mongrédien, Georges and Jean Robert. "Recueil des textes et de documents du XVIIe siècle relatifs à Molière." *XVIIe Siècle* 98–9, 1973.

Montaigne, Michel de. *The Complete Essays*. Translated by Donald Frame. New York: Doubleday Anchor Books, 1960.

————. *Essays*. Translated by J. M. Cohen. Baltimore: Penguin, 1958.

Moore, W. G. *Molière: A New Criticism*. Oxford: Clarendon Press, 1949.

————. *French Classical Literature*. London: Oxford University Press, 1961.

————. *Molière: A New Criticism*. New York: Doubleday Anchor Books, 1962.

Nicoll, Allardyce. *The World of Harlequin*. Cambridge: Cambridge University Press, 1963.

Palmer, John. *Molière*. New York: Benjamin Blom, 1970.

Provine, Robert R. *Laughter: A Scientific Investigation*. New York: Viking Penguin, 2000.

Racine, Jean. "Correspondance." In *Œuvres complètes*. Vol 2. Edited by Raymond Picard. Paris: Gallimard, 1950.

Racine, Louis. *Mémoires sur la vie et les ouvrages de Jean Racine*. In *OEuvres complètes*. Vol 1. Paris: Gallimard, 1950. (As quoted in V. Scott, *Molière: A Theatrical Life*. Cambridge: Cambridge University Press, 2001.)

Rey, François, ed. *L'Album Molière*. Iconographie choisie et commentée par François Rey. Paris: Éditions Gallimard, Pléiade, 2010.

Rosenberg, Pierre, ed. *France in the Golden Age: Seventeenth-century Paintings in American Collections*. New York: Metropolitan Museum of Art, 1982.

Schaeffer, Neil. *The Art of Laughter*. New York: Columbia University Press, 1981.

Scherer, Jacques. *La dramaturgie classique en France*. Paris: Librairie Nizet, 1959.

Scott, Virginia. *The Commedia dell'Arte in Paris 1644–1697*. Charlottesville: University of Virginia Press, 1990.

———. *Molière: A Theatrical Life*. Cambridge: Cambridge University Press, 2001.

Segal, Erich. *The Death of Comedy*. Cambridge, MA: Harvard University Press, 2001.

Sevigné, Marquise de. *La vie noble en province au XVIIe siècle: choix de lettres*. Paris: Union Générale d'Éditions, 1963.

Seyler, Athene and Stephen Haggard. *The Craft of Comedy*. New York: Theater Arts, 1946.

Simon, Alfred. *Molière, une vie*. Lyon: La Manufacture, 1987.

Sorell, Walter. *Facets of Comedy*. New York: Grosset & Dunlap, 1972.

Sypher, Wylie, ed. *Comedy*. New York: Doubleday Anchor Books, 1956.

———. "The Meanings of Comedy." In *Comedy*, edited by Wylie Sypher. New York: Doubleday Anchor Books, 1956.

Teyssier, Jean-Marie. *Réflexions sur Dom Juan de Molière*. Paris: Éditions Nizet, 1970.

Torrance, Robert M. *The Comic Hero*. Cambridge, MA: Harvard University Press, 1978.

Turnell, Martin. *The Classical Moment: Studies of Corneille, Molière and Racine*. New York: New Directions, 1946.

Vilar, Jean. *De la tradition théâtrale*. Paris: Gallimard, L'Arche, 1955.

Whitman, Cedric. *Aristophanes and the Comic Hero*. Cambridge, MA: Harvard University Press, 1964.

Wilcox, John. *The Relation of Molière to Restoration Comedy*. New York: Columbia University Press, 1938.

Willey, Basil. *The Seventeenth-Century Background: The Thought of the Age in Relation to Religion and Poetry*. New York: Doubleday Anchor Books, 1953.

WORKS BY MOLIÈRE

Selected editions and translations

Bartlett, Neil, trans. *The Misanthrope*. American version: *American Theatre* 7(4/5), July/August 1990.

———, trans. *The Misanthrope*. British version: London: Oberon Books, 1990.

Bermel, Albert, trans. *One-Act Comedies by Molière*. New York: Frederick Ungar Publishing, 1981.

———. *The Actor's Molière*. Vol. 2. New York: Applause Theatre Book Publishers, 1988.

Bishop, Morris, trans. *Eight Plays by Molière*. New York: Modern Library College Edition, 1957.

Bouvet, Alphonse, ed. *Le Malade Imaginaire, l'Amour Médecin*. Paris: Les Petits Classiques, Bordas, 1970.

Baker, Henry and James Miller, trans. *Molière's Comedies*. Introduction by F. C. Green. 2 vols. London: J. M. Dent & Sons, Everyman's Library, 1956.

Dear, Nick, trans. *Le Bourgeois Gentilhomme*. Bath: Absolute Press, 1992.

Forestier, Georges, ed. *OEuvres complètes* (French). Paris: Gallimard, Pléiade, 2010.

Frame, Donald M., trans. *The Misanthrope and Other Plays*. New York: Signet Classics, 1968.

———, trans. *Tartuffe and Other Plays*. New York: The New American Library, 1981.

Gregory, Lady, ed., trans. *The Kiltartan Molière*. New York: Benjamin Blom, 1971. (Three plays by Molière including *The Rogueries of Scapin*. Originally published in Dublin in 1910.)

Graveley, George and Ian Maclain, trans. *Don Juan and Other Plays*. Oxford: Oxford University Press, 1989.

Jouanny, Robert, ed. *Œuvres complètes*. 2 vols (French). With preface by R. Jouanny. Paris: Éditions Garnier Frères, 1962.

Marmur, Mildred, trans. *The Imaginary Invalid*. In *The Genius of the French Theater*. Edited by Albert Bermel. New York: Mentor Books, 1961.

Porter, Stephen, adpt. *Don Juan*. New York: Dramatists Play Service, 1972.

Rat, Maurice, ed. *Œuvres complètes*. 2 vols (French). With annotation by M. Rat. Paris: Bibliothèque de la Pléiade, Gallimard, 1956.

Waller, A. R., trans. *The Plays of Molière in French and English*. 8 vols. Edinburgh: John Grant, 1907.

Wilbur, Richard, trans. *Molière: Four Comedies*. English verse translation. New York and London: Harcourt Brace Jovanovich, 1978.

_____, trans. *Amphitryon by Molière*. New York: Dramatists Play Service, 1995.

_____, trans. *Don Juan*. San Diego, New York and London: A Harvest Book, 2001.

_____, trans. *The Misanthrope*. New York: Harcourt, Brace & Co., 1954.

Wood, John, trans. *The Miser and Other Plays*. London: Penguin, 1962.

_____, trans. *Five Plays*. Baltimore: Penguin, 1968.

INDEX

A

Actor Named Molière, An (Dussane) 67
actors: onstage and offstage relationships 16–
    19, 21–2; physical and psychological
    reactions of 113, 138; roles effect on
    identity 94–5; strands 142–3; tension
    between self and character, 122; and
    transformation 141–2
actors' vocabulary (selected): acting
    metaphor 120–2; action 70, 99; aside
    37, 124; beats (units and objectives)
    145–52; blocking 28, 37, 40, 54–5,
    59, 60, 81, 139, 142, 144; burlesque
    114–18; commedia dell' arte 12, 138,
    159; communion 135; cross-purpose
    38, 169; costume 103; design 34, 37,
    40, 57–8, 70–1, 73, 76, 89, 125, 137;
    diction 11, 46, 49, 61, 80, 149–50;
    entrances 16, 53, 68; exits 21, 24,
    69–81, 104–6; ecstatic experience
    (endorphin rush) vii, 107, 135; fly-
    catching 140; gesture 48, 61, 65, 113;
    given circumstances (situation) 7, 56,
    80, 97; "grand style" 144; ground plan
    70–1, 140–1, 168; hook 41; intention
    (objective) 35, 99, 146–50; "*les trois
    coups*" 4; *lazzi* 125; lightness of touch
    117; make-up 18, 75; "magic if" 141;
    mask 12, 24, 61–2, 79, 84, 94, 95, 111,
    146, 158–9; mimetic 113, 119, 144,
    171–2; mime 144–9; playing together
    19, 113, 135; passion 33; rhetoric 9,
    17, 35, 41, 61–2, 85, 135, 139–45;
    repetition 43, 60, 147; rehearsal 50,
    51; stage business 61, 63–5, 72–3,
    84, 86, 133, 139, 152–3, 158; subtext

37, 61, 93, 99, 102; tempo-rhythm
    113; transformation 141, 170; turn
    and go 144–5; voice and speech 17,
    37, 38, 42
Allen, Woody 37–8
L'Amour Médecin (*The Love Doctor*) 70, 95
Amours de Psyché et Cupidon, Les (La Fontaine)
    112–13
Amphitryon 119–22, **121**
Armande **27**; children 51, 158; daughter
    of Béjart 10; depicted in film 22;
    early relationship with Molière
    10, 11–12, 21–2, 23; marriage to
    Molière 26, 111, 131, 134; Molière's
    death 178, 179; other romantic
    liaisons 26; performances of
    47–9, 56–7, 87–8, 91, 95, 99, 113,
    130, 137, 159, 168; as subject of
    Molière's plays 24, 33, 62, 87–8,
    94, 95–6
Auberjonois, René **175**
Aulularia (Plautus) 122
Aumont, Michel **90**
L'Avare **121**, 122–5; La Jolla Playhouse
    production 123–5; popularity of
    122, 123; set design 125

B

Baron, Michel 101
Barrault, Jean-Louis 81, 87, 138, 141, 146,
    150, **151**, 159
Barrymore, John 52
Bartlett, Neil 100, 102, 103, 104
Bayser, Clotilde de **164**
Beauval, Mlle 152–3, 171
Béjart, Louis 57

Béjart, Madeleine **27**; death 158, 169;
    depicted as Venus **20**; illness 152;
    performances of 17–19, 24, 28,
    47–9, 57, 116; relationship with
    Molière 9–10
Bell, Marie **105**
Bérard, Christian 37, 140
Bergerac, Cyrano de 153
Bergson, Henri 146, 150, 170
Bermel, Albert 51, 114
Bertin, Pierre **151**
Bishop, Morris 177
Blanchar, Dominique 38, 43
Blunderer, The: see L'Étourdi
Boileau, Nicolas 112, 150
Bores, The: see Fâcheux, Les
Bourgeois Gentilhomme, Le 131–5, **133**
Brécourt 49
Bretty, Béatrice 118
Bridgett, Darren 89, **90**
Brie, Catherine de **36**; death of Molière
    179; love interest of Molière 10–11;
    performances of 21–2, 28, 33–4,
    38, 120, 159
Brie, Edme Villequin de 10
Brustein, Robert 94–5
Bulgakov, Mikhail 78

C

Carnovsky, Morris 122
Casile, Geneviève **133**
Cattrall, Kim 102, 104, **105**
Chapelle 23, 35, 106
character development influences 77–9
Charon, Jacques **133**
Charpentier 167
Chekhov, Michael 113, 141
Children of Paradise, The (Barrault) 87, 141
Clariond, Aimé 3–4, **105**
collaborators 127, 137, 167
Comédie-Française: chair used in *Le*
    Malade Imaginaire 168; *Dom Juan*
    production 74–7; *Le Bourgeois*
    Gentilhomme production 131, 132; *Le*
    Médecin Malgré Lui production 118; *Le*
    Misanthrope production 3–4, 101, 104;
    Les Femmes Savantes production 163,
    165; as memorial to Molière 179

comedy: importance of voice 37–8,
    40–2; Molière's success with
    12–13, 15–16; Pierrot the clown
    87–9; use of strands 142–3; value
    of 112–13
Conti, Prince de 49
Copeau, Jacques 138, 139–40, 142,
    144–9, **151**, 152
Corneille, Pierre 137
costumes: *Dom Juan* 74, 79–80, 87–8; *Les*
    Précieuses Ridicules 16–17, **20**
Cournot, Michel 75
Creyton, Barry **164**
critics: of Molière 15, 26, 49, 112, 150,
    167; Molière's response 46–52, 56
Critique de l'École des Femmes, La 47–9
cuckoldry as theme 23–4, 28–9

D

dance and music in Molière's work
    127–35, 167–8
Darlow, David 102, **105**
Dear, Nick 132
death: inspiration for plays 8; portrayed
    on stage 157–8
debate: on friendship 96–7; on human
    nature 99–100, 160; on hypocrisy
    173; influence of Molière's
    education 9; *Le Malade Imaginaire*
    173; *Le Misanthrope* 96–7, 99–100;
    Les Femmes Savantes 160
Dépit Amoureux, Le 12, 15
Descrières, George 101
dialogue, effective use of 61–2
Docteur Amoureux Le, 13
doctors in plays: influence of mother's
    death 8, 157; *Le Malade Imaginaire*
    167–78; *Le Médecin Malgré Lui*
    167–78; *Le Misanthrope* 95
Dom Garcie de Navarre 23, 24
Dom Juan; ou, Le Festin de Pierre 24,
    69–91, **82**, **90**; character
    development 77–8; closing
    scenes 84–6; compared to other
    plays 168; costumes 74, 79–80,
    87–8; Goldsby production 74,
    79–80, 84–6, 88–91; objective for
    character 70; reasons for closing

93; reflecting Molière's feelings towards Armande 87–8; San Diego production 73; set design 69–74, 75–7, 89

Don Quixote 77, 79

double entendres 61–2

Du Croisy 54, 56, **66**, 145

Du Parc, Mlle 11, 28, 47–9

Du Parc, René Berthelot 11

Dussane, Béatrix 67

Dux, Pierre 101

E

L'École des Femmes 24, 29, 33–46, **36**, 62

L'École des Maris 23, 24, 26, 28–9

Eigsti, Karl 57

Eine, Simon **90**

Eliot, T. S. 100

Enfants du Paradis, Les (Barrault) 87, 141

entrances, stage 53–68

Epp, Stephen **121**, 123

L'Étourdi 12, 15

exits, stage 69, 84–6

F

Fâcheux, Les 127

Falls, Robert 102

family as inspiration for plays 8

farce: critics of 150; description 130, 138; *George Dandin* 128–30; *Le Malade Imaginaire* 167–70; *Les Fourberies de Scapin* 138–53; Molière's development in 12–13

Femmes Savantes, Les 158–65, **164**; Antaeus Theater production 163, 165; Comédie-Française production 163, 165; compared to other plays 158, 159, 160–1, 162, 171; original cast 158–9; set design 159

Fernandez, Ramon 7, 11, 24, 34, 53–4, 96

Feydeau 111

financial pressures on Molière 69, 111

Flautino **25**

Fontana, Richard **115**

Fourberies de Scapin, Les 137–53, **151**; compared to other plays 169–70; Copeau production 138,

139–40, 142, 144–9, 152; farce demonstrated in 138–40, 142–3, 145–7, 150; set design 140

French public regard for Molière 3–4, 7

friendship, debated in plays 96–7

G

George Dandin; ou, le Mari Confondu 26, 49, 128–31, **133**; compared to other plays 171; first production 128; Goldsby production 128–31; National Theatre production 132; play interspersed with musical productions 128–31

Gillard, Françoise **82**

Girls with Ridiculous Airs: see Précieuses Ridicules, Les

Going to Pot: see On Purge Bébé

Goldsby, Matthew 129, 131

Goldsby, Robert W. 3–4, 74, 179–80; *Dom Juan* production 74, 79–80, 84–6, 88–91; *George Dandin* production 128–31; *Le Médecin Malgré Lui* production 116; *Le Tartuffe* production 54–5, 57, 59–61, 63, 64–5, **66**, 67, 68; *Les Fourberies de Scapin* production 138

Gorla, Marquise-Thérèse de 10–11

Gracieux, Vincent **115**

Grand Divertissement Royal de Versailles, Le 128

Greenblatt, Stephen 9

Gregory, Lady 138, 139, 141

Grimarest, Jean-Léonor Le Gallois de 77, 112

H

Hamlet (Shakespeare) 61

Hancisse, Thierry **164**

Heigel, Catherine **115**

Hernandez, Riccardo 125

Hervé, Marie 26

Herzel, Roger W. 101–2

Hirsch, Robert 132, 134

Hoffman, Ted 145

House, George 130

House of Molière: *see* Comédie-Française

Hubert, Monsieur 158
human nature, debated in plays 99–100, 160
hypocrisy, debated in plays 173

I

Imaginary Invalid, The: see *Malade Imaginaire, Le*
L'Impromptu de Versailles 49–51
influences on Molière: for character development 77–9; education 9, 119; family 8; human nature 83–4; mother's death 8, 157; *see also* Armande

J

Jodowsky, Brontis **66**
Jouanny, Robert 118
Jouvet, Louis **36**; *Dom Juan* 76; *Le Tartuffe* 60; *L'École des Femmes* 34, 35, 37–40, 45–6; *Les Fourberies de Scapin* 138, 140–1, 146, 150

K

Keaton, Diane 37–8
Keeper, Nathan 125

L

La Fontaine 71, 112–13, 180
La Grange **98**; accountant for Molière 16; death of Molière 178, 179; performances of 39, 78, 96, 99, 120, 141–2
La Thorillière 144, 172
Langton, Basil 65, 67
language, double meaning in 61–2
Lasalle, Jacques 74–7
Learned Ladies, The: see *Femmes Savantes, Les*
Leclerc, Catherine: see Brie, Catherine de
Leibman, Ron 54–5, 58, 60–1, 64–5, **66**
Lhuillier, Claude-Emmanuel: see Chapelle
Loret, Jean 71
Louis XIV, King of France: comments on *Le Bourgeois Gentilhomme* 131; demands on Molière 93, 125, 127–8; godfather of Molière's son 51; *Memoirs* 127; memorial for Molière 179; Molière's fears about 78–9; Molière's first performance for 12–13; portrayed in Tartuffe 67–8; support of Molière 51, 56
love, Molière's comments on 106–7
Love Doctor, The: see *L'Amour Médecin*; *Docteur Amoureux, Le*
Lovers' Quarrel, The 12, 15
Loves of Psyche and Cupid, The (La Fontaine) 112–13
Lucretius 161
Lully, Jean-Baptiste 127, 131, 137, 167
Lynch, Thomas 81, **82**

M

MacDougall, Robert 57
Mahelot, Laurent 159
Malade Imaginaire Le, 143, 167–78, **175**; compared to other plays 168, 169–70, 171, 172; critics of 167; music and dance interspersed in 167–8; set design 168
Mars, Mlle 104, **105**, 106
Marziano, Nadine 3–4, 159, 178
masks: representing death 157–8; use in theater, 24, 53, 62, 95
Mayakovsky, Vladimir 68
Mayette, Muriel **133**
Médecin Malgré Lui, Le 111–18, **115**; Comédie-Française production 118; compared to other plays 113; Empire Burlesque production 116–17; Goldsby production 116
medical profession: *see* doctors in plays
Memoirs (Louis XIV) 127
Menou, Mlle: see Armande
Meshkin, Shahrokh **66**
Meyer, Jean 118
Misanthrope, Le 24, 29, 62, 83–4, 93–107, **98**, **105**, 162, 178; closing scenes 104, 106; Comédie-Française 3–4, 101, 104; compared to other plays 113, 172; first performance post–World War II 3–4, 7; French cast 91; Hollywood performance 100; La Jolla production 102–4,

106; Molière's state of mind while writing 93–4; objective of Alceste 99; relationship between Alceste and Célimène 101–4; title explanation 94; translations less effective 100

Miser, The: *see L'Avare*

Mnouchkine, Ariane: film about Molière 8, 12, 21–2, 125, 157, 169; *Tartuffe* production 55, 58–9, 60, 65, **66**, 67, 68

Molière **5**, **20**, **27**, **36**, **98**, **115**, **175**; as actor 113, 122, 138; and Armande 10, 26, 62, 87–8, 94, 95–6, 111, 131, 134; burial of 178, 179–80; changing name 7, 10; childhood 7–9; children 51, 158; death of 4, 13, 158, 172–3, 177–8; early theatrical experiences 9–13, 15; financial concerns 69, 111; French public regard for 3–4, 7; generosity of 123; lovers 9–12; mother's death 8, 157; other career directions 9

Molière, roles played: Alceste 62, 91, 95–100, 107; Argan 168; Arnolphe 34–5, **36**, 62, 78; Chrysale 158–9, 161; George Dandin 128; Harpagon 122–3; Jourdain 128; in *L'Amour Médecin* 95; Mascarille 16–21; Orgon 56, 78; Sancho Panza 77; Scapin 137; Sganarelle 23–4, 25f, 26, 28–9, 78–9, 111–13, **115**; Sosia 120, 122

Molière (film) 8, 12, 21–2, 26, 157, 169

Molière (Moore) 150

Molière (Wilbur) 34

Montaigne, Michel de 96

Montfleury, Zacharie Jacob *dit* 15, 49

Moore, W. G. 7, 19, 150

Muse Historique, La (Loret) 71

music and dance in Molière's work 127–35, 167–8

O

Oliver, Anna R. 73

On Purge Bébé (Feydeau) 111

P

pacing in performance 139

Palais-Royal 71, 93, 111, 137, 178

Paton, Angela 50–1, 74, 129, 131, **164**

Pédant Joué, Le (Bergerac) 153

Petit-Bourbon, Le 12

Phèdre (Racine) 61

Pirandello 94, 173

Plaisirs de l'Île Enchantée, Les 53–4

Planchon, Roger 130

Pleasures of the Enchanted Island, The 53–4

Poquelin, Jean-Baptiste: *see* Molière

Pot of Gold (Plautus) 122

Pralon, Alain **133**

Prat, Pierre 71

Précieuses Ridicules, Les 16–22, **20**, 49, 158, 160, 162

Q

Quinault 137

R

Rabelais, François 18, 40, 117

Racine, Jean 49, 61

Racine, Louis 112

Raimu 168

Rehearsal at Versailles: *see L'Impromptu de Versailles*

relationships: actors onstage and offstage 17–19, 21–2; presented on stage 130

Renaud, Madeleine **115**

Richards, David 135

romantic passion as theme 33

Rosqui, Tom 59

Royal Grand Festival of Versailles 128

Rumbel, LeAnne 89, **90**

Rupnik, Kevin 73

S

Salles des Machines 137

Sancho Panza character's influence on Molière 77

scenes, use in other plays 143, 169–70

Schmitt, Olivier 55, 68, 75, 76–7

Scholar Fooled, The (Bergerac) 153

School for Husbands, The: *see L'École des Maris*

School for Wives, The: *see L'École des Femmes*
Scott, Virginia 7, 106–7, 112–13, 137, 180
Seigner, Louis 131, **133**, 135
Serrand, Dominique 123, 125
set design: *Dom Juan* 69–74, 75–7, 89, **90**;
    L'Avare 125; *Le Malade Imaginaire* 168;
    L'École des Femmes 37; *Les Femmes*
    Savantes 159; *Les Fourberies de Scapin* 140
Seweryn, Andrzej 74–7, **82**
Sganarelle; ou, le Cocu Imaginaire 23–4
Sheie, Danny 63
Simon, Jean 71
soliloquies 124
stage entrances 53–68
stage exits 69, 84–6
Stanislavski, Constantin 7, 19, 70, 135,
    141
strands in acting 142–3
Sun King: *see* Louis XIV, King of France

T

Tartuffe Le; ou, L'Imposteur 24, 52, 53–68,
    66, 67, 68, 83–4; banned in France
    67; as comment on royal court 78;
    compared to other plays 163, 168,
    170; double entendres in 61–2;
    entrances in 53–68; final acts 67–8;
    Goldsby production 54–5, 57, 59–61,
    63, 64–5; as response to Molière's
    critics 56; story about family in peril
    56; Versailles production 54, 57–8,
    59, 67; Vincennes production 55,
    58–9, 60, 65, 67, 68
Tempest, The (Shakespeare) 61, 170
theater as community 113, 135, 179
Théâtre du Vieux-Colombier 138, 140

Théâtre Illustre, Le 10
Torelli, Giacomo 71
tragedies: last play as 24; Molière's failure
    in 12, 15
transformation in action 141–2
Trapolino **25**
Traversi (Pirandello) 94
Twelfth Night (Shakespeare) 142

U

using scenes from other plays 143, 169–70

V

Varlet, Charles: *see* La Grange
Vaux-le-Vicomte 127
Vialla, Florence **82**
Vie de Molière, La (Fernandez) 53–4
Visé, Jean Donneau de 97
voice role in comedy 37–8, 40–2
Voltaire 112

W

Wadsworth, Stephen 73–4
Walters, Jessica 65, **66**
Weiss, Julie 79, 87
Wilbur, Richard 34; *Amphitryon* 120; *Le*
    Misanthrope 100; *Le Tartuffe* 54, 61;
    L'École des Femmes 42, 45–6; *Les*
    Femmes Savantes 159–63
Will in the World? (Greenblatt) 9
Wron, Emmanuelle **82**

Y

Yeats, W. B. 138

Lightning Source UK Ltd.
Milton Keynes UK
UKOW05n1213030315

247212UK00004B/42/P